THE
TODAY SHOW

THE
TODAY SHOW

*An inside look at 25 tumultuous
years...and the colorful and
controversial people behind the scenes*

Robert Metz

ꟼ⋆P
A Playboy Press Book

Library of Congress Cataloging in Publication Data

Metz, Robert.
     The Today show.

     1. Today show. I. Title.
PN1992.77.T6M4   791.45'7   77-22554
ISBN-0-87223-483-5

To Liz—and to our sea shell

Contents

Acknowledgments

Any writer who undertakes a book of this nature is essentially a reporter. Without the cooperation of nearly a hundred individuals who graciously listened to my questions and racked their brains for story and fact, I could never have completed the assignment. Those sources who were willing to be identified have been mentioned by name and the rest will remain anonymous. I thank all of them in any case. My special thanks to Pat Weaver, who was patient with my ignorance of the strange ways of television, and to his associate at NBC, Jim Nelson, who helped again and again and also lent me his copies of the famous Weaver memos. I thank Al Morgan, one of my most valued and persistent sources, and I thank Bob Cunniff, a former writer on the *Today Show* who gave me a prompt and expert reading, guiding me along the paths of accuracy. I thank Stu Schulberg, who suggested the book in the first place—after reading *CBS: Reflections in a Bloodshot Eye*. John Dunn was my best source and a fuller tribute to that fine gentleman appears in the Afterword. I accept full responsibility for all errors.

Introduction

Each weekday morning in the gray hours before the dawn, a special group of some thirty people in metropolitan New York are rudely awakened by alarm clocks carefully chosen for their loud, persistent clatter. It is essential, for millions of Americans, that none of this number roll over and go back to sleep. They dress in haste, fortifying themselves with instant coffee—no time to brew a pot.

Then it's out the door and into the dark and deserted streets. The muggers have retired by now. The pre-dawn hours are unproductive even for the ambitious thief. Some members of this company step into taxis in Manhattan, some into chauffered cars which arrive daily by prearrangement. Others drive their own cars in from the suburbs. A few hop the mail train, enduring the torturously slow stop-start ride in from the exurbs.

As each steps out the front door—whether from high-rise apartment or private home—he or she becomes part of the out-of-step world of the overnighters. They join the truck drivers

THE TODAY SHOW

rushing through empty streets to make deliveries or to pick up trash, with their compressors screaming; the nurses passing out medications to restless patients, preparing others for surgery; the cops and security men peering into the darkness, their vigil mostly made unnecessary simply because it is kept.

Soon the New York 30 converge on Radio City in mid-Manhattan to push through an unpretentious door on 49th Street, step gingerly through suds from a charwoman's pail, make their way to a bleak elevator bank dimly visible in the poorly lighted corridor, and enter a car to be carried to a windowless studio on the second floor.

For the television viewer, a make-believe world is soon to begin. Inside the studio, there is an artificial environment of carefully controlled silence and, as the camera sees it, a world of impeccable order, hiding from view vast expanses of empty space and a tangle of cables like snakes in some strange zoo. The staff, still blinking, clutch coffee—or something stronger —in styrofoam cups. Most of them watch on the sidelines, holding cues or moving cameras, while the stars of the show— scrubbed and coifed, tailored and pampered—face the TV cameras.

This is *Today*, the National Broadcasting Company's early morning news and entertainment show. As television productions go, it is a granddaddy, with a record of a quarter-century of continuous production—the longest-running weekday network television program in history.

This televised morning ritual begins the day for more Americans than any other single news source. It is one of the entertainment world's all-time top revenue producers, which has also served scientists and charlatans on the inside looking out, and Senators and Presidents on both sides of the camera. On the viewing side it has served traveling salesmen in lonely hotels, harried mothers and commuting fathers, and even the

xiv

kiddies for one improbable period when an ape shared the platform as co-host.

It is a ritual so old that NBC no longer knows how it works and, more important, *why*. It is durable enough that some say Mickey Mouse could host the show without killing it.

Yet just short of its twenty-fifth anniversary the show was as weak as it ever had been. It looked for a while as if *Today* might lose in 1976 to ABC's *Good Morning, America* as the nation's favorite video eye-opener. Had ABC its full complement of stations—several key ABC affiliates run their own successful morning shows, and ABC has fewer stations than either CBS or NBC—*Good Morning, America* might well have taken the lead.

It didn't happen. *Today* perked up like an old coffee pot over a blazing campfire. After years of rather stodgy programing, it is once again a morning delight—the dominant TV influence at the breakfast table. *Today* marches on and probably shall for a long time, until new patterns of communication and audience response emerge in ways as yet unpredicted.

This, then, is the story of a particular television show. It is a story not only of the show itself and its victories and disasters, but also of its people and their personal triumphs and tragedies; their involvement with the show and with each other in the odd world of the early morning. This is also a story of television as a reflection of all America, its work ethic, its preoccupation with success and with the people who succeed. This is the story of *Today*.

THE
TODAY SHOW

CHAPTER 1

As the Queen Lay Dying

It was the spring of 1976, and Barbara Walters, the queen of broadcast interviewers and a familiar figure on NBC's *Today* for twelve years, was threatening to leave the network if she couldn't have what she wanted.

Precisely what this intense and enigmatic *Today Show* doyenne wanted was unclear. It was out of the question that she become co-anchor on *The Evening News* with John Chancellor. Ironically, Chancellor had failed earlier in his career as *Today* host. Now, however, in the shifting currents of broadcast popularity, Chancellor was a hot property too. He occasionally topped Walter Cronkite as the nation's favorite news teller. In broadcast terms, that's like beating Bobby Fischer at chess. Maybe Chancellor wasn't doing quite well enough to run the show unaided—he was to be joined in time by David Brinkley—but he was certainly strong enough to veto Barbara as co-anchor.

NBC was obviously in a quandary about Barbara. She had stated publicly that her milkmaid's hours were burdensome.

She had to be up at 4 A.M., which usually meant slipping into an early bed while friends were still at the theater or enjoying a dinner party. The deep cushions of a chauffered limousine in the pre-dawn hours of Manhattan and a few other perks—a hairdresser and a costumer—were no substitute for a social life. Barbara was single, intensely interested in dating and in being seen.

If you counted nearly four years of writing for *Today* before she became an on-camera personality, Barbara Walters had lived in an early morning limbo for almost sixteen years. She had reached the pinnacle on *Today* in 1974, when she received a coveted television Emmy and was named "Woman of the Year" by the *Ladies' Home Journal*. The time had come to parlay fame and accomplishment into a choice new assignment—if not at NBC, then someplace else.

And none too soon, either. Barbara had surprised network officials when *Today* host Frank McGee died by pointing to a clause in her contract which they had forgotten. The clause guaranteed her co-host status with the departure of McGee, in effect conferring divine right on Barbara. During an extended search for the queen's co-host, it was clear to all that Barbara could veto any candidate not to her liking. The assertive Miss Walters chose pliable, unassertive Jim Hartz and the viewers promptly went to sleep. *Today*, which at its best enjoyed a rating of 6—roughly 6 million viewers—had dropped to 3.9 in the spring of 1976, while ABC's increasingly attractive *Good Morning, America* with David Hartman was pulling 2.5. Meanwhile CBS, which had bombed against Barbara and company with blond and vapid Sally Quinn, had also begun to make inroads with Sally's old co-host, the funny, astringent Hughes Rudd.

Barbara's popularity was a curious phenomenon to begin with. Hundreds of thousands of viewers—millions even—didn't particularly *like* Barbara. Many had stayed with the show while the hard-nosed McGee was alive to watch the two strike sparks against each other. The veteran newsman had little affection for his somewhat abrasive junior, and he showed it.

By contrast, the airwaves marriage between Barbara and Jim Hartz was decidedly uninteresting. Hartz was amiable and pleasant—a great favorite with the mercurial *Today* staff and almost no one else. Before long, the ratings had dropped by 25 percent. Barbara, always on top of things, figured it was time for a change. She had lots of momentum not only from *Today* but also from a highly successful syndicated show, *Not for Women Only*, which followed *Today* locally in the NBC-TV morning line-up in New York. As the most-honored woman in broadcasting—and perhaps in the nation itself—she had enormous bargaining power. Barbara would find a new challenge, a new platform. The obvious move was to become an anchorwoman on the evening news; no woman had yet anchored a network news show. CBS, of course, was out. Uncle Walter was king.

As Barbara was aware, things had been happening at ABC, the third network. A few years earlier, Barbara might have bridled at the suggestion that she consider ABC, traditionally the weak sister in network broadcasting. Now, however, ABC was decidedly on the march. First it had become highly successful with its innovative sports programing, including *Wide World of Sports* and *Monday Night Football*. Then, emboldened by its success over NBC and CBS in this one key area and sparked by young and imaginative new leadership, ABC set its sights on a better-than-third finish in the lucrative prime time hours—7 to 10 P.M.

Youthful Freddy Silverman, CBS's programing wizard, was hired by ABC in 1975, and he quickly turned the prime time race upside down. ABC climbed into first place late in the

1975-76 season, on its way to becoming a runaway prime-time leader in 1976-77. Awash with profits, the ABC executives decided it was time to do something about its news programing. While news may not be as lucrative as situation comedy, the news leader does win solid profits, plus prestige—in short supply at ABC.

Some spectacular coup would dramatize a strong news thrust at ABC, and Barbara Walters quickly became ABC's target. The network's quietly amusing Harry Reasoner appealed to sophisticated viewers, but he lacked appeal for the mass viewer. Harry needed help—whether he wanted it or not, and he most assuredly did not. ABC was a poor third in the evening news ratings with a 9, compared with CBS's 14 and NBC's 12. A rise of one rating point for ABC would mean an increase of $2 million in ad revenues for the program.

ABC executives reasoned that they could afford to pay Barbara Walters a fortune if she brought a respectable number of her fans to ABC. And there were additional pluses. If Barbara joined ABC, the network would enjoy the prestige of having hired the first national anchorwoman. Less important, perhaps, but certainly equally intriguing was the impact Barbara's decision would have on *Today*. Even if Barbara fizzled as Harry Reasoner's co-anchor, her departure from *Today* could cripple the show, which was proving vulnerable to the challenge of ABC's *Good Morning, America*—the first serious contender to *Today*'s dominance of the early morning in a quarter-century.

Barbara, in short, was in the catbird seat—even as the *Today* ratings drifted lower. While the sky was not the limit, perhaps, the money needed to power Barbara's departure from NBC would be astronomic by broadcast standards—or by almost any other standard.

Meanwhile, hoping to continue with the network that had made her famous, Barbara had begun informal discussions with her bosses at NBC in December 1975—a full nine months before her contract was to expire.

It was typical of Barbara Walters to begin things early; preparation had always been her first rule of action. She can become so deeply engrossed in what she is doing that associates have complained of snubs, charging that she has walked right past them without so much as a nod. Her defenders insist that this reflects an eye condition, myopia, and the fact that Barbara is invariably lost in thought. "That mind is going twenty-four hours a day," comments an old associate, who adds, "During commercials while on television, Barbara mulls over letters and memos; even scribbles replies while the camera is on the product."

NBC's senior vice-president of television, Al Rush, received Barbara's formal demands from top people at the William Morris talent agency—Lou Weiss, who headed the agency's television division, and Barbara's own representative, Lee Stevens. Barbara, they said, wanted a seven-year contract—$7 million for a package to include veto power over major changes in the *Today* format, reimbursement for extensive home entertainment expenses—NBC executives were frequently among her guests—and NBC to pick up the tab for Barbara's long-employed personal press agent. Barbara also wanted to do product endorsements without prior network approval. The latter was a perk no other NBC personality enjoyed.

The Hollywoodesque money demands were shocking enough, but there were serious problems with the other demands as well. Could NBC permit the star to run the show, as it were—do what the show's first star had done with disastrous consequences decades earlier?

NBC's top brass were deeply troubled, but blissfully ignorant, it appears, about the aspirations of ABC. As the NBC negotiations dragged on, NBC received a telephone call from William Morris, who said they wanted to "test the market" for Barbara's talents; take Barbara's demands elsewhere—to ABC. The agency had broached the idea to ABC months earlier at a Westchester country club where Lou Weiss and Fred Pierce, ABC's president, often played tennis together. It was one of those casual "You wouldn't be interested in Barbara Walters, would you?" kind of tentative remarks so common in business, but the outcome was predictable.

Before long, the Morris agency and ABC were involved in intense negotiations. Finally, on April 19, 1976, ABC offered Barbara a $1-million-a-year contract to become co-anchor with Harry Reasoner on the ABC *Evening News*.

NBC News, meanwhile, made a counter-offer that matched ABC's "about dollar for dollar," according to an unnamed NBC official. NBC also assured its superstar that eventually she would be relieved of the early morning *Today Show* grind and that she would receive first consideration if NBC ever decided to team anchorman John Chancellor with another correspondent on the evening newscast.

It was a thrilling coup for a woman in a field that had always bestowed its highest favors on men. Either contract offer would have about doubled what Barbara earned from *Today*, special NBC assignments, and from *Not for Women Only*. And either contract would send her base pay soaring above what Walter Cronkite, the dean of television newscasters, was believed to earn.

But Barbara let it be known that "a new way of life" was what she was really turning over in her mind. The evening job at ABC would mean a more normal existence and, presumably, a richer social life for America's most prominent woman broadcaster.

Meanwhile, with typical thoroughness, Barbara evidently asked everyone she knew and trusted what they thought about the idea. She even asked opinions of people she didn't know well. The author, for example, in the course of an initial telephone interview, was asked his views regarding the advisability of moving to the also-ran network.

As she mulled all this, Barbara responded to NBC's request that she hear them out—after ABC's formal offer became known. She had lunch with Herbert S. Schlosser, president of NBC, telling reporters, "This is still my company, and I owe them that."

Obviously, NBC didn't want to lose Barbara Walters and might have been happy to offer her a co-anchorship if this had been possible. An NBC official told the press at the time: "If we had offered her such a position on the NBC news, there would have been no negotiations, no contest."

There was an amusing irony to the ABC offer. Years earlier, just before Barbara got her on-camera break on the *Today Show*—after three and a half years as a writer on the show—an ABC news executive had rejected her request for a job, saying, "You'll never make it on the air."

On April 22, 1976, Barbara Walters accepted ABC's $1-million-a-year offer, signing to become co-anchor with Harry Reasoner. Her five-year contract would make her the world's highest-paid newscaster and the first woman ever to present the evening news over a major television network.

Suddenly, Barbara was the most envied woman in journalism and, for some at NBC and elsewhere, an object of sudden contempt. Her long-time employer began griping that Barbara was a spoiled child—demanding a limo, a publicist, and other privileges. Some of the demands they complained about, she had, of course, already been enjoying for years at *Today*. Later, with the network's obvious acquiescence, she became "Baba Wawa," as the wags on NBC's irreverent show *Saturday Night* made fun of the lisp that had become a trademark of the star known to the millions of *Today's* avid viewers. To outraged print media in particular, Barbara became the "million-dollar baby," and even Walter Cronkite raised his voice in the chorus of those who complained that Barbara's switch was a media event, a regrettable descent from serious journalism to show business hoopla.

As Barbara Walters prepared to begin a new career, the *Today Show*, wake-up companion to millions, faced an uncertain future, one that would tax the ingenuity of the network just to keep it alive, now that its single most important personality was leaving to join the competition.

ABC had its superstar—for better or worse—and at a super salary. An era at *Today* had ended, and a new one was about to begin.

CHAPTER 2

The First King of the Morning

David Cunningham Garroway, who was to become the first host of the *Today Show*, graduated from the NBC announcers school at Radio City in 1939, twenty-third in a class of twenty-four. Despite the low rating he received from his instructors, he was soon able to give up his $16.65-a-week job as an NBC page to take a job covering special events for an important regional station, Pittsburgh's KDKA. He reported from almost everywhere, including an airborne blimp, the depths of a coal mine, and a submerged sub. At six foot two and well over two hundred pounds, Garroway was large but gracefully athletic. He once played a round of golf with the Pennsylvania amateur champion and described the action stroke by stroke on a portable radio hook-up; he so unnerved the champ that Garroway won the match.

After Garroway moved to a more important job at Chicago's WMAQ, A. A. "Abe" Schecter, NBC's canny news chief, noticed the young broadcaster and sent him on a special assignment for the network to Shreveport, Louisiana. NBC was covering Army maneuvers staged in 1940 by a lieutenant colonel named Dwight D. Eisenhower.

It was 6 P.M. and Dave was broadcasting live when he spotted a platoon of farm boys marching up as the sun went down, carrying sticks to simulate rifles. As Dave described the scene and stood by with an open mike, they began singing "Onward Christian Soldiers." Radio news competitors John Daly and Eric Severeid were also there covering the maneuvers, but neither of them caught that dramatic episode. Dave's three-minute broadcast drew wide attention. The network later offered Garroway a job as war correspondent, but he said no and spent the war running a yeoman school in Pearl Harbor.

Garroway got permission to broadcast a disc jockey show in nearby Honolulu while off duty. Too tired after his daytime chores to plot a radio program and write continuity, he just played jazz and filled in the breaks with casual talk and patter—"As though I was talking to a friend over a highball," he described it. "I'd reminisce about astronomy, or jazz, or oysters, or the good old civilian days back in Chicago or St. Louis or New York."

Thus began the eccentric Garroway style—out of weariness in wartime Hawaii. Back at WMAQ after the war, Garroway became host of a two-hour midnight jazz and talk show called the *11:60 Club*. He continued his rambling commentaries in a curious start-stop cadence that made his words seem at times poetic. Garroway was seemingly never at a loss for words. Sometimes he did material suggested by others, but rarely more than a thought or an idea, upon which he built elaborate word pictures. Writers say Garroway always made material seem better than it was.

While his style was simple and direct, he liked to send listeners to the dictionary with offbeat introductions of guests

"Welcome my esoteric Peruvian," he would say. Or he'd refer to a singer as "a gossamer thing, an incandescent woman."

Garroway borrowed that style from Dick Maney, Tallulah Bankhead's press agent. "I thanked him for it many times and all he did was grunt. I later knew Tallulah, asked her about Maney and she said, 'That's all he ever did was grunt.' "

One of Garroway's fans was Charlie Andrews, a droll, sad-faced native of Wisconsin and a writer for WMAQ who created the station's hit *Studs' Place* with Studs Terkel. Charlie had once written Peter Pan Peanut Butter television commercials for a then-obscure broadcaster named Mike Wallace. Mike, done up as a circus side-show barker, in straw hat and bamboo cane, would deliver such lines of Charlie's as "Now here's the strong boy—strong because he eats Peter Pan Peanut Butter." Or, "Hey, gang, how about some Peter Pan Peanut Butter? It comes in smooth and it comes in crunchy. Now here's Bobo the two-headed boy—one likes smooth and one likes crunchy."

Like Garroway, Charlie was a jazz buff, and as he got to know Dave he began feeding him material for the *11:60 Club*. The two men became friends and discovered they had similarly eccentric turns of mind. Once they agreed on the proposition that lunch with a pretty girl was bliss—if you didn't have to talk to her. To test out their idea, they rented two models the next day and instructed them to join them for lunch but not say a word, and just smile and eat while looking devastating in silence. The caper backfired though. The girls withered the two men with frigid stares all during the luncheon.

Dave took Charlie along after he agreed to a terse request from Jules Herbuveaux, an NBC vice-president in Chicago, who had wired from out of town to ask Garroway, "Can you fill TV net 9-9:30 P.M. EST on Sundays?" Garroway recalls that Andrews wasn't enthusiastic: "Television was kind of a

13

nuisance. We both thought radio hot stuff." But if the program was successful, it could be exciting since the NBC-TV network was expanding rapidly that year, 1948.

Garroway said, "Sure, Jules, we'll fill."

Once committed, Garroway and Andrews lost no time putting their stamp on the program, which became known as *Garroway at Large*. They brought the viewer backstage—a TV first. There amid the twisted cables and studio props, Garroway mixed informal humor with live entertainment. Charlie Andrews recalls their concept of the show: "We were only attempting to entertain one person—some guy sitting in a living room somewhere out there in television land. If we entertained him we were doing good. We never tried to make anyone laugh ... only tried to make 'em chuckle."

Once, in a song calling for a soda fountain setting, Dave was to be dressed as a soda jerk and to set up the number by making a malted milk. Andrews thought it might be funny if Garroway got his necktie caught in the spinning mixer shaft so that it would pull his head down. The idea worked twice in rehearsal. With Garroway held fast by the mixer, comedian Cliff Norton reached over with a pair of scissors and cut the tie . . . fade to song. With the cameras recording the scene live for viewers, everything went well at first. The tie tangled with the mixer, drawing Dave's head in close. But when Norton reached over with the scissors, the heavy knit tie resisted. Norton whacked away repeatedly without effect. Dave and mixer were then waltzed away to be disentangled. When the song was over, Garroway came back laughing and giggling. *Voilà* ... a charming bit of Garrowayana.

The tag lines for the show were called "Milk Bottles" since the first one followed a torch song called "Black Coffee." As the credits appeared, milk was seen being poured into black coffee to overflowing. As it splashed to the floor, Garroway said, "This program came to you from Chicago . . . the neatest studio in the world." On another occasion, "This show came to you from Chicago . . ." and with that he whacked a cable with a hatchet and the screen went black. Or, "This show came to you from Chicago . . . the friendly city," and with that he turned to reveal a knife in his back.

In those early days of television in Chicago, new tools meant new flexibility and excitement. Most were expensive, but at least one special effects device cost nothing at all. One day cameraman Bob Haley walked by a construction site and discovered a broken, discarded hollow glass brick. He carried it back to the studio, held it in front of the camera, and discovered it would repeat the image thirty to forty times. After he used it in one number with singer Betty Chappel, NBC called from New York and asked where it had come from. "Zeiss made it," Haley said, referring to the noted lens-maker.

"Could we borrow it?"

"Not a chance . . . too valuable."

Garroway soon became the hottest property on NBC, outpaced only by Arthur Godfrey on CBS. In addition to his *Garroway at Large* show, he also had a half-hour show sponsored by the United States Army, plus a local call-in show, *Dial Garroway*, appropriately sponsored by Dial Soap. Charlie Andrews, a farm boy who had never earned big money, was making upwards of $800 a week by writing for all three shows. Garroway, of course, did even better. Living costs were low in the late 1940s in Chicago. Andrews found a downtown apartment for $80 a month with a two-story living room, balcony, stained glass windows, and a place directly outside for his car. Garroway, who lived nearby, rented a garage in an alley for his four classic cars, including his favorite Jaguar and a Rolls-Royce he was rebuilding. Life was exciting, frenetic, and exhausting.

Though Garroway didn't smoke and rarely lifted a social glass, he turned to an occasional stimulant for instant energy.

So did Charlie. Dave knew a show business doctor who mixed vitamin B and molasses with a liquid pep-up, which he found worked faster than pills.

Thus, though he was keeping crazy hours, Garroway managed to maintain his hobbies. Sometimes he raced his 1937 Jaguar XK 100—after a fashion anyway. No fool, Garroway would start slow and, when about to be lapped by the pack, would reach down, turn off the water, and retire from the race heroically with steam pouring out of the cowling.

He spent most of his free time on his back on a mechanic's sled, working on his cars. Parker Gibbs, one of Dave's producers, would pace nervously at the studio as Garroway's time of arrival would pass; then he would say, "Go get him, Charlie." Andrews would take a cab to Dave's alley garage and find him under the Rolls. "He would come to the studio in his overalls with oily rags sticking out of his pocket," Andrews recalls. "He would wiggle out of the work clothes and do the show."

In time, though, things slowed down considerably. The Army show was canceled, and so was *Dial Garroway*. Garroway and Andrews concentrated on the big one—*Garroway at Large*. When its sponsor, Congoleum Nair, gave up the show, Armour, the meatpacker and maker of Dial Soap, bought it for even bigger money. The future seemed assured.

Garroway, Andrews, and Dave's agent William "Biggie" Levin went to Europe together to celebrate for three weeks. Traveling by car, the three men arrived in Switzerland late one afternoon and drove through the gathering darkness to a hotel at the base of a mountain. They were tired and each went immediately to bed. In the morning, Dave went to Charlie's room and woke him up.

"I want to show you one of the most thrilling sights in the world," Dave said. With that he walked to the window and announced, "Here is the Matterhorn at dawn," sweeping back the heavy drapes with a flourish. The rising sun bathed the mountain, and the awestruck Andrews said, "Dave, that's just beautiful."

Then Garroway added the news he had just learned by telegram: "Our show has been canceled."

Dave Garroway learned of the *Today Show*'s forthcoming debut by accident. Back in Chicago one morning he wandered into the Pump Room in his resident hotel, the Ambassador East, and decided to order breakfast, something he almost never did. While waiting for his order he discovered a discarded copy of *Daily Variety*, a show business trade sheet, which someone had left in the booth. He read the headline and immediately telephoned Biggie Levin.

Biggie weighed 110 pounds—a cadaverous figure in a cashmere suit. A slight bulge over Biggie's heart was telltale evidence of his secret weapon—a wad of crisp one-dollar bills. If a restaurant's poor service threatened to make Biggie late for his next appointment, he would peel off a greenback and snap it with a loud pop, instantly riveting the attention of the waiter.

Dave told Biggie on the telephone that morning about NBC impresario Pat Weaver's forthcoming early morning television show. Dave argued that it cried out for the Garroway touch. Garroway—chess whiz, amateur astronomer, vintage car collector, gadget fancier, jazz buff, offbeat conversationalist, and all-around charmer—was a natural, he continued.

Garroway at Large had not been canceled for lack of popularity. It was taken off the air because mighty Procter & Gamble, broadcasting's biggest advertiser, coveted Garroway's prime time slot. According to Garroway, P & G persuaded NBC to cancel, cashier everybody, and pay off Armour. P & G supplied the dollars and Garroway walked. Now, his talents unemployed, Garroway wanted Biggie to convince Pat Weaver that a comedy host for the *Today Show*—Fred Allen, Bob Hope, and Milton Berle were all said to be under consideration—would lay an egg. Garroway kept telling Biggie, "The spot was made for me," and Biggie kept saying, "We'll see."

It was agreed that Garroway would telephone Mort Werner, a *Today* producer, and ask for a meeting in Chicago. Dave promised Werner dinner. Garroway picked him up at the airport and drove him to the Ambassador Hotel. Instead of heading for the Pump Room, Garroway took Werner to his room and offered two cans of cold baked beans and bottles of warm root beer. They talked until dawn.

Dave stressed his newscasting experience and charmed Werner with his rambling commentaries. A day later, after Werner had returned to New York, he called Garroway and asked him to come to Radio City. In New York, Garroway was told to read a piece of hard news copy. After he did so, the NBC people said only "Thank you," and Garroway flew back to Chicago to wait. Two days later, Biggie called Dave and said, "You got it."

Garroway's blues over the loss of *Garroway at Large* evaporated, and the soon-to-debut *Today Show* had a host.

CHAPTER 3

The Man Who Invented Today

Sylvester "Pat" Weaver, a 6-foot-4-inch, jug-eared redhead with a smiling, open face, was brought to NBC in 1949 from the advertising business. As NBC vice-president in charge of television, he was given carte blanche to help the network recover the initiative from CBS, which had taken the lead in prime time ratings, mainly by having snatched away NBC's biggest stars in 1948—Burns and Allen, and Jack Benny. Weaver was picked because of his reputation as an expert in nearly all facets of show business.

The son of a wealthy Los Angeles roofing manufacturer and unsuccessful candidate for mayor, Pat had been a gifted and studious child. An inveterate reader, he ran through Edward Gibbon's monumental *Decline and Fall of the Roman Empire* at age thirteen. As a teen-ager, he cut a dashing figure in a Ford roadster he customized himself—a gift from his father for high marks. Social as well as bookish, he developed a love for performers and performing. He Charlestoned to trophies in dance contests fairly regularly, occasionally with such

Hollywood comers as Carole Lombard, Loretta Young, and Joan Crawford. Pat attended Dartmouth College, where he was seen behind the wheel of his speedy Marmon so often that he baffled classmates with his straight A's and his election to Phi Beta Kappa in his junior year. After graduating *magna cum laude* in philosophy, he sailed for Europe to study ancient ruins in Italy, Greece, and Egypt. When his money ran out, he returned to New York City. It was 1931, with the Depression well underway. A couple of unrewarding sales jobs convinced him that the West Coast was more hospitable to a man of ideas. He gravitated into radio in L.A., selling advertising spots and producing shows.

One program, designed to perk up citizens battered by the Depression, began with an inspirational: "America unconquered, America unafraid, America victorious." A few weeks of that and the irate advertiser turned up at the studio to intone: "America unconquered, America unafraid, America unsponsored."

But there were triumphs too. During a disastrous Long Beach earthquake, Weaver stayed up all night coordinating the station teams that covered the quake and writing the continuity himself. By this time, Pat had impressed his boss, Don Lee, who had helped establish the infant CBS by affiliating the radio stations he owned with that network. Lee sent Weaver to manage his station KFRC in San Francisco.

Radio was still in its formative stages, and Weaver produced, directed, and acted in many of the station's shows. Once he conceived a half-hour show for the CBS network, to be broadcast on the anniversary of the San Francisco earthquake, which would describe the quake as though it were just happening. But a vice-president in New York vetoed the idea. Later in his career, according to Weaver, he worked on a pilot of a show to be called "I Was There," years before Goodman Ace developed the show *You Are There.*

The pilot was built around the Battle of Gettysburg. The producers took the show to an old soldiers' home and found a cavalry subaltern who said he had fought at Gettysburg. They explained to him that at a certain point in the show they would turn to him and he was to say, "I was there," the aged voice to cap the broadcast with an authentic touch. The ex-cavalry man was ancient and foggy, but the three-word assignment seemed within his range. While potential clients listened to the live pilot broadcast, the show reached its climax. The announcer then described the old man, thrust the mike in his face, and said, "And now, here is subaltern Smith." At the cue, as Weaver describes it, "Smith sort of slipped into his coma." Dead air. The announcer, in a near panic, prompted, "Ah . . . *Lieutenant Smith*. This is Gettysburg, and *you were there*." Suddenly roused, Smith said, "Oh God, no! I wasn't there. I was posted north on a scouting mission and didn't get there until the next day—after it was all over."

Weaver eventually moved back to New York, where he worked for Young & Rubicam. The advertising agency had a rich roster of radio talent in the era when the ad agencies produced the important shows for their clients. The agency chose Weaver to produce Fred Allen's *Town Hall Tonight*, then starting its first full season on NBC. Allen despised representatives of agencies, clients, or networks because of their inevitable attempts to pull the barbs of his jokes when they struck any target that had clout. Weaver's first official act as Allen's producer was to throw two men out of the control room of the studio as the show started. Weaver didn't know them, and perhaps it was just as well. They turned out to be Lee Bristol, president of Bristol-Myers, which sponsored the show, and Deke Aylesworth, president of NBC. Weaver commented later: "If anything was needed to cement my relationship with Fred Allen, this maneuver proved to be the real stickum. From then on, Fred and I never had a cross word."

Weaver's success with Fred Allen caused Y & R to regard him as something of a miracle man, which was the way Weaver unabashedly regarded himself. In 1937, two years after the Weaver-Allen collaboration began, Weaver was named supervisor of all Young & Rubicam radio programs.

A former colleague recalls: "Pat just breathed confidence. He would grab a client and get him so excited over a show—even a dog of a show—that he would hardly know what he was doing."

The agency handled a minor product of the American Tobacco Company, and this brought Pat to the attention of its president, George Washington Hill, one of advertising's fabled characters. Sidney Greenstreet played a character modeled on Hill in the film *The Hucksters* and shocked moviegoers with a scene in which he hawked and spit on a polished conference table, saying, "Gentlemen, you have just seen me do a digusting thing."

After Hill's Lucky Strikes dropped into third place in national sales, below Chesterfields and Camels, Hill decided that Weaver's flair could put Luckies back on top, and he hired him.

When Weaver worked there, Hill would arrive for his daily staff meetings with his advertising assistants seated apprehensively around a conference table. From beneath his black eyebrows, Hill stared long and menacingly at each man in turn while fishing two packs of Luckies out of a pocket, slapping them on the table, and snapping, "Tobacco is what it's all about, gentlemen!" While the others sat in ramrod stiffness, Weaver stationed himself off Hill's bow, feet on the table, tipped back in his chair. Occasionally, Weaver would part his feet to fix Hill in his sights and to make a comment or even to argue, after which he would bring his feet together again, closing the gates in relaxed satisfaction.

Weaver steeped himself in tobacco and advertising lore and

batted out a twenty-four-page, single-spaced memo, which traced advertising back to "the first social contact that man had with man," then through the voyages of Minoan merchants, the rise of medieval guilds, the beginnings of the machine age, up to American Tobacco's latest commercial, which he then critiqued. Hill gave the Weaver memo his supreme accolade, reading it in its entirety at his next meeting. He adopted Weaver's suggested softer-sell pitch: "The finer, the lighter, the naturally mild Lucky Strike tobacco," and within three years Luckies sailed into the lead over Chesterfields and Camels.

By the time Lucky Strike's slogan became "Lucky Strike Green has gone to War," so had Weaver. A weekend sailor with a 56-foot yawl, Weaver applied for a Navy commission, shortly after marrying a pert English actress, Elizabeth Inglis. Soon he sailed as skipper of a convoy escort vessel. Never attacked, he was soon bored as he languished on deck in swim trunks, feeling ashamed as a steward freshened his drink in all-out war. He welcomed reassignment to the West Coast as director of programs for Armed Forces Radio Service—called the Y & Rmy for its heavy nucleus of Young & Rubicam people. Weaver's programing included the much-admired *Command Performance*. Weaver had developed a conviction that broadcasting owed culture as well as entertainment to its public, a theme that would deeply affect his later work at NBC.

After the war Weaver returned to Hill's service and found the tycoon ailing, but smoking as resolutely as ever. Hill died in 1946 without naming Weaver to the expected vice-presidency at $250,000 a year. Saddened by the loss of a man he regarded as a friend, Weaver went back to the agency business.

Increasingly bored with narrow client concerns, Weaver jumped at the challenge offered by NBC in 1949. Once at the network, Weaver turned his back on his agency friends and began wresting control over programing from the advertisers. Weaver wanted "quality" productions with a dash of culture —a famous pianist to leaven a comedy hour, for example. Placed end to end, quality productions would draw and hold a national audience for the entire evening, he reasoned.

To accomplish that goal, Weaver led the network to produce its own attractions, particularly "spectaculars" and other shows lasting more than an hour. Such lengthy productions were extremely costly; no one advertiser could bankroll such a show for long. Thus, he was able to sell "participations"—as though each advertiser were buying pages in a magazine.

Weaver's advertising concept began to take hold, and he established network control over a number of popular attractions, to the whimpers of old friends on Madison Avenue who regarded him as a turncoat. He was cutting their contacts in the glamorous world of show business and reducing the ad game to commercial production, a dull business by comparison.

Weaver's signal success, the one that paved the way for the *Today Show* and other experimental numbers, was a strong Saturday night line-up that included *Your Show of Shows* with Sid Caesar. As a result, the usual night out became a stay-at-home evening for millions of Americans, alarming movie and restaurant owners.

Weaver encouraged his people to think of television as an entirely new medium with a totally different potential from that of radio. But when he designed a show to fill the then-unused morning hours, he approached it quite differently from his other productions. It would indeed be radio with pictures. It even carried the working title "Rise and Shine," which he lifted from a successful radio show. Weaver's ambition was to woo millions of listeners away from the radio wake-up shows that played to 75 percent of the nation's homes between 7 and 9 A.M. with an amalgam of music, news, patter, time checks, weather reports, and helpful tips. In one memo, Weaver, one of the great memo writers in the broadcast business, said:

"We cannot and should not try to build a show that will make people sit down in front of their sets and divet their attention to the screen. We want America to shave, to eat, to dress, to get to work on time. But we also want America to be well informed, to be amused, to be lightened in spirit and in heart, and to be reinforced in inner resolution through knowledge."

But in fantasizing on the potential of the television screen for imparting knowledge, Weaver got carried away. He began to see "Rise and Shine" as spewing forth information in a verbal-visual omelet that would be bound to cause indigestion at breakfast.

As first conceived, the show was to feature wire service reports, regional newspapers on a rack to be scanned by the camera so that the nation could see what headlines were currently in each population center, clocks giving the time hither and yon through world time zones, and television monitors showing pictures of the world at large, while the latest, hottest bulletin walked across the bottom of the TV screen.

The host—"the Communicator," as Weaver styled him—was to somehow bring it all together. Weaver had Russ Hughes in mind, a broadcaster who talked very fast but was nevertheless "easy to understand." But then Dave Garroway suggested himself for the role. And the more Weaver thought about it, the more he leaned toward Garroway's easy-going style. "A calm relaxed guy in the middle of that maniac setting would be better than another maniac," Weaver decided.

Though making one decision in favor of sanity, Weaver continued to befuddle aides at NBC briefings with his grandiose plans. Charlie Andrews remembers his first meeting with Weaver:

"Dave and Biggie Levin sat near his kidney-shaped desk, and I sat in back with the writers who had been working on this concept of Pat's for six to eight months in the fall of 1951. Pat had been writing all these fabulous memos. As we all sat listening, he would say, 'Norman Bel Geddes will design the studio. It will be huge—glassed-in so the sun can shine down on the set, and there will be balconies where people can stand and watch the news room below.

" 'The Communicator will pick up the telephone and there will be Moscow with instantaneous pictures from the Russian capital coming in over the wires . . . This man will be the news center of the world . . .'

"When we walked out my head was spinning. I fell back with Charlie Spear, one of the writers. I knew the show was to start in a few months and I told him how confused I was."

Andrews asked Spear to explain how it would all come together, and Spear said, "Well, to begin with, we'll have to share studios with *Howdy Doody*."

Even before Weaver had begun setting up the staff for his new morning show, he had already hired a manager of television planning, a glib and engaging executive named Richard A. R. Pinkham.

Dick Pinkham—"Tom Triumph" to Weaver after some early mistake had briefly caused Weaver to dub him "Frank Failure"—was a former newspaper executive who fled that "narrowing" industry to become a part of the "exploding" world of television in 1951. Pinkham's last job had been as circulation manager of the New York *Herald Tribune*. Pinkham believes himself to have been the first person in 105 years to resign from that paper's board of directors.

As a Weaver assistant with seemingly vague responsibilities, he was deemed an unnecessary "dangling executive" by a management consultant team that reported to RCA chairman David Sarnoff. Weaver had to supply a safe label, so shortly after the show aired, Pinkham became executive producer of *Today*.

In assuming that title, Pinkham replaced Abe Schechter, a portly, street-wise, and respected newsman who had built NBC's reporting stable in the old radio days. At *Today*, he proved to be an ineffective executive and he also proved unable —as were his successors—to obtain cooperation from the NBC-TV news department. Abe had frequently argued with Pat Weaver and regarded the show Weaver wanted as a "hodge-podge." Schechter, however, stayed on for some months after *Today* went on the air.

The man who was to function as line producer for *Today* was Mort Werner. Mort had been producer of an NBC comedy show Pat had set up for his zany brother, Doodles Weaver. Doodles had gained fame doing comedy routines with the Spike Jones City Slickers, a band specializing in laughter and cornball jazz. Doodles' specialty was a frantic version of "Cocktails for Two," which he punctuated with gulps, Bronx cheers, and hiccups.

After Doodles flopped on NBC, Mort Werner was left without a job, but not for long. A former radio station owner and program executive, Mort had been a Pat Weaver associate during the war, and Weaver quickly put him on the *Today* staff.

When Pinkham got the title of executive producer, he worried that Mort might feel slighted. He thus made the decision which he terms his best in a forty-year career. He moved Werner into his big corner office to make the communications between them easy and informal.

Mort Werner's quiet talents quickly became obvious. It was Werner who brought Dave Garroway to the attention of Pat Weaver. Werner then selected the seasoned and astute Jim Fleming as newscaster and smiling Jack Lescoulie to do sports and be resident clown.

Pinkham recalls that Werner was indefatigable. Most of the *Today* staff, weary at noon after an eight-hour day, would quickly disperse. But Werner stayed on, often well into the afternoon. And he was good at getting to the heart of things. When conferences wandered, Pinkham remembers, Mort "would throw out his hands, like an umpire calling 'Safe!' and say, 'Wait a minute, let's cut through the baloney,' which he quickly did."

Equally important, Mort had a "marvelous rapport" with Garroway. "That was very helpful, because Dave, like any guy carrying that kind of weight, needed all the reassurance he could get," Pinkham adds.

As the deadline approached, the title the *Today Show* was selected and a target date was set—January 7, 1952. Weaver's plans, though now more specific, were still grandiose. One month before "T-Day," as Weaver called it, he wrote his best-remembered memo on *Today*, addressing it to all members of the NBC news and special events departments. He began with typical enthusiasm, proclaiming that *Today* was "about to inaugurate a new era in television programing.

"These words mean what they say. *Today* is a big undertaking in every sense of the word . . . Seven to nine A.M. will be no 'Siberia' as one columnist surmised; it will be the Sun Valley, Palm Springs, and Miami Beach of TV."

While there would be no glassed-in studio with sun streaming down, Weaver had by now convinced RCA that *Today* needed a showcase where it could be observed. The studio of Howdy Doody wouldn't do. Instead, a store front featuring RCA's latest television sets in the heart of Radio City was to be home base. It was a location that would pick up and reflect the weather, the crowds, and the excitement of Manhattan:

"We are building TV's first communication studio on the

floor space of the RCA Exhibit Hall on 49th Street. The camera will see a working newsroom with [tele]printers, wirephoto, facilities for trans-Atlantic communication—every device needed for news coverage on the broadcast scale."

Then, more of the Weaver hyperbole:

"*Today* is in every sense a vast undertaking. It is a top priority program. I urge you to destroy any mental image you have of just another morning program. We are building a program that will change the listening habits of this nation. We are setting standards that will bring distinction to every man and woman who joins in this project.

"The proudest order of journalists has always been that select group who made the old New York *World* in its heyday. Now we are in an era where newsprint has lost its force to the electronic wonder of television. I have a commission for each one of you. It is simply this:

"To make of *Today* not merely a good program but the finest news presentation in history. We have the resources. We have the opportunity. Now we go to work and do the big job."

To the introductory report, Weaver attached a six-page "discursive" memo that discussed the philosophy of *Today* and how it was to be done. There was to be no attempt at "visual impact of a high order," he wrote. "We also freely admit that we are going into something highly auditory when we do so and encourage lack of interest in the picture."

To advertisers would go "an honest admission" that the *Today* selling strategy differed from most, emphasizing "to advertisers the value of continuous association, of preparing advertising material which is good in either or both media, sight and sound, and sight or sound. We need not fear an uninteresting picture, as radio-trained men fear silence."

Weaver went on to picture the show's typical audience:

"Let us imagine a family at home. The set is presumably in

the living room, and is turned on by the wife who beats her husband to that room. Wife, kids and husband now all hear the audio of the show until they arrive in the dining room. Meanwhile, the wife has called out the time, and the news flash if important.

"The audience begins to build. Should Dave be going into a special, or the briefing period, or something of unusual interest to that family, the group may come before the tube before they are ready; i.e., before they are dressed and ready for breakfast and school or business . . . Therefore, the listener will become a viewer whenever his interest in the audio reaches a point where it interrupts his preparation for work or school and replaces it in importance to him. This period, however, is followed by another period in which there is attention to picture and sound, the period probably at the breakfast table in most homes."

Weaver recognized that *Today* would play to a "turnover" audience and that the average viewer-listener might hear no more than an hour, see no more than half an hour. He continued:

"We are not trying to get people to rise earlier to see the show, nor to stay at home and be late . . . We therefore must repeat key information . . . all important hunks or points should be made in each of the two hours . . . We are not trying to get a 10 rating for two hours, but we are trying to get sixty per cent of all sets to turn on the show, with time from the viewers varying between a fast two-minute look at the time and the headline from a bachelor who eats out and has a big apartment . . . to a longish hour from a large family . . . where the father hits the road at 7:50 and the kids leave for school at 8:40. We will learn as we go just how to vary our pattern to be sure that all families have at least two chances on the briefing period, plus a chance at every major hunk, but without losing the smaller audiences that would stay with us longer."

Weaver's memo went on to discuss remote news pick-ups, human interest stories, music spots, and comedy. In short, Weaver was, as he put it, publishing a magazine every morning. "It has sections on news, books, entertainment activities, records, performances . . . it is a bird's eye view of the world and its happenings."

In brief, staccato segments and without being "jerky," *Today* was to provide people with "an extremely literate, energizing program service . . . sugar-coated, and . . . [well] paced . . . We want rounded human beings, who will emerge into higher types in due time to join us mutants, but there must be fun with the stuff."

Before the fun could begin, Weaver had a final hurdle to clear: convincing NBC's affiliate stations to pick up the show. Doubting that there would be much of an audience, the affiliate owners were concerned over the prospect of marginal operations early in the morning. If they didn't schedule *Today*, they could telecast test patterns till noon, avoiding the additional overhead and a potential drop in profits. Affiliates were spoiled by their substantial and easy profits.

Having a network franchise, even in a small community, was roughly equivalent to owning a toll booth on a busy turnpike with no responsibility for maintaining the road. There was little local television production. The affiliates—"filling stations" to cynical network officials—pumped *network* news and *network* entertainment and pocketed most of the resulting advertising revenues. (Until recent years, CBS earned more money on its five owned-and-operated television stations—the limit for a single corporation under federal regulations—than it did on all affiliation revenues.)

Some affiliate owners were appalled that *Today* would end at 9 A.M. while the network feed wouldn't begin again until 10 A.M.—an embarrassing gap for those with nothing to contribute. They would have to fill the void with local shows, or forget *Today* and continue their late starts. Pat Weaver wooed them with a potent argument: "Fellows," he said, "money will take care of all problems." He finally convinced the stations that *Today*'s two hours had prime commercial potential, but he was not sure how to split the revenues with the local stations, and his early suggestions met with considerable resistance. Some stations would not accept less revenue from the network ads than they would receive for local advertising spots. They demanded that Weaver up the network ad rates in order to boost the local stations' share.

Weaver knew he would have enough advertiser resistance to overcome without overcharging them. He also knew that if enough local stations refused to clear air time, he couldn't even promise a national audience to potential advertisers. He warned the affiliates that they might wind up being identified in the press as "the greediest character[s] on the American scene." Finally Weaver worked out a plan offering *Today* advertisers reasonable rates and local stations a big concession. The affiliates could have five minutes for locally sponsored newscasts at the hour and at the half hour for each of the two hours of the show.

The filling stations had managed to wring their extortionate price from the network, and Weaver could get on with the *Today Show*.

CHAPTER 4

"T-Day"

The *Today Show* made its debut at 7 A.M. on Monday, January 14, 1952, a week later than Pat Weaver had planned.

In that era television was almost exclusively an evening pastime for those who watched the nation's 15 million home screens. After dinner they would sit down in front of their sets, perhaps to view the *Texaco Star Theater* with NBC's "Mr. Television," Milton Berle, or *Your Show of Shows* with Sid Caesar and Imogene Coca. On CBS, the public saw *Toast of the Town* with stone-faced Ed Sullivan. Television offered the kiddies *Kukla, Fran and Ollie,* and bona fide adults watched *Philco Playhouse.* And there was this redhead—Lucille Ball in *I Love Lucy,* seen only in black and white, of course, like every other attraction.

Morning television was available here and there, but watching it was a taboo in an America dedicated to the work ethic. It was acceptable to listen to morning radio but, like sex and alcohol, television was deemed proper only after sundown. Getting viewers to spend time in front of the set even before leaving for work would take some doing, as Pat Weaver well knew.

On that bleak wintry morning just before seven o'clock, a small crowd gathered to shiver outside the window of the RCA Exhibition Hall, awestruck by Weaver's bristling electronic studio with its news-gathering machines and TV monitors. NBC publicity releases called the studio the "World Communications Center" and "The Nerve Center of the Planet."

Some television critics had already commented on NBC's inflated promotion of the *Today Show*. John Crosby wrote in the *Herald Tribune* that NBC vice-presidents were "drunk on their own prose." The entire NBC press agent staff, it seemed, had been influenced by Pat Weaver's bubbling enthusiasm. Weaver had promised that the show would be a "milestone in the social history of this country," and, on another occasion, said that after five years of *Today* all the nation's children would know the statesmen and the customs of all the countries of the world. Amused by the hype, Crosby commented that even the NBC interoffice memos were "couched in such sweeping grandeur that the tendency among the more timorous of us is to flee to the hills before this shattering enlightenment is thrust on us."

Today's top command realized that they would face a hostile press if the show didn't measure up to advance claims. They were understandably nervous.

Dick Pinkham, soon to be named executive producer, stayed in town before the opening and slept little in his bed at the Yale Club. Mostly he worried that the two-hour broadcast would offer a static picture as host Dave Garroway and his team ran out of things to say. Awakening in the dark, Pinkham rose, dressed, and lurched into the studio at 4 A.M., wan and anxious.

In the early hours of T-Day near his Scarsdale home, producer Mort Werner encountered a cop who wanted to know why Werner was loitering on a corner at 3 A.M. When Werner explained that he was waiting for a friend to drive him to NBC for a TV show to air at seven o'clock, the cop said, "You must be out of your mind."

At the studio, many of the staff questioned their own sanity as they yawned and blinked, fortifying themselves with coffee. There was to be a 50-minute dry run at 6 A.M. Dress rehearsals are always a technical nightmare and an emotional strain, but this concern paled beside the tensions and hazards of the show itself.

Newscaster Jim Fleming had driven in from Greenwich, Connecticut, making it in minutes on car-free roads. Yet he too was "*very* nervous," he admitted. The engineers muttered as they worked, complaining that the Exhibition Hall—officially the Johnny Victor Theater—would look terrible because of the light from the street and all those people standing outside shifting from foot to foot, looking at the cameras.

Abe Schechter, who continued to clash with Weaver over how the show should be done, stationed himself in front of a monitor down a ramp below street level in the advertising clients' booth. During the dry run Schechter constantly expressed dissatisfaction with the picture, shouting, "Pan over, pan over—*come on*, pan over!" as helplessly as a fan watching Ohio State play Michigan on TV. When nothing happened—the cameramen couldn't hear him—Schechter would run up the ramp to give instructions which were already too late. He'd return to his position below, then see something else he didn't like, then it was up the ramp again, huffing and puffing in a pattern that he would continue every morning while he was with the show. It came to be known as the "Schechter Ramp Dance."

The star of the show, Dave Garroway—the man who should

have been feeling the greatest pressure of all—stood in the midst of the confusion minutes before 7 A.M. looking, in Pinkham's words, "fantastically relaxed."

Pinkham asked Garroway how he could be so at ease. Garroway hauled out a bottle of dark fluid and said, "Have a spoonful of The Doctor." Pinkham did and suddenly things "began to look wonderful." They weren't.

The second hand ticked toward 12, the countdown began, and then the cameras rolled. The result, well, it was silly. Garroway, who has always been fascinated by gadgets, stood in awe of his equipment and said so—again and again. It was all largely wasted. Telephone pick-ups from abroad brought vacuous reports. Garroway didn't ask much. When he got Romney Wheeler, the NBC man in London, on the phone he said, "All we want you to do is start our next record." "I hope it's 'Domino,' " said Wheeler. "It's very popular over here." The next record was "Domino."

"Hello Ed Hasker in Frankfort," said Garroway in another phone hook-up. "Tell me the news in your part of the world."

"The big news is the weather," said Hasker, his voice ringing clear as a bell, which one critic called a triumph of communications over content. "We had our first big storm of the year. We're really chilly."

"You're not alone," said Garroway. "Good-bye, Ed."

While the banality of the interviews probably did not result from the news department's hostile attitude toward *Today*, it didn't misrepresent that attitude. *Today* had raided the NBC roster for talent: Weaver's clout at work. Cooperation, in the news department's view, meant loss of status, new chores, and early morning calls.

The only notable cooperation *Today* received on opening day thereafter was provided by Washington bureau chief Julian Goodman, then a little fish in the NBC News pond and later NBC president. But the Washington report that morning was perhaps the silliest feature of all, with the possible exception of shots of empty parking lots gradually filling with commuter automobiles. Goodman's remote unit was parked outside the Pentagon, where the reporter managed to collar Admiral William Fechteler, Chief of Naval Operations. "How's the Navy going these days, Admiral?" the reporter asked.

"Guess it's all right," replied the Chief of Naval Operations. "It was there last night all right, when I left it."

"Thank you very much, sir," said the correspondent as the Admiral sailed on. "Ladies and gentlemen, you have just heard from Admiral William Fechteler, Chief of Naval Operations down here at the Pentagon in Washington. And now we return you to Dave Garroway in New York."

The TV critics seemed to enjoy deflating the *Today Show*'s pretentions. One brainstorm, "Today in Two Minutes," which offered headlines and pictures from newspapers across the country, was seized upon by John Crosby, who wrote:

" 'Today in two minutes,' said Mr. Garroway and showed us the headlines of the day. 'Indochina Rebels Get Red-Built Radar Guns: Down Ten French Planes' from the New York *Herald Tribune*. The Trend of the Day (a picture of Justice Douglas, who had said he didn't want to be President) . . . A picture of Jimmy Demaret, winner of the Bing Crosby golf tournament, being kissed by Bob Hope. . . .

" 'That's Today in capsule. Cut to two minutes,' said Mr. Garroway. 'That is the day you are going to live.' Having seen it, he implied we were better equipped to face the world, to breast the slings and arrows of outrageous fortune. I don't know, though. About the only useful bit of information I gleaned from this capsule, repeated four times during the two hours, was a warning against inflammable sweaters, which I never wear anyway."

Crosby then tackled *Today*'s problems with its equipment: "Mr. Garroway wandered from machine to machine trying hard to make them fulfill their function. 'This is the telephoto machine,' he pointed out and asked the operator, 'Anything coming in?' 'Yes, the 25th division,' said the operator. Garroway tarried a bit waiting for the 25th division to spill out. It didn't and he moved away. . . . 'We're still waiting for Secretary of the Army, Frank Pace—expected any minute,' said an offstage voice. He never showed either. So we returned to Garroway seated at his huge horseshoe desk surrounded by clocks showing what time it was in, say, Tokyo. (Who the hell wants to know what time it is in Tokyo?)"

Jack Gould, the dean of the television critics, held his fire until Sunday in *The New York Times*. Gould was kinder than most of the other critics but still had some cutting observations. He said that in the "jargon of show business [the show] needs a lot of work." But while he found *Today* a disappointment, the troubles, Gould argued, could be overcome.

"Thus far, *Today* has been excessively pretentious and ostentatious and unreasonably confusing and complex," Gould wrote. "With all the variety of equipment around them, the Messrs. Garroway, Fleming and Lescoulie give the appearance of baffled fathers on Christmas morning who are intrigued with a new set of electric trains but are not quite sure how they work. . . . *Today*, in short, is the slave rather than the master of its own inventiveness and ingenuity."

About the only critic who liked the show was the Cleveland *Plain Dealer*'s man, and that was of little help in New York City, home of Madison Avenue and the nation's leading advertisers.

The poor reviews only added to the *Today* staff's major worries: viewer tune-outs and advertiser turn-offs. Perhaps no one would join the show's single sponsor, the Kiplinger magazine *Changing Times*, and fill the "recesses" built into the two-hour format to accommodate commercial messages. General David Sarnoff's own review summed up the nervous mood that permeated the show that bleak January morning and for months thereafter. Quoth the General: "Everyone smoked too much."

Pinkham and others at NBC dismissed the critics' reactions as a conspiracy by newspapers to undermine a competing advertising and news medium. And the enthusiasm and confidence of Weaver and Garroway helped reassure those connected with the show that *Today* would weather the storm. Garroway had such faith in the show that two months before its debut, with, according to him, "no financial resources to speak of," he rented a penthouse on Park Avenue, signing a four-year lease. Garroway still insists that the reviews did not alarm him.

Though Weaver weighed the constructive criticism in the reviews, he ignored the bad-mouthing, such as one critic's caustic suggestion: "Do yourself a favor, NBC, roll over and go back to sleep." Very much awake and thinking, Weaver remained the show's cheerleader and idea man, and its defender on the corporate level.

When he called an urgent meeting that first week, those who understood him knew that he would exude more charm than venom. James Nelson, who left book editing for the higher pay of broadcasting, was for years Weaver's amanuensis, paid to do for Pat "whatever routine tasks he didn't want to do himself." Nelson says that Weaver's magnetism was such that even the skeptics would "go along, thinking, 'Maybe he knows.'"

Weaver had no quarrel with the critical judgment that no one would watch *Today* for two hours. But despite uninspiring initial ratings, he believed that a million people would watch at least fifteen minutes and that another million would then get out of bed and turn their sets on. That was all he needed for success—fifteen minutes per customer. If morning radio could work, so could morning television. All he had to do was get the formula working right for TV and *Today* would succeed.

Unlike many corporate executives, Weaver managed to have fun on the job, and a limping morning broadcast wasn't going to change that. "Pat never gave the impression of being an executive," Nelson says of the man who was then NBC Television's chief executive and would become NBC president in 1953. "I was more at ease with him than with the NBC vice-presidents. One day I told him about a mistake, saying, 'Well, I loused that one up . . .' and he said, '*Well*, Nelson, *once more* and who do you know at Dumont?' "

Weaver kept a bongo board—a seesaw for the feet—in the office and often jumped on it, rocking back and forth to work off nervous energy while speaking to Nelson, other executives, and even to startled outsiders. He once told Nelson, "This character who is coming in next is a dreadful fellow. I'll have him try the bongo board and maybe he'll break an ankle."

Weaver even approached sticky discussions with relish. When a diminutive agent named Lastvogel—"Firstvogel" to Pat—came to complain, Weaver, who towered over the 4-foot-10-inch agent, reported back that "Firstvogel got so mad he bit me on the kneecap."

With Weaver conducting it, that urgent *Today* meeting during the first week went without recrimination or bombast. In recollection, Pinkham comments: "We all knew what we were supposed to do. We knew we were pioneering and didn't expect instantaneous success."

Weaver maintained his infectious enthusiasm, offered suggestions, and even followed up with a memo of congratulations: "You have done well in the first week. I have just read through a large assortment of fan mail, most of the critical press reviews, some inter-department information on the subject, and what I can find of the reaction from the stations.

"As usual, the public in part at least has sensed what we are trying to do for them; while the critics find us preoccupied with the miracles that the public wish. The recurring 'mountains labor and mouse emerges' note from the critics fails to realize that we bring mice to people who have only heard of mice hitherto, people whose letters thank us for showing them at last mice, for giving them a new horizon where mice will be commonplace. All this, before the fact that in addition to mice, we are and shall be bringing elephants."

Weaver gave his own critique of the show, conceding that "we are far from doing it right." Noting the criticism of inane remote pick-ups from abroad, he cautioned that "an interview should have a point," and that London shouldn't be called in to introduce a record. Planning would solve that problem, he said, for there were a "hundred interesting points-of-view" from London and other foreign capitals—human interest, obituaries, book publishing news. When in doubt, he said, just remember that the basic theme of *Today* is "what the people should know today, which is what happened yesterday as reported today plus what is actually happening now and is going to happen momentarily."

Weaver was unhappy with the use of the newspapers collected from across the land. The "right way" was to pass through at least some of the papers, identifying them, "cover the basic headline stories in some quickly understandable way . . . then show the regional and local differences." That idea would soon be abandoned as too unwieldy, quickly following the demise of the printed bulletin which marched across the bottom of the *Today* screen, adding to the confusing three-ring-circus effect of early broadcasts.

A note of exasperation crept in as Weaver noted that he had reread his original *Today* memo and suggested that all executives do the same: "Mark the things that are not being done, and which you are not trying to do. Unless reported back to me as abandoned, I am expecting that these things be done. I see no evidence of a book department as suggested . . . We did not show Falmouth or the Sierras or Ottawa well . . . No features were done on people as suggested which is also ok, because we are starting, but are we working on that?"

Weaver saw the need of the equivalent of a newspaper city editor, "who will make assignments including the story line to take, including the directions to both crew and reporter on what is to be done . . . with of course full authority to change for better presentation given to the man in charge of the remote."

Impatient with the lack of advertising support, Weaver spoke of the need to put "real pressure" on coffee, cigarette, orange juice, and "other naturals" among the companies who were logical advertisers for *Today*. He offered a selling approach tailored for the *Today* audience—his idea better than his syntax: "At this time, selling adroitly aimed at the all-family audience in terms of getting all-family approval of trademark brands, for purchase that day by the housewife, as she is preparing her thinking, at least, for marketing adds up to a new kind of selling opportunity. The kind of commercials that talk about the dinner that's coming up that night and the sort of things that could be used for dessert or dinner, the main course or the soup, etc., all leads to a possible family order with the woman, instead of doing the buying on her own initiative, now doing the buying on a family approved order. I think you see what I am driving at."

Weaver concluded with fervor, saying that he had been looking through the Hammond *Atlas* and an almanac and "couldn't help but feel" that the *Today* unit should be "bursting with projects" that will give "the full picture of our world . . . the cities, the rivers together with our solar system, etc., and a way of making it relevantly included in the *Today Show* whenever it comes up in the news."

CHAPTER 5

Shakedown Cruise

By the time television critics came around for a second look at *Today*, a few weeks after the launch, the show had improved considerably. In the New York *Morning Telegraph*, a racing newspaper, Leo Mishkin said that the show "actually does try" to give the customers some idea of what's going on in the world and what the coming day will be like. No longer was Garroway preoccupied with the gadgets: "Not once on those two mornings when I looked in did Mr. G run his fingers over an electric typewriter with an astonished look on his face, not once did he pause in front of a teletype machine to gaze at the copy in mute wonder, not once did he forget to have that trick microphone around his neck."

Yet a remote from the Fulton Fish Market, Mishkin said, produced more shots of the back of the commentator's head than of fish and fishmongers. If the helter-skelter quality was gone, it hadn't quite been replaced with sure-footed professionalism, in Mishkin's eyes.

John Crosby commented in the *Tribune* on Garroway's

aplomb among the miracles of technology and a new sophistication in execution: "Now Garroway and his two assistants, James Fleming and Jack Lescoulie, telephone Frankfurt to find out what's happening there rather than just for the sake of wasting NBC's money," Crosby wrote. "There are still occasions when Mr. Lescoulie says, 'Come in, Milwaukee,' and Milwaukee doesn't. This leaves Mr. Garroway, Mr. Lescoulie and the communications business with egg on its chin, and the rest of us devoured with curiosity as to what Milwaukee had on its mind."

Crosby was still complaining about those clocks and NBC's determination to tell him what time it was in Tokyo despite his "passionate protest" that he couldn't care less. Commenting about a remote from the Bureau of Engraving showing dollar bills racing out of the printing presses, Crosby wryly observed that most of that money was probably destined "to line Garroway's pockets." This was a tacit prediction by Crosby that *Today* would probably become quite profitable, though there was as yet little evidence of this at Radio City.

The Bureau of Engraving feature might have been a sore reminder to NBC cost accountants of the rate at which the *Today Show* was spending money, while making surprisingly slow headway with major advertisers. Small fry saved NBC the embarrassment of a totally unsponsored two hours, but didn't fill major commercial gaps. There was an Appian Way Pizza spot, an example of Weaver's theory that the little guy could afford *Today* even if he couldn't afford other television. The dry-mix pizza was made not far from Radio City, and the owner journeyed in at the end of each accounting period to pay the tariff in person.

Knox Gelatine, another early advertiser, captured the audience's attention with its commercial: Mrs. Gladys Malm, the well-padded wife of a Brooklyn minister, melted away almost before the viewers' eyes on a Knox Eat and Reduce Plan. Bank-rolled by NBC, Mrs. Malm would diet all week, pay a precautionary visit to the NBC doctor, then have her hair done. As the fat fell, she would buy new outfits before her regular Monday appearance on *Today*. Each week she mounted the scale as the camera watched and then silhouetted herself against a chalk rendering of her former 171-pound self. In one week on the Gelatine she dropped a satisfying six pounds and lost a full two inches around the hips. She was weighed and measured by Bess Myerson, a former Miss America, for a subliminal message, perhaps, that only a boxcar figure stood in the way of a glamorous career. Knox Gelatine and the *Today Show* eventually went through three fat ladies in one year.

But total advertising revenues continued to lag behind projections. A dog food commercial was a big plus, raising spirits and giving Garroway something more to talk about. Unlike the network newscasters who sailed above the commercial world on a contamination-free magic carpet, Garroway pitched products and pitched them well. The commercials—all of them live—were not without hazards, however, for Garroway and everybody else.

One day a puppy was placed as usual on a big white card to have his sponsor's breakfast, as Garroway talked his way up to the commercial. Just before the camera turned to the dog, the pup did what he should have done before he arrived at the studio, depositing a lump so large in the middle of the white card that the production crew was astonished. The young floor director in charge of the commercial panicked, but producer Mort Werner simply leaned over and scooped with his hands. As the camera moved in, the puppy was seen serenely gobbling his favorite dog food.

Mort quietly walked over to the badly shaken floor director —low man on the production totem pole—smiled, and said, "I want to show you the difference between floor director and producer." With that he opened his hands and said, "To be a producer is to have the ability to handle this."

Mort Werner was a pragmatist who was as unimpressed with the quality of the early shows as were the critics. Restless and quietly impatient, he felt the show "just died on the air" in those early months. Werner's creative instinct and willingness to try anything brought a variety of changes, weekly and sometimes daily, as he improvised to save Weaver's morning dream. A succession of pretty girls was provided by press agent Jim Moran for light relief. Garroway would do, say, an obituary of a world-famous scientist and be deeply moved, then shift gears smoothly, unabashedly introducing "Miss E. Z. Pop," a buxom blonde, or "Miss Concrete Life Preserver," a well-endowed brunette.

Some things worked well from the beginning. Despite the clutter, Garroway and company managed the camaraderie Weaver had hoped for. It was early morning "happy talk" as then news editor Gerald Green described it—"long before ABC News ever thought of it."

One pert and fresh-looking girl on the show was given to genuinely impulsive gestures like straightening Garroway's bow tie. She was charged with calling Washington for weather bureau reports, which she then wrote on the studio blackboard. Garroway, if momentarily stumped for something to talk about, would often say, "Estelle, you know more about this than I do, you tell 'em!" or "Hey, Estelle, what's going on there?" and Estelle would interrupt her chores and give Garroway a flip or amusing answer. As did most of the on-air staff, she thrived on informality and improvisation. Once when Ava Gardner skipped a *Today* appearance at the last minute, Garroway interviewed Estelle as though she were the temptestuous actress.

Estelle sang with dance bands on Long Island on weekends

during her *Today* years. She eventually made it big not on television or the bandstand but as a movie actress. In 1967 her role in *Bonnie and Clyde* led to an Academy Award: "To Estelle Parsons for Best Supporting Actress."

With NBC News as supportive as an aging rodeo champion teaching a talented greenhorn the ropes, *Today* had to develop its own news staff and techniques. And it did, rapidly, for *Today* staffers were hungry, talented, and creative. Newscaster Jim Fleming, formerly a foreign correspondent and editor of an excellent radio program, *Voices and Events*, was a broadcast journalist of distinction. Fleming had hired Gerald Green away from International News Service to be *Today*'s news editor. Green, a Phi Beta Kappa, got on well with Garroway. He fascinated the star by poring over the *Journal of the American Anthropology Association* in his spare minutes. Later Green wrote the novel *The Last Angry Man*. But for now he had his hands full. Backed by Mort Werner, who "helped hold things together," Green fought the trench coat brigade from NBC News. Green describes himself as the "point man" in the battle—an infantry term for the man who draws the enemy's main fire.

It was an uphill fight. As early as March 1952, the ratings were so bad the staff thought *Today* would be going off the air. From the beginning, Green recalls, "the NBC news department hated *Today*, tried to discredit and sabotage it. They really wanted it to die. We'd have been better off if we had been a part of the news department instead of a rival, separate entity. I had to meet with them every morning."

During those sessions, Green says, News blatantly worked to destroy *Today*. "We couldn't get NBC films," he says. "There were always convenient ways of keeping exciting news footage off the *Today Show*." Often they would be "reserved" for John Cameron Swayze and the *Camel News Caravan*—at 7:45 P.M.

47

Green drummed up an effective news routine, deciding to do both "A" and "B" news. The "A" news was to be an on-the-hour report, featuring the lead stories of the day. If there were good pictures, fine. If not, Fleming could always read the hard news without illustration. The key element in choosing items for the spot was their importance. The "B" news came on the half hour. Those who missed the on-the-hour report got an update. There would be a minute to a minute and a half of headlines and then the softer stuff—films of routine fires, minor riots, etc.

"I did it that way because I knew I was competing with radio news on the hour," Green explains. "Not a great invention, perhaps, but I think it was mine."

Green watched NBC's prime news feature the *Camel News Caravan*. The show would run a news film with a voice-over, a disembodied narration from a staff announcer. Jerry felt he could improve on that technique. He began sending reporters right to the scene of the story—Joe Michaels, who now does television editorials for NBC's local station in New York City, or Paul Cunningham, who left *Today* recently to become London correspondent for NBC. Michaels would take a mobile unit to a disaster area—a midnight fire at Wanamaker's perhaps —film the story, and return to the studio to develop and edit it with Green, who worked all night. During the *Today* broadcast, Michaels would come into the studio and say to Garroway, "I was on a terrific story earlier today," then give his eyewitness account with *Today*'s own footage.

Green insists *Today* scooped the NBC television news department in using reporters' own live narrations with film stories. The only other show doing that, he says, was Edward R. Murrow's *See It Now* on CBS. He adds that NBC finally got around to it with the *Huntley-Brinkley Report*. "We pioneered and I don't give a shit who says we didn't, it's true."

The *Today* reporters sometimes worked on features that

took as much as two weeks' preparation. But it was the overnight work that exhausted the staff. Burroughs Prince—"Buck" in a business impatient with jawbreaker names—once arrived at 2 A.M. for his overnight editorial assignment, glanced at the schedule left by the day side, and read the words "Cleveland, Armory." Buck figured it was another of Pat Weaver's going-places-and-doing-things ideas, and he called the NBC traffic department to ask whether everything was set for the Armory remote in Cleveland.

Traffic said, "What?"

Buck replied, "I said Cleveland Armory."

Traffic: "I've got nothing for Cleveland."

Buck: "Well, you better get on the ball, because there's one there all right."

Traffic: "The day side won't even be in at Cleveland. I'm not waking anybody at 3 A.M."

It wasn't enough that the whole news department was fighting the show, now Traffic was making waves. Buck called Cleveland himself. The station knew nothing about the remote, but since Cleveland was one of the five television stations NBC owned and operated itself, Prince was able to order a producer, reporter, and mobile unit to the armory, plus the necessary telephone lines to bring the remote broadcast into the New York studio.

When Mort Werner walked in at 4 A.M., Prince, who had to write a lead-in for the story, asked the producer, "What's this pick-up from the Cleveland Armory all about?"

Werner was baffled, so Buck showed him the schedule. "That's Cleveland *Amory*, the author!" said Werner, some $3,000 into the phantom Ohio remote.

Those early morning hours were hard for everyone to get used to. Once *Today* planned a remote telecast from the George Washington Bridge. *Today* staffer Len Safire, whose brother Bill is now a *New York Times* columnist, woke with a start that morning with just half an hour to make it to the bridge. Unshaven and uncombed, he ran out of his midtown apartment into the pre-dawn, drawing a coat over his pajamas. Racing to a cab with his slippers flapping, he yelled into the driver's window, "Take me to the George Washington Bridge!"

"Which end?" asked the driver.

"Neither," said Safire. "Take me to the middle!"

Looking at the wild-eyed disheveled figure before him, the cab driver replied, "Not in this cab, you ain't!" He roared off, leaving Safire at the curb.

It was during this period that Buck Prince received a visit from a young woman just out of college. She walked into his office one day to ask for a job. Buck said he didn't have one, but she persisted.

"She and I talked for a long while," he recalls. "Finally she got up and said, 'One day everyone is going to know about me at NBC and I hope you're going to be around to remember this visit.'" With that parting shot, Barbara Walters rose and left Prince's office.

Buck Prince was also the man who got former President Harry Truman on the show—almost. Truman was invited to appear on *Today* while visiting New York City. He was only one of many—fashion designers and fashion queens, artists and actors—who balked at *Today* invitations in those early days. The show wasn't regarded as important, at least not important enough to awake at dawn and appear on television with blinking eyes and body chemistry out of whack. Early riser though he was, Truman politely declined.

But someone in the *Today* company knew a man in Truman's entourage. Figuring that Truman would take his usual early morning constitutional while *Today* was being broadcast, the staffer asked the Truman aide to guide the Chief past the RCA Exhibition Hall window. As the former President approached, Buck Prince aimed a camera through the window and waved the ever-present sidewalk superintendents aside so he could focus on Truman's brisk approach while a young reporter rushed outside with a mike.

As the reporter approached, Truman realized he had been tricked, but laughed and prepared to submit to the interview good-naturedly. Jerry Green signaled frantically for Truman to come in. The young reporter caught the signal and said, "Mr. President, Dave Garroway would love to say hello to you." But as Truman obligingly stepped forward, his companion, old friend George Jessel, took his arm and reminded him that Jessel's television variety show was on the rival ABC network. Truman deferred to his friend and declined the interview, and *Today* had to settle for half a scoop that morning.

Some guests were far more eager than Truman, even in the beginning. After author Fleur Cowles appeared on the first *Today Show* broadcast, her book *Bloody Precedent* did so well that it started a legend in publishing—justifiable to a degree—that *Today* was the best single medium anywhere for selling books. Authors clamored for a *Today* gig in the hope that their books would land in that tiny bull's-eye of best-sellers reached by the merest handful of books out of some 20,000 published each year.

Part of the problem from the guests' point of view was that they couldn't just do a brief spot and then go home to sleep. The show was aired live from New York. But 7 A.M. in New York was 6 A.M. in Chicago—the western terminus in the early months. There was no video tape then, and a film of the first hour couldn't be developed in time to repeat in the Central Time Zone. Thus, if *Today* billed a guest for 7 A.M. in New

York, he or she would have to wait around to do a repeat performance of that first hour at 9 A.M.—8 A.M in the Central Zone.

Norbert Wiener, the mathematician and logician who had an important role in developing high-speed electronic computers, found himself sharing that time-killing problem with Yankee star Mickey Mantle, who had been booked for a guest appearance on the same show.

As absent-minded as he was brilliant, Wiener once stopped to chat with someone on campus. He then asked where he was coming from when they met, and when told from the faculty club, commented: "Oh, good. Then I've had my lunch." Wiener had just completed his book on cybernetics, a subject that fascinated Garroway. Asking in passing about baseball during the 7 A.M. interview, Wiener told Garroway that while the other boys were swinging bats, he was flipping pages of Plautus and the comedies of Terence. During the recess between the first and third hours, Richard Pinkham took Wiener and Mantle to the Cromwell drugstore in Radio City, where NBC provided breakfast for its *Today* guests. Pinkham was nervous with Wiener, since every time Pinkham started a sentence Wiener would know what he was going to ask and answer before Pinkham could finish his question.

"Imagine how disconcerting this was to Mickey Mantle, who didn't know himself how he was going to finish his sentences!" Pinkham says. Somehow Mantle got through breakfast without striking out, and the three men—a baffled trio, or duo at least—returned for the reprise.

While *Today* was basically a news program, Garroway's informality and willingness to improvise allowed humor to creep in. Everyone knew this was a big plus for the show. Besides, humor was a Pat Weaver dictate. And Weaver believed that it takes three to tangle.

"You need a stooge," he says. "A third person to kick off little pieces of business. You get more laughs than you do with just two people talking garbage."

The man who provided the needed third person for the humor role was Jack Lescoulie. Years earlier, when Lescoulie was about twenty, the tall, blond, open-faced man originated a radio show called *The Grouch Club*, which Jerry Green remembered as "very funny." Green thought it funny enough that "Lescoulie probably should have been chosen for a situation comedy."

Not everyone agreed with Green's assessment. Pinkham calls him "one of the nicest men alive, whose single talent is a nice smile. When Dave took a day off and Jack had to take over the broadcast, the first thing he always did was to go to the nearest blackboard and say, 'I want you to know what my name is,' and he wrote it on the blackboard with a piece of chalk."

Pinkham would have to agree that even *his* Lescoulie wasn't a bad choice for the *Today* buffoon. Green explains how Lescoulie filled that role: "Dave would have little things to read. If the last item was to be about a boomerang, I would grab Lescoulie by the seat of the pants and say, 'Think of a boomerang joke.' And he would be funny."

The show's format included skits to further leaven its heavy diet of news. Lescoulie was seen in a takeoff of George Bernard Shaw's *Caesar and Cleopatra* in a Roman toga and crowned with a laurel wreath, the much-commented-on *Today Show* lavaliere mike, more than a foot long, rising from his waist, "looking as though it was part of him," as one critic remarked. The siren of the Nile was played by the voluptuous Jayne Mansfield.

Slapstick, imitations, and parodies abounded, perhaps justifying the critics' misgivings about *Today*'s serious purpose. Jerry Green would do his impression of Groucho Marx doing *You Bet Your Life*. The show parodied man-on-the-street interviews with disguised members of the cast. Garroway's gag writer, Harvey Bullock, now in Hollywood, would take news off the wires and write amusing variations, sometimes building skits around them.

It was all part of a continuing effort to brighten up the show, and some of the leavening worked well. But with a $2-million annual budget, *Today*'s advertising revenues remained anemic, and heavy losses continued to pile up.

CHAPTER 6

Selling the Show

Despite the improving quality of the *Today Show* through its first year, the NBC front office was unhappy, very unhappy. Big advertisers remained indifferent, and leading ad agencies yawned at the idea of a morning television show as an advertising vehicle.

One of the first weapons *Today*'s staff seized upon in their efforts to open sponsor coffers was the response the show was eliciting from the public. In its first two weeks the show received 65,000 unsolicited letters, many of them from towns and cities poorly served by newspapers. Surely there ought to be some way to make this broad base of support work for the show, turn some national advertisers from print media to *Today*. For the letters weren't the usual complaints from soreheads and malcontents, but raves and thank-yous. And their diversity was heartening and impressive.

"Twenty of us on the faculty now meet every morning at the Faculty Club for breakfast," wrote the dean of the School of Architecture at a southern university. "We watch the show in its entirety and we are well up on current events—much more so than when we read our local newspaper."

That same day, a woman wrote from Providence that she'd like to watch all two hours but electricity was too expensive. "And please, Mr. Garroway, say something about the kiddies —they've got to get dressed and get out to school or they'll be late."

Some of the few complaints had their positive implications. School principals reported tardiness when *Today* featured a jet plane tracing the historic flight of the first Army bomber to fly from Washington to New York. While the original flight took three hours, the jet reached Mitchell Field on Long Island in only sixteen minutes. But some of the kids who stuck around to see it land missed buses or were otherwise late for classes.

At meetings between *Today* executives and ad agency account executives, NBC page boys would march in and, with dramatic flair, dump postal sacks full of unopened *Today* mail on a large conference table. The *Today* people then passed out letter openers and let the advertising men slit the envelopes and read for themselves. They were told that if they didn't like what they read, they could forget *Today*. Otherwise they'd have to listen to the pitch that Dave Garroway would then deliver.

Garroway was NBC's main weapon in the intense effort to interest national advertisers in *Today*. Pinkham, wanting to expose potential clients to the phenomenal Garroway, could occasionally become overeager. He once invited an advertising prospect to be a guest at a golf outing with Garroway at Pinkham's club, Apawamis, in Rye, New York. Pinkham improvised, telling the man they would go to Rye in Dave's car.

The advertiser, a "straight kind of guy" according to Pinkham, stood with the executive producer on a Manhattan street corner as Dave drove up in his beautifully maintained Jaguar

XK 100, a vivid yellow roadster with chromium-plated super-
chargers jutting from the sides of the hood. Pinkham then
noticed in dismay that the car had only two seats for the three
big men. When they arrived in Rye, thirty miles away, Apawamis club members saw Garroway at the wheel, his executive producer at his side, and "this dignified and important
man" crouched on Pinkham's lap.

Pinkham and Garroway got on well, Pinkham believes,
partly because of an evening early in their relationship. Garroway had invited several friends and associates to his Park Avenue penthouse to play chess. Garroway is said to be a chess
whiz, while Pinkham says he plays erratically and by instinct.
Dick had serious misgivings when Garroway announced that
Pinkham would be his first adversary that evening. Pinkham
figured Garroway wouldn't respect an executive producer
who fizzled at chess, but he never got a chance to find out.
Pinkham got lucky, polishing off Garroway three times in a
short span of time.

There was more gamesmanship later when Garroway and
Pinkham flew to the West Coast to pursue those elusive advertisers. They played Scrabble, for money, all the way, and
when they landed for a stopover in Salt Lake City, Pinkham
led wordmaster Garroway by $200. But on final landing in
Los Angeles, Garroway had pulled even. Pinkham never told
Garroway that under a deal with NBC, Pinkham kept his
winnings while his losses to Garroway were underwritten by
the network.

The West Coast trip was part of an exhausting show-and-
tell routine for Garroway. Under the format, Garroway led
off, jollying the crowd in his pleasantly eccentric manner, often
telling his favorite story to illustrate what a good line could
do to get attention. He had seen a man with a cane on the

street one day, he'd say, with a sign reading, "It's spring and I'm blind." The hard sell was then done by Pinkham. In Los Angeles things went according to plan. Garroway sat down and sank into a half-awake state as Pinkham recited his carefully written text. But Garroway's subconscious was evidently at work. When they arrived in San Francisco, Garroway rose for the warm-up and to Pinkham's dismay recited a Garrowayan treatment of Pinkham's Los Angeles speech, unaware that he was using, and using up, all of Pinkham's material. This time, when Garroway introduced his colleague and sat down, Pinkham was speechless.

It would not have made much difference. Advertisers remained indifferent no matter what Dave and Dick told them. They all knew that the ratings for *Today* were awful—even by the minimal standards set for early morning hours—and were getting worse. Potential advertisers were skeptical, and they needed more than fan mail and a Garroway-Pinkham pitch to be convinced to take the plunge. They received little further urging, for there was no follow-through by the NBC sales staff.

Today's staff believed that the NBC salesmen were more interested in the Milton Berle show and other hot NBC attractions because they were easy to sell. On the way out of a prospect's office they were inclined to say, in effect, "Oh, you don't want to buy *Today*, do you?" That way they were in the clear when Pat Weaver's lieutenants asked if they were offering the show.

Meanwhile, Weaver was extremely busy with the entire NBC programing schedule and had less time to give to *Today*. John Kingsley Herbert, formerly a magazine publisher, was brought in and given overall responsibility for the morning show. His big job was to get *Today* out of the red, and he knew it would not be an easy matter. After seven months on the air, *Today* was losing money at an annual rate of $1.7

million. And Herbert knew he would receive no help from the NBC news department. They wanted no share of the blame if and when *Today* failed.

In August, Herbert called Pinkham and said, "There are two ways to make a go of this thing. One is you've got to get the ratings up, and the other is we've got to assign a salesman specifically to sell it. I've handled the latter by hiring a guy named Matthew J. Culligan, a supersalesman from the magazine field. He lives out your way, in Rye. Matter of fact, he's a member of your golf club."

When Pinkham finished a round of golf at Apawamis that Saturday, he decided to look for Culligan. He went to the caddy master and said, "Do you know a member named Joe Culligan?"

The caddy master said yes, and Pinkham asked for a description. "He's a nice-looking guy," said the caddy master. "About your size, about your age."

Pinkham figured the description fit dozens of members and asked if Culligan had any distinguishing characteristics.

"No . . . just another guy," said the caddy master. But as Pinkham walked away, the caddy master had an afterthought. "Oh, wait a minute. One more thing. He's got a black patch over one eye."

In the waning moments of the Battle of the Bulge, a German lobbed a plastic egg grenade toward Joe Culligan, and he was hit with twenty-two pieces of shrapnel, losing an eye. Thinking himself reasonably lucky, Culligan explained to his buddies that if he had to lose one of all the things he had two of, he would rather it was an eye.

The eye patch eventually led to a secondary career for Culligan as the Hathaway Shirt man. Those who saw the Hathaway ads noticed first what the caddy master nearly forgot to mention. But it wasn't Culligan's dashing appearance that led Jack Herbert, who had once been his boss at *Good Housekeeping,* to hire him. It was his sales ability and his optimism—equally important qualities in those gloomy days of *Today.*

Jerry Green remembers his first encounter with the man brought in to head *Today*'s sales. "I walked into this little office next to mine," says Green, "and there was this nice-looking Irish guy with a patch on his eye. He had gotten up brochures to show why *Today* was a great buy. Meanwhile, we were in a panic over the low ratings."

Culligan and Green exchanged introductions, and Green said he thought Culligan had boarded a sinking ship. But Culligan, according to Green, came back ebulliently to say, "I'm not worried. All we need is a couple of big ones. Get a GM and a food company, and the show will be a success."

Green didn't believe Culligan could do it, but he was encouraged. He liked Culligan and hoped he would carry it off: "We were both typical New Yorkers and had good vibes right away."

If Green and the others had known Culligan's orders, they might have been scrambling for the nearest exit. Culligan had been told: "Save it or we'll scuttle it."

Culligan remembers that Jack Herbert was under "terrible pressure" from Pat Weaver to get *Today* out of the red. Culligan signed on because he was anxious to switch from magazines to television. He thus took the job for less than half the $25,000 he had been making as advertising director for Ziff-Davis publications. Herbert could only afford to pay $12,000.

Money didn't bother Culligan. What vexed the man was that he had been hired without the knowledge of his new boss, NBC sales executive George Fry. "Fry was so mad that he wouldn't approve me for the payroll. I had no office either. So I went to Pinkham and he got me on the talent payroll. I used to line up with the actresses at NBC and get paid cash in a brown envelope."

It was more than four months before Culligan finally appeared on the regular payroll. NBC officially records Culligan's hiring on January 1, 1953. Meanwhile, Pinkham got Culligan his cubicle next to Jerry Green. A young producer, Greg Garrison, who recently produced NBC's fiftieth-anniversary show, used to drop by to enliven dull mornings by serenading Culligan's secretary Ethel Smok with the ballad "On Top of Old Smokey." After one of those morning sings, Miss Smok muttered to Culligan, "If he wasn't such a good source of free tickets, I'd kill the s.o.b."

Realizing it was hopeless to depend on the NBC sales staff, Culligan hired three NBC guides as trainees. They were Bob Bonagura, who now sells for CBS, Bill Asip, now on Wall Street, and Dick Sewell, now a marketing manager at a large package goods company. The three youngsters, said Culligan, had no experience but "lots of personal charm and dedication." They would need it. And, of course, there was Garroway to help with sales. Culligan would call old friends in advertising agencies and ask for time to make a presentation before the media department.

"When they all assembled, I would walk in with Garroway. He would lean on the podium and talk with such charm and literacy about what he was intending to do with the *Today Show* that we got the first nibbles."

It would be months, however, before Culligan and his youthful sales force clicked. The show limped on, looking for scoops and attention-getters, working overnight to add to the show's growing news reputation. But something was clearly missing, some little touch that would grab and hold audiences, make the nation wake up and take notice.

That something walked into an NBC elevator on February 2, 1953, wearing a diaper.

CHAPTER 7

The Ape and the Eye Patch

In late January 1953, Dick Pinkham was sitting in the big corner office he shared with Mort Werner when Len Safire entered and announced, "There's something next door you've got to see."

Pinkham followed Safire to the NBC casting office's waiting room, and there, Pinkham says, was "a young guy with the most adorable animal I ever saw sitting on his lap and sucking formula from a plastic bottle." It was a baby chimpanzee, owned by two young men, Carmine "Buddy" Menella and Roy Waldron. Both owners were former NBC pages.

"He's great, put him on tomorrow," Pinkham said. "But Len suggested, 'How about putting him on every day?' " They did put J. Fred Muggs on every day, and thus began a new era in the *Today Show*. The critics were appalled to see an ape sharing honors with *Today*'s serious newsmen, and that feeling was shared by some members of the news staff as well. But most of the *Today* team were delighted as the show began to get heavy press coverage. And not a moment too soon.

By its first anniversary, two weeks before J. Fred loped into television land, *Today* was being seen in forty cities—up from the initial thirty-one. Its audience was a dedicated one. The folks at home were learning to dress with one eye on the box and one on their socks. Some mounted their TVs on casters, others rigged mirrors to see around corners, and one man used main force, knocking down a wall between his breakfast nook and living room. And they weren't just watching for fifteen minutes at a time, as Pat Weaver had expected. After a poll showed that male viewers devoted forty-five minutes to *Today* and female viewers fifty-three minutes, Garroway and associates stopped repeating themselves every few minutes and did one show from the 7 to 8 A.M. rush and a second for the more leisurely 8 to 9 crowd. There was clear-cut evidence that the show was reaching rural America and that rural America cared. On New Year's Day 1953, Dave Garroway wondered out loud who on earth would be looking at TV at 7 A.M. that morning. A plea for postcards brought Garroway over 8,000 pieces of mail. He once offered a free issue of a magazine and got 20,000 requests.

And yet, the show was still struggling. Devoted as it was, the total audience wasn't large enough to impress advertisers. The show had forty-four sponsors, including seasonal ones—not enough to make the show a money-winner for NBC. Then came Muggs.

As Pinkham sees it, J. Fred Muggs served the same purpose for *Today* as a comic strip serves for a newspaper. Just as the children would grab the comics when the daily newspaper landed on the doorstep, they began monopolizing the television set from the moment Muggs made his appearance. Everyone was entranced, it seemed, except for J. Fred Coots, a member in good standing of ASCAP and the composer of "Santa Claus Is Coming to Town." Coots sued, charging a deliberate effort to embarrass him. He might better have suffered in si-

lence. He lost the case, while winning unwelcome publicity.
The nation's kids, meantime, were ecstatic as J. Fred (Muggs)
cavorted through the studio, dismantling Jack Lescoulie's desk,
leaping from here to there, hooting at the sidewalk observers.

Young viewers guarded the TV dial like goalies protecting
the nets at Madison Square Garden, threatening tears or may-
hem if a parent tried to change channels. Consequently, parents who had shunned *Today* the whole first year suddenly
became involuntary regulars. Though captive at first, many
became fans, discovering that *Today* was a good news show.
The ratings went up like a rocket. J. Fred Muggs captured
that elusive audience the advertising prospects had demanded.
Now it was up to Joe Culligan and his boys to convince them
what a good deal *Today* was, particularly for the small advertiser.

"It was like Weaver said," Culligan explains. "If an advertiser bought a half-hour program on, say, a Friday, he might
reach 10 million people in the course of half an hour's exposure
of prime time—once a week. But an advertiser could get the
same low cost per thousand viewers on *Today* and without
spending a fortune. For example, Goodyear paid $3.6 million
to buy thirty-nine weeks of alternate sponsorship on a half-
hour show in prime time in the early 1950s. But a small company could be on national television with a budget of less than
$250,000 if the company chose *Today*.

"No other medium offered the *Today* exposure," Culligan
continues. "What we had to do was to persuade the advertisers
that they were reaching enough people for their purposes and
also that they got a screened audience with a high potential
for needing their product."

Dow Chemical was one of the first of the national companies to take the bait, at an affordable quarter of a million dollars. Culligan explains that Dow was just introducing Saran
Wrap. Ads for the new product reached the housewives at

breakfast, when they might be removing leftovers from the refrigerator to make, say, a ham omelet. What better time to show them a new transparent wrapper?

"Garroway would hold Saran Wrap over the camera lens to show how clear it was," Culligan recalls, "and he then smiled through it and into the TV lens. Saran Wrap thus became a dominating national brand on the strength of a modest advertising budget on the *Today Show*."

Other advertisers soon followed. As Culligan sees it, *Today* became the minor league of television advertising. Scores of advertisers got their first experience with TV advertising on *Today*, as did dozens of small advertising agencies through their small clients. Culligan became a hero to the *Today* staff as more and more advertisers joined the show through his efforts and those of his young trainees. In time, Polaroid joined the family of sponsors. Garroway, Culligan, and other members of the production staff bought stock in the picture-in-a-minute company and "made lots of money," Culligan adds.

Garroway, who did commercials from the beginning, was an accommodating man. When Fedders advertised its air conditioners on *Today*, two tons of shaved ice were dumped on the street outside the studio in midsummer. Dave then walked outside to do his live commercials for Fedders sitting on the ice.

Easy to work with though Garroway was, he did set limits. Once Culligan got a letter from a sponsor complaining in a nice way about a slighting reference Garroway had made concerning their product, Rennit junket—"a most unattractive food," as Culligan admits. They were an important advertiser, so Culligan wrote to Garroway saying, "Look, Dave, I've got a problem . . ." The next day Culligan got a note from Dave that said, "Look, Joe, if I can't say I don't like Rennit Mix, I can't say I don't like anything."

Culligan says he bothered Dave with a special request only once after that. The following Christmas the ad agency Batten

Barton Durstin & Osborne appealed to Culligan to get Dave to wear a Santa Claus hat. Culligan wrote Garroway again, stating, "I've got a problem . . ." Garroway wrote back, "Dear Joe: It took me twenty years to get to the point where I could make a decent living without wearing funny hats. But I'll do it if you really want me to." Says Culligan: "Of course I withdrew the request."

Garroway was also regarded as being very careful about commercials that might be deemed offensive at breakfast. Win Welpen, who was in charge of commercials at *Today*, remembers that Tuffy Pads, a plastic cleaning product, had an advertising line that read: "Tuffy Pads remove icky dirt." Would Garroway say it? Welpen knew even before he asked Dave. There was simply no way Dave Garroway was going to say such an ugly word as "icky" to the orange juice and corn flakes crowd. Welpen recalls that Dave and he attended a heavy advertising agency meeting to discuss the pros and cons of the word "icky" in the slogan.

"No matter what point the agency guys put forth, Dave felt so strongly about the word, he wouldn't say it—even if Tuffy canceled," Welpen says. Finally, it was agreed that Dave would say, "Tuffy Pads remove *sticky* dirt," though the line on the TV screen read "icky."

The ads continued to roll in. Smuckers, a tiny jam company, became a well-known national brand, and the metamorphosis was seen again and again with other companies. *Today* was, at last, beginning to make it in the ratings, with a powerful assist from J. Fred Muggs. Pinkham says that "wretched little ape" did more to put *Today* over the top than *Today*'s news coverage.

If Dick Pinkham and Mort Werner had known more about the effect of the flow of testosterone on adolescent male subgorillas, they might have thought twice about making ten-month-old J. Fred Muggs co-host of the *Today Show*.

In the beginning, J. Fred lived up to his promise as the show's comic strip. His studio capers brought an army of infant fans and a mass captive audience of their elders. *Today*'s commercial success assured by the increased ratings, the show's staffers abandoned their morale-sapping on-the-set habit of reading the help-wanted ads every thirteen weeks as cancellation time rolled around.

J. Fred showed up every day between his two owners, his trainer Buddy Menella and Roy Waldron. The two ex-NBC pages kept Muggs clean-shaven and diapered (chimps grow beards early in life), and dressed him as a little boy. In no time, Muggs was earning upwards of $500 a week; Buddy and Roy had paid only $600 for him upon arrival from West Africa. Mostly, Muggs was lovable, delightfully unpredictable, and intelligent—far brighter than other chimps that did guest appearances from time to time. In four years of *Today* broadcasts, the maturing Muggs grew to understand (and sometimes to ignore) the meaning of five hundred words. He could count with his fingers, do cartwheels, raise his arms to be taken to the toilet, play the piano—or at least "ape" guest star Steve Allen's ivory-tickling—and, as one news magazine put it, "perform numerous other monkeyshines, including raising TV ratings." He could even spank himself, though some say he didn't do that often enough.

Typically, Muggs would be found by *Today*'s cameras sitting next to or on the lap of Garroway, his leash mostly concealed and held tightly by Buddy or Roy, who hid under Garroway's desk. Dave would talk with Muggs, interview him, and generally appear to enjoy him, though it was an open secret at Radio City that the two were on-again, off-again pals. Garroway discussed his differences with Muggs philosophically and illustrated his ambivalence toward the chimp in a story. Once, after a series of exasperating escapades, J. Fred climbed atop a camera and teetered over high-voltage wires,

68

threatening unwittingly to fry himself at any moment. That left Garroway alarmed and hopeful by turns, until Muggs finally climbed to safety. Garroway was not above mild teasing. On one occasion, Muggs sat on Garroway's lap and as the chimp looked away briefly, Dave donned a fright mask. Muggs looked at Garroway again and screeched in terror. Garroway removed the mask, and Muggs threw his arms around him in joy and relief—an impulsive act that Garroway found irresistible.

As Muggs' importance grew, the writers looked for ways to put him in skits. Muggs had friends in for his birthday party, and the three chimps demolished a birthday cake with perverse glee, throwing pieces of it across the studio. Lower lip thrust forward, Muggs imitated Popeye the Sailor Man—in a Popeye suit—and impersonated a Hollywood director done up in a plaid jacket, beret, and cigarette holder and seated in a director's chair. He eventually accumulated 450 outfits, not counting diapers. Though he was billed as housebroken, he occasionally made mistakes and was changed like any damp infant. Among other costumes, Muggs acquired a set of tails and what men like to call a monkey suit—a tuxedo—not to mention the inevitable gorilla suit.

The formal attire was useful for dedicating supermarkets, which J. Fred Muggs was constantly being asked to do. He also whacked newly commissioned naval vessels with champagne at the behest of admiring naval officers. But that was freelance. What he mostly did was run amok at *Today*, developing a shrewd sense of his importance and power. He mastered the uses of the red "tally" lights that indicate which camera is on, and he did it in a fraction of the time Sally Quinn would later require on a competing CBS morning show. Muggs quickly discovered that nobody could punish him when the tally light was on, so he'd bang Garroway or grab his glasses by the tally's red glow and duck as soon as it went off.

His trainers tried behavior modification, rehearsing Muggs while flicking the tally lights on and off at random, punishing Muggs when the lights were on and not when the lights were off. But they didn't fool him for long. Soon he was back to his old tricks, battering Garroway with impunity and ducking only when the camera was off.

The chimp was not without a memory and some sense of logic. Paul Cunningham, a *Today Show* writer and reporter who liked Muggs more than some, explained: "He was a friendly little guy and would come by and shake hands every day. But one day I was busy typing and as he came by gesturing and reaching out for me, I said, 'Go way, don't bother me.' He didn't forget it. When he came back, approaching me from behind, he banged me with the back of his hand and nearly flipped me into my typewriter."

That was the trouble. Muggs was somewhat uncontrollable, even in the beginning. His antics even caused an international incident. It was during Queen Elizabeth's coronation in 1953, a few months after J. Fred Muggs joined the show. There was no satellite pick-up then, and *Today* was using direct-sound broadcast of the procession, supplementing it with newly received news photographs. From time to time, J. Fred Muggs was seen cavorting around the studio. Then at a moment of high drama in London—one *Today* staffer believes it was at the precise moment Her Majesty was crowned—Fred bounded over a chair and the studio camera flashed on him just in time to catch his rump clearing the barrier. Garroway added the frosting when he walked over to a sofa where the chimp was sitting and asked, "Ah, don't you wish that you too could be a king in a far-off land where you originated?"

Was it all inadvertent, as Garroway and others insist, or a calculated parody in poor taste, as *New York Times* critic Jack Gould and some others believe? Either way, the impact surprised everybody. A terrible uproar ensued in the House of

Commons. Some said the British were so appalled by the episode, and the commercialism that made it possible, that television's arrival on the shores of jolly old England was delayed for several years. Notes Paul Cunningham with a grin, it was the *Today Show*'s first world-wide publicity.

A year later, when Muggs went on a world tour, London, originally scheduled as his first stop, was bypassed and Muggs landed in Paris instead. The British, still fuming, had made it clear that Muggs was chimpana non grata. It wasn't only the British who were put out about Muggs. In Rome, former King Farouk of Egypt left a night club in a huff after he was upstaged by the magnetic chimpanzee.

Mary Kelly, a valuable *Today Show* staffer, adored Muggs and was therefore chosen to go on the good-will tour. She had her hands full. Once J. Fred excitedly jumped out of his sneakers at a zoo, and an elephant ate them. One night in Beirut, Muggs, in the room adjoining Mary's, got out of his harness, knocked a telephone off the hook, and escaped from the room when a hotel employee came to investigate. Mary wound up chasing the screeching ape through the lobby of terrified guests, dressed in her bra and skirt. The episode ended peacefully when Mary, a plucky sort, used her upper register to order everyone back. She then carefully walked up to Fred, who was as frightened as everybody else. Recognizing Mary, Fred put his arms around her and the two went calmly back to harness.

Muggs' popularity was world-wide. In Hong Kong, such a crowd surrounded the store where Muggs was "shopping" that a riot squad had to rescue him. In Japan, his welcome was exceeded only by that accorded Marilyn Monroe, and fifteen geishas fanned him while he napped.

There was some hostility, too. *Time* magazine reported a "typical man-in-the-street" reaction by an elderly Roman lady. "I never thought that I would live to see the day when a chimpanzee earned more money than most humans and was sent on a grand tour," the woman said. Then she spoke of an occasion in 1944 when a U.S. war relief organization tried to feed her canned clam chowder: "What can you expect of a people who make soup out of shellfish and boiled milk?"

The money, of course, went to Muggs' owners, Buddy and Roy. J. Fred, who pocketed not a dime, received criticism at home too. Some on the show had questioned from the beginning the wisdom of having a half-tamed anthropoid on the set. It was during the J. Fred Muggs publicity build-up that *Today Show* newscaster Jim Fleming, who had joined the show to work in electronic news, quit in disgust, concluding that *Today* had definitely gone ape.

Some expressed relief, saying that next to Muggs, Fleming, a nervous man with a mustache, was the jumpiest animal on the scene. He was succeeded by Frank Blair, a clean-shaven newscaster with an easy delivery and unflappable manner. And the *Today Show*, ape and all, continued merrily on its way to becoming an established part of America's morning routine.

CHAPTER 8

A Team Effort, from the Quarterback to the Scout

The *Today Show* was many people—and one wild animal—who worked strange hours with great esprit to bring off Pat Weaver's conception of morning television. For most viewers, though, one man was the key. It was Dave Garroway they welcomed into their homes. With his quiet, slow-paced delivery and impeccable manners, Garroway was, as a nurse who lived alone wrote in, "someone wonderful to have into the house for breakfast." Viewers not only ate breakfast with Garroway, they even woke up with him—those who had electric alarm clocks hooked up to their TVs.

It might have been worthwhile for Garroway to have taped the show's sound portion for use the next morning as a self-help alarm clock. As it was, to return himself to consciousness at 4 A.M. he invented and installed a personal Bakelite control board to synchronize various alarms. Since he wasn't due at the studio until 5 A.M., it wasn't essential that he answer the first call to action—a radio, on at 4, that was interrupted every five minutes with an annoying buzz. He could, and sometimes did, still the radio's buzzer by flipping a lever. Then at 4:25, the second alarm sounded, this one also a buzzer, but a more insistent, "urgent must-get-up signal," as Garroway explained. Sleeping through that one brought an ultimate wake-the-dead signal from a clock that went off at 4:35. To still its cacophonous rudeness, Garroway had to leave his bed and cross the room. One can imagine an apprehensive Garroway lying half-awake and enduring the countdown before hopping out of bed to beat the final alarm's angry report.

Next came breakfast, a curious Garrowayan brew of orange slices floating in orange juice. Garroway then dressed, stepped through the front door of his Manhattan digs, and entered a cab which awaited him daily by prearrangement. He then rode through his "tunnel," as he termed the unchanging route to RCA, in silence to the studio, where he would rouse himself with coffee and perhaps a doughnut.

At 5 A.M. rehearsals began. Rehearsals? Well, not really. The show was basically unrehearsed, Garroway's calm manner in a precarious live-broadcast setting being one secret of the show's appeal. Most guests did not appear until the show was about to be broadcast. What Garroway did, amid yawns and sips of coffee, was to rehearse the commercials, talking to the camera as though to an old acquaintance about a garden product perhaps. In the words of one commentator of the period, the manner in which he "brings his little talk to a close, by laying his hand in a friendly way on the shoulder of a big bag of fertilizer, is an affecting thing to watch."

Under Garroway, the style of *Today* was a rambling serendipitous journey through the day's highlights . . . interviews of famous people . . . performances by jazz groups . . . light patter with busty models touting anything from peanut brittle to a gadget that caught Garroway's fancy . . . amiable remarks about this and that . . . filmed features . . . live farcical skits featuring Jack Lescoulie . . . weather reports and time check . . . national and international news . . . and, say, a round-up with NATO generals on the defensive posture vis-à-vis the Russians. Garroway was the glue holding this amalgam together. Even while J. Fred Muggs aped his precise moves, Garroway handled all kinds of rattling assignments with amazing calm. He would, for example, report from inside a plastic garment bag to warn parents that children could suffocate in these dangerous "playthings."

In contrast to radio's frenetic disc jockeys and talk show hosts with whom he competed in the morning, Garroway spoke quietly, in a mellifluous baritone. He was informality in a formal age, intelligent, casual and, at all times, sincere—even with the commercials. He pitched products well but refused to pander to a sponsor. Nor would he eat a product on camera, having once tasted frosting on a sponsor's cake and discovered it was shaving cream. A reservoir of factual information, he was dignified in presenting his knowledge and was somehow handsome, peering owlishly through his gigantic horn-rimmed glasses.

As he shifted from set to set, Garroway moved with a grace that belied the 240 pounds his 6-foot-2-inch frame sometimes carried. While he often walked at a brisk pace, such was his on-camera style that he appeared not to rush. Rather, he moved in a kind of vague manner that matched the mood of those in his audience who tarried before the set on the way to breakfast. Struggling to capture the slow-motion quality of a Garroway in transit, *The New Yorker* commented: "Sometimes, while watching Garroway, the viewer has the illusion of peering not so much at the screen of a television set as at a twenty-one-inch tank of water."

Garroway sensed that the waking populace was in no mood for jokes, particularly side-slappers. He could be quietly droll, though, in imparting his odd bits of information. He might explain equestrian statues: when the horse has all four feet on the ground the military figure seated on it died of natural causes; if the horse has one foot off the ground, he died of his wounds, and with both front feet aloft the man died in the heat of battle. In Garroway's understated delivery, punctuated by pauses, the explanation was delightfully amusing.

Most television professionals agreed that Garroway was the perfect host for the *Today Show* and its unique requirements. They marveled at the way he could shift smoothly from a chat with, say, Miss Pasta Fazool—"Thank you [pause] my dear [pause] for being our queen [pause] and for bringing us this delicious snack"—to a serious conversation with an erudite visitor, to an amusing transition that seemed to be spur-of-the-moment invention: "Of all the earth's inhabitants, man is the one most likely [pause] to take a station break [pause] and we take one [pause with a meaningful look into the camera] right now."

Once, on a remote broadcast, Garroway demonstrated how to overcome a transition that was inherently in bad taste. Checking out landmarks in a field, he looked finally onto a military leader's tomb. Turning toward the camera, he said, "Ah yes, a magnificent monument," and without so much as a nervous cough was off on a seemingly casual but very-much-to-the-point chat about a sponsor's Rock of Ages Monuments, a switch calculated to put a normal communicator into an early grave out of sheer embarrassment.

In extremis—or the broadcast equivalent thereof—Garroway was given to abrupt action as the least painful way out. When a sponsor's watch, certified shockproof, broke into pieces after he dropped it a short distance to a table, he deadpanned, "Well [pause] that didn't work," and went on imperturbably to the next item of business.

Garroway did those features that fell somewhere between a commercial and a soft news item with similar grace—such as the time he went to the Waldorf-Astoria to show the Kitchen of Tomorrow.

"It's almost more than two old eyes can stand," said Garroway as he peeked into a freezer built vertically rather than horizontally—an innovative wonder in 1954. Garroway marveled at a sink built into the middle of the room, then turned to push buttons on a microwave oven that amazed viewers by cooking a turkey in less than an hour and crisping bacon before their eyes. "It's beautifully complicated and at the same time simply practical," said Garroway, adding, "Looks like the control panel of a B-29."

In a featured interview with a Westinghouse engineer about the nuclear submarine *Nautilus*, which was being launched that day, an awed Garroway said, "The ramifications of this are infinite. The submarine can stay submerged indefinitely. It has to come up every four years so the sailors can re-enlist. That's not my line." (Said a critic, reviewing the program, "No, it isn't. It's Herb Shriner's.")

Garroway and the Westinghouse man pondered the long-range prospect of supplying all the nation's energy needs from the atom. "Got to get three hundred more barrels out of my oil well before that happens," Garroway said briskly, of an event that proved to be far more remote than a microwave oven in every household.

Many of Garroway's lines were as spontaneous as they seemed, but in one situation he was not permitted to ad-lib—during his infrequent *Today* interviews with the RCA head, General David Sarnoff. Questions and answers were prepared in advance by the General's aides for direct transcribing on video cue sheets. Thus, the General would say exactly what he meant to, including occasional responses that began, "That's a *very* good question, Dave ..."

Dave Garroway's on-camera aplomb was in odd contrast to his off-camera timidity. His millions of viewers, who knew him to be a man never at a loss even at calamitous moments on camera, would have been amazed to hear him described by a friend as an "essentially decent man who tries to get through to people and just doesn't know how."

His best friend, Charlie Andrews, said Garroway found it difficult to have fun. "He was not a conversationalist, not a party guy. He was at his best in front of a mike."

To many of his associates, Garroway seemed unreal when off camera. In one disastrous attempt to establish a better rapport with associates, Garroway threw a party at his home. Some members of the *Today* staff drank too much, ground cigarettes into the carpeting, and damaged a prized Garroway possession, his telescope. After that, few got past the barrier Garroway placed between himself and associates. As one of them remarked much later: "How should I know what Garroway is like? I've only worked with him for eight years."

To some on the show he seemed on a "disconnected plane" as he immersed himself in a page-by-page reading of the *Encyclopaedia Britannica* or in leafing through his favorite light reading matter, mail order catalogs. He thus cut himself off from chances to converse with most of those with whom he worked.

Despite his social isolation, however, Garroway managed to work very well with the *Today* staff. He recognized that *Today* was not a one-man show and that all parts had to function together smoothly for the show to work. Far more than most shows, *Today* was a team effort. And many members of the team made essential contributions in the early days of the show.

Mary Kelly, for instance, did far more for the show's success than just keep J. Fred Muggs happy on world tours. Mary was an attractive and amusing young woman who happened to be single. That, in her opinion, "probably helped my career, though my pre-dawn hours on the *Today Show* probably killed my chances." She was certainly a helpful person to have around in the wee hours. Garroway used to say Mary was the only one who walked into the studio at 4:30 A.M. wide awake.

Mary Kelly was determined to have a satisfying career, in an era when most girls who began as secretaries either got married and had families or simply remained secretaries. Mary had begun as a secretary to a comedy producer on the old Dumont network in 1948. When her boss left Dumont for NBC, Mary went with him. Soon she was picked to help with the dry runs of *Today*. Interested in writing, Mary took courses at the Columbia School of Journalism. As part of her responsibilities at *Today* she often wrote out questions for Garroway to ask guests. When Garroway and the guest clicked and her questions weren't used, she was philosophically cheerful about it. It was a good learning experience to watch a pro at work.

Working up interview questions led Mary into a much more important function, one that few were aware of as the result of an early *Today Show* deception. Mary often traveled to distant cities with a crew to film a Garroway "interview." When, for instance, Shirley Booth opened in *The Matchmaker* in Philadelphia, Mary Kelly and film crew journeyed to the Keystone state. Off camera, Mary asked her questions. Shirley would answer with a "Yes, Dave," or a "No, Dave," or "It was this way, Dave . . ." When Mary got back to New York City, she carefully edited the film. On the show Dave would pose questions live, and then the camera would shift to the film as Shirley gave her answers. At the time the live-to-film-and-back-to-live technique was new, and viewers were not aware of the trick. It became a popular way for *Today* to get busy celebrities on the show, and Mary carried much of the load. Thus, it didn't matter that celebrities wouldn't get up for a 7 A.M. call, or that they balked at traveling to New York for an in-person interview.

Another niche that Mary carved out for herself—scouting for guests—led producer Mort Werner to nickname her "the Procurer." When someone difficult was arriving, Werner would dispatch Mary, saying, "Her Irish charm will win him over."

"It was up to me to line up the unusual for the show," Mary explains. "When a ship came in, I would take an NBC limo to the dock and say, 'Get in, I'll drive you to the studio right now.'" She usually brought her quarries back to the studio alive, after convincing them that people were actually watching television at 7 A.M.

Mary Kelly's most important procurement was of a former Russian premier. When news of the Soviet dictator Joseph Stalin's death reached *Today* early in the morning on March 5, 1953, the show had the makings of an important scoop, for the morning papers had already gone to press. News editor Jerry Green wanted more than just a news item, which morning radio news shows would be carrying. He wanted some kind of in-depth report which could be gotten quickly.

Green then remembered that Alexander Kerensky, the premier of the Provisional Russian Government who was overthrown in Lenin's October Revolution, now lived in exile on Manhattan's Upper East Side. He assigned Mary to fetch the former premier. Mary rode to the address, a Russian monastery, rang the bell, and quickly persuaded Kerensky to do the show with Jim Fleming and the revered old NBC newsman H. V. Kaltenbourn.

Jerry Green remembers that Kerensky was a "sensation" as he stood in front of a huge blow-up mural of the Kremlin, "quivering with righteous rage." Fleming and Kaltenbourn analyzed the significance of the passing of the great leader and tyrant. Kaltenbourn, who still had a following but was out of favor at NBC, enjoyed his rare moment in the spotlight, and Green was happy to have him.

"He was a wonderful old man," says Green. "Nobody at NBC would touch him though," as Kaltenbourn's era of journalism, in which he and others expressed strong opinions, had faded. Green remembers "this marvelous moment when Kaltenbourn said, 'Yes, Fleming, you and I were in the Kremlin many times.' He then turned and stood there as though the whole show, as reflected in the mural, had suddenly and miraculously moved to Russia."

Garroway's informality, J. Fred Muggs' antics, hard work by staffers like Mary Kelly, and important news reports like the one on Stalin's death: somehow it all came together well enough to establish the *Today Show* as an important part of America's morning.

CHAPTER 9

Gofers and Girls

The *Today Show*, like any organization, had its hierarchy. The top of the pyramid was occupied by the show's star and the key executives. Below them were dozens of staffers of varying importance, on camera and off. And the base of the pyramid was made up of those known as "gofers."

In any field where one learns as much by observing as by doing, there is a period during which the neophyte is essentially an errand-runner—someone who, among other menial chores, is expected to "go for" coffee. At *Today* the gofers who succeeded became writers, producers, and even stars of the show. Many quickly acquired the rather grand title of associate producer, but these staffers were still gofers. "Associate producer" was put into perspective by a *Today Show* producer—a vastly more important person—during rehearsals of an animal act. Someone asked, "Suppose the animal urinates on camera—then what?" The producer snarled, "Let the associate producer clean it up. That's what he's paid to do."

In the beginning the *Today Show* was crawling with gofers

—ambitious young men and women who took the job hoping to become writers on the show. With its combination of news and entertainment and its unstructured beginnings—producer Mort Werner was constantly adding and throwing out ideas, adjusting and fine-tuning—the show was an especially popular place for television hopefuls to work. Upward mobility was the rule, and anyone with talent could reasonably expect to get both opportunity and recognition. Mary Kelly was one example. Starting with coffee-fetching, she worked her way up to "procuring" guests and ape-sitting, then writing and on-camera interviewing. It all paved the way for a career, years later, as the star of her own television show in the Bahamas, *Mary's Paradise*.

Alan Smith is another example. A would-be writer who came to the show in the early years, Al had worked for the New York *Daily Mirror* and had done some radio work in Syracuse and Utica, New York. He also had a brief stint in the NBC news department. But when he transferred to the *Today Show* he was not qualified to be a writer and began as a production assistant—a gofer. He had several responsibilities. One was to arrive at the Exhibition Hall bright and early. Real bright and early. An NBC operator called to wake him up in Queens at 2 A.M., and he rode the subway to Manhattan to become one of the first on the scene at 3 A.M.

The initial thing he did was to draw the weather report on the blackboard in blue chalk, which didn't show up on the television picture. When Garroway would later do the weather, he appeared to be writing it there himself—tracing over the blue with visible white chalk. Al also prepared the so-called weather crawl, a print-over that gave a one-word definition of the weather in each city in which an NBC affiliate was carrying the *Today Show*.

Smith's personal life was turned upside down. Fortunately, Al says, his wife was working on an NBC news show and "she understood." He would arrive back in Queens at about 2 or 3 P.M., hop into bed, and be awakened by the smell of dinner, which his wife—who worked the noon-to-8-P.M. shift—generally put on the table at a little after 9 P.M. They'd spend the evening together until about midnight, when Al went to bed for a two-hour nap prior to the next show.

Al Smith's ambition to be a writer never ceased. He began by writing those little tidbits of information called "pad" material which Garroway could throw in from time to time as a gap appeared: "On this day, *x* years ago, the first typewriter was invented by . . ."

Smith began to seek visual items to pad out the show. He would find some new toy or gadget. Gadgets were very big on the show, and aspiring writer Smith loved them as much as Garroway did. Al also made a deal with a museum whereby the show could put borrowed works of art on camera for thirty seconds at a time.

Al finally convinced the producer to give him a shot as a writer. It would be a ticklish business, though. He would write some scripts for the show, but the managing editor's initials would appear at the top rather than Al Smith's. Otherwise the union would insist he be paid as a writer, which would have made the producer much more reluctant to give him the try-out. "I was breaking the regs," Smith admits, "but it was the only way to do it."

He was given two weeks to prove himself. "If I didn't work out it was understood that I could go back to what I had been doing," he says. "But that's horseshit. Once you failed you never got a chance again. It was a tough two weeks, but I made it. The man in charge of the shows I was writing for was sufficiently impressed to battle to keep me as a permanent writer."

Al Smith's gofer days were over. He had made it as a writer. Eventually he became *Today*'s managing editor.

85

Some who had solid writing backgrounds, though little or no television background, joined the show as writers without having to go through the gofer period. But they too were on trial. They quickly learned that writing for television was like nothing else—or they didn't last long. One who did learn was Ric Ballad, a newspaperman with five years' reporting experience. Ric—short for Richard and "an adolescent affectation I'm now stuck with"—had banged around the country reporting for the Houston *Post* in Texas and the *Hudson Dispatch*, located across the street from the Hudson Burlesque, the only landmark in Union City, New Jersey. Ric turned his back on burlesque city and came to NBC News to break into broadcasting as a writer. Instead, he became an assistant to William R. McAndrew, then director of NBC News.

Ric comments that he "didn't know how to be an assistant to anybody. I was the world's worst." Befriended by Joe Michaels, a *Today Show* reporter, Ric got a berth on the still-evolving show. Ric joined "the base drum and piano show," as the news department contemptuously called *Today*, on December 6, 1956. At the time he had never written a line of radio or television copy, nor had he even seen a TV camera. When he arrived he was handed a sheaf of copy and was told, "This is what a script looks like. Get to work."

Ric muddled through somehow, and a week later he was sent to pre-Castro Cuba to write copy for a film story of J. Fred Muggs, who was "being his usual charming self, screaming and carrying on in Havana," Ric remembers. "When we got back, film editor Tom Galvin put the skit together. He still twitches when I mention it.

"Sometimes we got into the story itself, functioning as writer-reporters, doing on-the-air spots," Ballad adds.

It was catch-as-catch-can, but some of Ric's assignments were fairly important, for the producers soon recognized his competence. It was Ric who was chosen to interview Soviet foreign minister Andrei Gromyko. Then there was a "Jacques something or other" who was promoting skydiving when the sport was young.

"He wanted us to put him on the show early in 1957," Ric recalls. "Nothing fancy, he'd dive out of the plane, assume a swan position and drop, opening his parachute later. Conditions were primitive in the sport then, but when I got to Orange, Massachusetts, I said, 'How about teaching me?' I was about to become the first reporter ever to try it.

"We got into an old four-seater plane," he continues. "We had a camera on the ground and a crew in the ship. They bailed me out and I skydived. Unfortunately, I had one of those rare experiences. The chute opened inside out and the shroud lines tore the hell out of it. I looked up and saw rips, but I was still floating. I hit hard but was okay. The instructor walked over white-faced and said, 'Why the hell didn't you open the emergency chute?' I was afraid it would foul the main chute. Obviously, I survived."

Ric also had a breathless feeling in his first on-the-air spot with Garroway, who may have decided to show Ric who was boss.

"Garroway fouled things up to a fare-thee-well that morning," Ric remembers. "We were writing a complete script for everyone then. He would read his part of the script *and* my line and say, 'Oh, that was *your* line, wasn't it?' "

After his skydive, action pieces became a Ballad specialty. Once he filmed on a racing iceboat, in essence a sailboat with skates, on Michigan's Lake St. Claire. Ric and the iceboater were on their backs in the traditional sailing position and Ric's cameraman, "overage but with guts," was strapped to a bar stool bolted to the prow. The iceboat took off "like a bat" and was soon doing sixty miles an hour, skimming the ice on one runner, the cameraman grinding away. When they were at least a mile from shore, the ice suddenly broke. One bolt on the bar stool parted, and the cameraman was tossed about like a rag doll as the boat plowed through the icy water and began to sink. There were no other craft around, and Ric was convinced they were finished.

"We were going to swim for our lives," Ric says, "when we discovered that there was more ice about two feet beneath the surface of the water. The surface ice had melted during a warm spell and then refroze." The iceboat spot was a great success on *Today*—right down to the last scene when the camera went under, still grinding and filming bubbling water.

Another writer who joined the show at about the same time Ballad did was Bud Lewis. Lewis had written for Garroway on NBC's weekend *Monitor*, a radio show, and came to *Today* at Garroway's request. Impressed by Lewis' style, Garroway told the other writers that thereafter he wouldn't do lines that Lewis hadn't approved. It was some time before Lewis learned why he was getting the cold shoulder from his colleagues. Like all the writers, though, Lewis had a variety of writing assignments to do.

"We all had to write for the ape," Lewis says. "You'd devise something to happen between Garroway and Muggs, and the trainers would try to get Muggs to do it. You'd sit down and write a script to go with the action."

The sad-faced and quiet Lewis is not likely to be mistaken for a comedy writer, but often comedy was what he had to write, even for animals other than J. Fred Muggs. When *Today* did a remote in St. Louis near a reflecting pool, Lewis was assigned to do an animal spot at the zoo to tie in. Like the Mary Kelly interviews, the animal spot would be filmed, then merged with Garroway's live broadcast.

"I prepared a skit about a 'talking' seal," Lewis recalls, with some pain. There was relatively little actual writing. The film crew lensed seal footage and recorded their barks. Lewis stayed up all night doing a short script for Garroway, calling for lots of "yes" responses. Whenever Garroway got to such a spot, he'd pause and the "talking seal" would say, "Arf!"

With so little dialogue called for in many of the spots, the job was "iceberg work," as Ric Ballad sees it. The writing played an important role, but usually beneath the surface of what was actually heard on *Today*. The writer was expected to provide "background," and the on-the-air personality was encouraged to ad-lib whenever possible, based on a review of the material provided by the writer. Scripted shows were abandoned early.

The writers for *Today* made it or didn't make it depending upon their adaptability to a function that little resembled any other kind of writing. As routine as it was at times for *Today* writers, at least they did not go for coffee.

Estelle Parsons found another route up from the gofer level, and by so doing she created a permanent on-camera role that later became known as the *"Today* Girl." Estelle began in 1952 as a $75-a-week production assistant whose first chore was to telephone Washington unobtrusively and essentially off-camera to get the weather report. Soon she was chatting amiably with Garroway, and eventually her role was enlarged. She interviewed important guests, including Eleanor Roosevelt (who fell asleep and then awoke with a start when Estelle asked her the next question). By the time she started filling in for vacationing Dave Garroway, she was making $1,000 a week and "then much more than that."

When she left the show to pursue her acting career, Estelle was followed by a succession of *Today* Girls. *Today* was a man's world, and a female was a "girl"—it was no accident that she *wasn't* called the *Today* Woman. The girls were chosen for their wholesome, pretty faces and their ability to pour tea and make light conversation. In the *Today* "family" the girl was the bright, young homemaker—involved with food, fashion and, well, feminine things. Ideally, the *Today* Girls would also be witty and talented performers. But they weren't chosen for sexiness—that would be the wrong note. A sensuous woman around the house at 7 A.M. could be threatening to the couple at breakfast.

Pat Weaver hadn't originally thought of a female regular, but he had always felt that in addition to a communicator and a stooge (Lescoulie), a third person was necessary "to get the action working." And after Estelle, the third was inevitably a woman. Not all of them, however, were successful in the role.

There was a miscast, less-than-attractive woman who drank. She got the job because of a powerful patron connected with the network. She wasn't very good when sober. When suffering from one of her "absolutely staggering hangovers," as a source called them, she misread scripts, and the reasons for her distress must have been painfully obvious to some viewers. When she was drunk—it happened often enough that she was known as "The Stiff"—she was impossible. For The Stiff, it was a good deal. Call it occupational therapy at $50,000 a year, the going rate for *Today* Girls.

One *Today* Girl had difficulties on the show not because of her boozing but because of her husband's. When he was in his cups, he became violent. More than one *Today Show* appearance had to be canceled when the woman showed up battered and with a black eye.

Singer Helen O'Connell became the *Today* Girl in late 1956. She was famous from the Big Band days of the 1940s, and she was good on the air. She often lip-synched the old numbers because she knew the viewers wanted to bathe in nostalgia, but she was also perfectly capable of doing her numbers live, and sometimes did. The crew regarded her as somewhat temperamental and sensitive.

Early in her stay, a *Today* director told Helen to "go to Siberia" and, none too sure of herself at the time, she walked off the set thinking she had been fired. No one had told her that

"Siberia" was anywhere out of camera range; the command was simply a stage direction to clear performers who were not to appear in the next *Today* item.

Helen was not only a pop singer of distinction. She was also smart and quick-witted, and could ad-lib. She interviewed guests when the topic fell within her sphere of knowledge, and she was not afraid of Garroway.

Actress Betsy Palmer, another *Today* Girl, may have been afraid of the host. At least Garroway could befuddle her, and she once burst into tears as she told a *Today* writer that she couldn't take Garroway at that hour in the morning. Betsy's husband, an obstetrician in New Jersey, wasn't anxious for Betsy to do the show anyway. She had a game show with Gary Moore at the time and really didn't need the aggravation. Finally, she left. The writer, speaking of Betsy, says, "God, I loved that woman. She was wonderful, sweet and kind. She would come back for a *Today* party and the whole place would light up."

Florence Henderson brought her own special brand of light-hearted warmth. The musical comedy star was clever enough to do interviews on subjects she knew. Her songs were done live with only a piano for accompaniment. Feisty as well, she didn't take guff from anybody. So tiny she needed a pillow for her chair, she once pulled it out and smacked Garroway in the face during a live *Today* broadcast, her blunt way of answering what she felt was a nasty remark.

The *Today* Girls came and went. There were beauties like former Miss America Lee Ann Meriwether, former Miss Rheingold Robbin Bain, and Beryl Pfizer, whom Garroway thought the perfect woman. Garroway first spotted the dazzling Miss Pfizer on a New York City bus. Before he could make her acquaintance, she disappeared into the crowds of Manhattan. Never expecting to see her again, Garroway was astonished one day when Beryl showed up at the studio to join the show.

She became the *Today* Girl with the host in hot pursuit. But soon Dave learned that she was not interested.

The *Today* Girls, a mixed group, were part of the mix that made the show a success. In later years, as the mores of the society changed, the *Today* Girls evolved into women.

CHAPTER 10

Success Spawns Competition

Shortly after Pat Weaver came to NBC to be vice-president for television, he was asked by a higher authority at parent RCA how much it was costing the network to broadcast the NBC Symphony. Weaver, who is not an accountant, called a financial aide and asked him. The accountant, rather more droll than some of his breed, answered with a question: "How much do you want it to cost?"

Weaver asked, "What kind of an answer is that?"

The accountant then explained that in broadcasting, as in other enterprises with numerous so-called profit centers, how much a particular segment of the business earns or loses depends on how you assign *general* overhead expenses. How much of the building's depreciation and heating expenses do you assign to the Symphony? How much of the salaries of the NBC vice-presidents and pages, cleaning women and security guards do you lay on it?

As it was for the NBC Symphony, so it was for the *Today Show.* Currently the official line at NBC is that *Today* was unprofitable through the first six to eight years of its existence. If that's the case, NBC must have assigned heavy news department expenses to *Today* and God knows what else, for as early as its second year the show began to develop spectacular momentum with advertisers. NBC's reluctance to call *Today*'s early years profitable may simply stem from the desire of RCA founder and chairman General David Sarnoff to justify pushing Pat Weaver, who conceived *Today*, out of NBC in 1956.

In fact, *Today* got a rave financial notice in *Variety*, the show business bible, as early as September 1953. The article said that in 1953—*Today*'s second year—the show would earn more money than any other TV show on the networks. So commercially anemic just months earlier, *Today* boasted 115 different advertisers through September 1953—at a rate of $3,861 for a one-minute participation. In December alone, the show was "booked solid with $1,200,000 in sponsors' orders." Total annual billings would therefore top the $7.5-million mark, surpassing *Your Show of Shows*.

Variety went on to say that "whereas the Saturday night Sid Caesar-Imogene Coca display represents a weekly talent-production nut in the neighborhood of $55,000 a week, *Today* is brought in for about $24,000." NBC was apparently the source of those cost figures. It certainly appears that no one at the network or at RCA complained about *Variety*'s frothy report.

Variety also said that the critics' early barbs and advertisers' indifference had initially threatened Pat Weaver's concept of selling pieces of individual shows to different sponsors. But the *Today Show*'s eventual success with this technique put over the idea of segmented sales in television generally.

Beyond that, "*Today* established that there's an early morning audience, which thus far in '53 averages 1,265,000 homes reached in its 47-market spread, with an average rating of 7.9 comparing favorably with later morning and afternoon ratings. For the 8:30 to 8:55 A.M. segment, the rating goes as high as

9.4, and on special occasions, as with the atom bomb explosion pick-up, *Today* hit the jackpot—25.7. Many a nighttime entry would envy such a rating."

Variety added that because *Today* allowed five minutes of each half hour for local sponsorship cut-ins, the stations on the hook-up had been "cutting an additional early-morning melon adding up to a sizeable chunk of coin on an annual basis."

Whatever their later view of the show's profitability, NBC certainly seemed to know that it had a hit on its hands by late 1953. And things were to get even better—or worse, depending on one's tolerance for commercials. Joe Culligan, who headed the sales force and should know the figures, said that J. Fred Muggs' publicity value coupled with star Dave Garroway's appeal got the show the necessary momentum: "The net result was we turned from a loss of $1.7 million a year to a profit of $2 million on a gross of $10 million on the first full fiscal year—after six months of getting organized."

In calendar 1954, the *Today Show* made a profit, Culligan states, of $2.4 million, on a gross of over $11 million. That figure made the once-troubled attraction the biggest one-year grosser in the history of radio and television broadcasting. *Billboard*, another respected trade sheet, put the case in even broader perspective, estimating that *Today* was "probably the largest-grossing venture in the history of show business within a period of one year"—surpassing even *Gone With the Wind*, at the time the benchmark by which the success of all entertainment efforts were measured.

The flood of new commercials wasn't without its drawbacks, at least as far as some viewers were concerned. Wrote critic John Crosby in a *Herald Tribune* column entitled "Garroway Two Years Later": "Listening to [*Today*] you get the idea it has at least one hundred sponsors. Along toward the middle of the second hour here in the East—the first hour in the Mid-West—the commercials come roaring at you one after another.

"Jack Lescoulie will mix up some Amazo, 'the fastest instant mix dessert in the world,' the sight of which at 8 o'clock in the morning will make you a little ill. Then a girl on film palpitates at us to eat more Florida grapefruit if we want to avoid winter colds. And Steve, the Alka-Seltzer urchin, tells us how to get fast relief from headaches, and Arlene Dahl blinks her pretty eyes and whispers the virtues of Pepsi-Cola, and Garroway sells toothbrushes and demonstrates a detergent and shows off a Polaroid Land Camera and—oh, brother!"

Crosby added that in those rare intervals between commercials, *Today* was a pretty good show.

Once Pat Weaver proved morning television could be profitable, CBS began to plan a competing program to be called "The Morning Show." Proud of its strong news division, CBS hoped to steal some of *Today's* audience in part by offering better news coverage in the morning.

One incident before the debut of the *Morning Show* should have warned CBS that competing with Dave Garroway even on news coverage could be very difficult. The occasion was a "media event" at Yucca Flat, Nevada: the press's first look at an atomic blast in the United States. While NBC planned live coverage for the *Today Show*, CBS sent out a news crew headed by Walter Cronkite and Charles Collingwood, also for live coverage. High winds caused repeated cancellations of the test. Each morning Jerry Green, Dave Garroway, and other members of a remote *Today* crew would drive from Las Vegas about a hundred miles to the viewing area, a series of trenches and other shields on the desolate flats.

One morning news editor Green and one of *Today's* directors, Dick Schneider, were on a rise with the cameras and the Atomic Energy Commission's Ralph Graves, a respected scientist-administrator. Charles Collingwood and the CBS cameras were also there. Two minutes before the bomb was to go off, the wind rose and the blast was canceled, just like every other day.

It was dark and bitter cold, and it was show time in New York. As the cameras were about to go live, Collingwood began to interview Graves. Garroway, meanwhile, was nowhere in sight. New York was ready to go with alternate programing if necessary, as it had been for days. Jerry Green turned to Schneider and said, "We're screwed, we'll stay off the air"—or else Collingwood would appear on NBC as well as CBS, since the only focus of attention was Graves.

"Just then a jeep appeared and began laboring up the hill," Green recalls. "Garroway was a huge man then. He got out of the jeep, wearing a white duster with goggles and a tweed cap, for godsake, and carrying two huge lunch boxes so the rest of us wouldn't go hungry.

"The cameras were going live and Collingwood was being trenchant about atom bombs. Graves said, 'Hi, Dave,' and Garroway said, 'Dr. Graves, should nuclear physicists be allowed to express strong political views?' It was during the Oppenheimer flap. [Accused of being a Soviet agent because he opposed a crash program to develop the H-bomb, atomic scientist J. Robert Oppenheimer lost his security clearance.] Graves blinked once and said, 'Yes, they should. But we shouldn't attach any more weight to their opinions than to those of anyone else.'

"Collingwood looked like someone had shoved an icicle up his ass, and said, 'Er, what about the Bandung conference?' Garroway looked so comical in that outfit, but, typically, though he was show business oriented, he came up with the big one. Everybody wanted to know the answer to Dave's question."

The *Morning Show*, competing with *Today* in the same 7 to 9 A.M. slot, aired on March 15, 1954, with Cronkite and

Collingwood handling news and an obscure wit named Jack
Paar acting as host.

The news coverage on the *Morning Show* offered tough
competition to *Today*, as Jerry Green freely admits. But the
rest of the show was largely improvised. For that reason, and
because the *Today Show* was so well established, the *Morning
Show* never got off the ground. In the fall of 1955 CBS turned
the 8 to 9 A.M. period over to Bob Keeshan as Captain Kangaroo, who proved to be as durable, though not as profitable,
as *Today*. That left CBS with an ailing 7 to 8 A.M. format, for
which they tried various improvements and hosts, including
Dick Van Dyke.

Garroway's writer Charlie Andrews had little to do on the
Today Show, and he eventually gravitated elsewhere. Then
one day Charlie got a call from CBS executive Lou Cowan,
who said that Will Rogers, Jr., son of the famous humorist,
would soon be coming in to take over the show from Dick
Van Dyke. Cowan asked Charlie to come in right away and
produce for thirteen weeks.

"It was a funny period," Charlie explains. "They had tried
several people. There was no audience and no budget. They
would book any asshole who wrote a book—obscure books
that couldn't get on *Today*. Since nobody cared, we did silly
things. There was a girl who could eat underwater. So we
decided to use her. We got a glass tank, filled it with water, and
put her in it. There was a weather map on the glass. Dick would
say, 'There's a cold front over Colorado,' and she would circle
it—underwater and with her cheeks puffed out. Another time
we had an archer come in. She stood at the end of the studio.
There would be a cold front over Colorado and she'd shoot an
arrow across the studio and into the map at Colorado. We
found a lumberjack who could throw an ax. There was a cold
front over Colorado and this big double-bladed ax whizzed half
the length of the studio and landed in Colorado."

Andrews remembers giving an attractive young woman a

job. A graduate of Sarah Lawrence College, she had worked for local television stations. Hired by Andrews as a writer and talent coordinator, the twenty-seven-year-old Barbara Walters took another early step toward what would be a spectacular career in broadcasting. She soon had a chance to prove her worth, on a major news story in competition with *Today*.

In the foggy waters off Nantucket shortly after dawn on July 26, 1956, the *Andrea Doria*, pride of the Italian passenger fleet, was knifing through the water, speeding toward New York, when the *Stockholm*, a Swedish ship, appeared out of the mists. Unable to stop or alter course, the two ships collided, the prow of the *Stockholm* opening the side of the *Andrea Doria*. The *Stockholm* remained afloat, but the Italian liner was fatally stricken and soon sank to the bottom with nearly fifty passengers still aboard. The rest of her passengers had scrambled safely aboard lifeboats.

Among the first to hear about the disaster were Mary Kelly of the *Today Show* and Barbara Walters at CBS with the program recently renamed the *Good Morning Show*. Barbara was dispatched by Jim Fleming, late of *Today*, who had been brought in to help CBS save Will Rogers, Jr., already foundering opposite Dave Garroway. Fleming remembers that on the morning following the collision, Barbara had thirty survivors of the *Andrea Doria* in the CBS *Good Morning* studio.

Mary Kelly had even better luck. Mary showed her credentials to the Coast Guard and boarded a cutter that took the press to the scene. She transferred at sea to a passenger liner that had been diverted to rescue duty. A tourist recognized Mary from stories she had done on the *Today Show* and handed her a roll of 8-millimeter film he had just shot. Mary later took the film back to NBC, where it was blown up to 16 millimeter and shown on *Today*. The tourist had caught the *Andrea Doria* as the great ship sank beneath the waters, apparently the only filmed record of the sinking.

Also aboard the rescue ship was a distraught actress, Ruth

Roman, who had been a passenger on the *Andrea Doria*. Her son, age six, was missing. All the reporters were crowding in, trying to get Miss Roman's story. Mary, who recognized the actress, shielded her from the other writers. Ruth Roman took an immediate liking to Mary Kelly.

"I told her that I would do anything I could to help her learn the details about her son," Mary says. "I got Ruth to agree to let NBC have her story. When we landed, I took her right to the NBC suite in the Warwick Hotel—it was early evening by then —and again I was being bugged by reporters. We sort of locked her up and I stayed with her there. People were calling from California, and a guy and a woman she knew dropped by. No one had any idea whether her boy was dead or alive."

Finally, during the evening—Mary thinks it was at about 9 or 10 P.M.—NBC called to report that Ruth Roman's son was alive. The boy had been scooped out of his bunk on the *Andrea Doria* by the prow of the *Stockholm*, and when the two ships separated he had wound up on the *Stockholm*—uninjured.

By this time, Ruth Roman was in a state of shock and in no condition to be a *Today Show* guest the next morning. Mary didn't pressure her. Instead, she just related the story to Garroway on the show herself. It was that unusual instance in journalism in which the reporter puts sentiment ahead of a great story. In effect, Mary missed the story she had sat on for nearly twenty-four hours.

Ruth Roman later told her story to a magazine. In it, she said that "if it hadn't been for that marvelous girl from NBC, I don't think I could have gotten through the evening."

"Sure I wanted the story. But looking at it as a human being, I didn't get it," Mary comments.

Despite the great success of his brainchild, the *Today Show*,

Pat Weaver's demise at NBC was inevitable. He was too unconventional an executive, too outspoken, and, most important, General David Sarnoff was not his father.

Pat Weaver never functioned as a proper organization man. He has always believed that the way to make things work is to find talented people, give them the authority to do their jobs, and to hell with titles and executive ladders. Now a television consultant whose clients include ABC's *Good Morning, America*, Weaver recently paid a call on NBC president Julian Goodman. Good-naturedly, he suggested to Goodman that he drop the tough security precautions at Radio City, since a berserk gunman who made it to the executive floor and succeeded in bumping off a dozen vice-presidents would do wonders for NBC's efficiency.

NBC has been VP-heavy since it was set up half a century ago, and Weaver was often in direct conflict with General Sarnoff over how things were to be run. "Fangs," as Weaver recklessly referred to the General, had a passion for executive organization. In part it offered a useful blind for elevating favorite son Bobby Sarnoff to the top of the pecking order at NBC and, at the General's retirement, to the top rung at RCA.

RCA was sprinkled with evidence of the General's blood ties. In addition to the nepotism that brought Bobby along so rapidly at Rockefeller Center, son Tom Sarnoff, regarded by Weaver as a better executive than Bobby, held a high position in NBC on the West Coast. Son Eddie's position with a station in Bakersfield, California, was perhaps not a prime case of consanguinity on the march. But brother Irving was clearly a beneficiary of the General's largesse as head of a company called Bruno New York Industries, RCA distributor for the Eastern Seaboard.

The instrument of General Sarnoff's father-to-son executive campaign was the respected management consulting firm of Booz, Allen & Hamilton, which Weaver insisted on calling

Booze, Idiot & Simpleton. Under the direction of an RCA hatchet man nicknamed "Mack the Knife," Booz, Allen conducted a management investigation and recommended dividing all responsibility for the network among five division heads. They were all to report to an executive named Robert Sarnoff. Implementation of this plan would cut off Pat Weaver, by now president of the network, from his departments, from the decision-making and financial controls.

Possibly because of his enormous prestige in broadcast circles, Weaver was elevated to the post of chairman of the board of NBC in December 1955. He was instructed, however, to "work as a team" with Bobby as the newly elected president. In typical flip fashion, *Time* magazine reported that Weaver "soon discovered that his part of the teamwork gave him a lot of spare time for balancing exercises on the bongo board."

Weaver explains that he had expected Bobby to become president. "That was no problem for me, but [Robert Sarnoff as] chief executive officer was. I wouldn't agree to that until I got a commitment that they would not do anything about my people without consulting me. The top personnel who had built NBC-TV with me could not be bounced without my agreement."

One of Weaver's people was Frederick William Wyle, an associate from Weaver's Young & Rubicam days. When Weaver first came to NBC, he had installed Wyle as head of programing. A typical no-nonsense Weaver lieutenant, Wyle was both abrasive and colorful. He would pace his enormous office barking into a phone with a thirty-foot cord on calls that sometimes lasted for hours. Once an NBC executive was asked why he had flown to NBC's West Coast offices and back within twenty-four hours. "Well," he explained, "Fred had the tie line." In time, Pat Weaver sent Fred Wyle to the West Coast to head television operations there.

General Sarnoff's strategy when he was ready to ease out Weaver was simple. Remembering his commitment to Weaver concerning Pat's personal cadre of executives, he simply disregarded it and relied on Pat to supply his own withdrawal. Sarnoff sent one of his executives, Emanuel Saxe, to the West Coast and, according to a source, "Manny fired Wyle out of nowhere."

Since Weaver didn't get the news in advance as promised, he was unable to place Wyle in a new job and spare him the embarrassment of a very public swift kick to nowhere. And Wyle was only the most conspicuous Weaver lieutenant to get the ax suddenly and without warning. While most believe the General deliberately used this technique to get him to resign, Weaver himself is not convinced the General even knew "my people were fired.

"But [the firings] showed me what I already knew," Weaver explains, "that I couldn't get along with the General and that Bobby, who I had sort of trained, was becoming a Little General himself. Therefore I was finished."

With a fat severance check for his unexpired contract in his pocket—a $200,000-plus settlement—Weaver resigned. Says Weaver's man Friday at NBC, James Nelson: "The best message—and there were scores of them—came from Jackie Gleason's agent, Bullets Durgom. The wire just said, 'Pat, NBC has lost its class.'"

Pat Weaver was gone, but his most innovative programs, *Today* and *Tonight*, survived his regime by two decades.

CHAPTER 11

Goodbye Mr. Chimp

The most important contributions to the *Today Show*'s early success were made by Pat Weaver, who thought up the idea and midwifed its birth, Dave Garroway, whose telegenic personality set the show's style, and J. Fred Muggs, who drew audiences and therefore advertisers. Of the three, Weaver was the first to depart NBC. Next to walk the plank was the chimp.

The first disquieting notes in the J. Fred Muggs story occurred during the height of his popularity. As the *Daily News* reported in tongue-in-cheek style, J. Fred began to leave his mark on more than the nation's children:

"Martha Raye, the last person in the world you'd expect to find on the receiving end of a bite, was sulking in her tent yesterday, her professional pride shattered. The girl you'd expect to do all the biting had been beaten to the punch—by a chimpanzee.

"The only redeeming factor . . . was that the chimp is a star in his own right . . . J. Fred Muggs . . . and not just any little old chimp who just happened to wander by."

Also "consoling" was that Muggs didn't pick only on the "amply dentured" Miss Raye, but also nicked the understudy of her Saturday night show, Vicki Carlson. Martha was bitten early Saturday evening on the left elbow during a dress rehearsal of the show, "for which Muggs had been lend-leased from Garroway." Miss Carlson was bitten above the left eye after the show as she was about to board an elevator to her dressing room. Miss Carlson commented to *The News*: "All I did was turn around to shake hands with Muggs. All I said was 'Goodnight, Fred,' and he grabbed my hair and bit me."

Neither bite was regarded as serious, but the NBC doctor who treated Miss Carlson warned her that she might have a permanent scar.

Executive producer Dick Pinkham collected a scar to his psyche when he arranged a show with Marlon Perkins, star of NBC's *Zoo Parade* and a director of the Chicago Zoo. J. Fred was commanding extraordinary space in the newspapers, and the NBC publicity department had decided to ride the crest. Muggs would go to the Chicago Zoo for a visit with other chimps and be a guest at a birthday party. In an excessive burst of enthusiasm, NBC hired Cadillac limos to take Muggs and twenty eager representatives of the press to a send-off at Idlewild (now John F. Kennedy) airport. The whole retinue was waiting when Marlon Perkins suddenly telephoned and asked, "Has J. Fred Muggs been wormed? If he hasn't, I can't have him out here associating with my chimps because he might infect them."

Suddenly the amateur quality of the Muggs back-up was exposed. Said Dick Pinkham, who took the call, "My God, *I* don't know." He turned to Muggs' co-owner Buddy Menella and asked the question. Buddy didn't know.

Meanwhile, the pressures were building, with the press waiting to follow Muggs to the airport and Chicago warming up a similar welcome on the other end. Pinkham, in a "masterful executive attempt" to solve the dilemma, said to Perkins: "I'll have to worm him here. How do I do it?"

"First place the monkey face down on the desk," said Perkins, "and spread his buttocks..."

With that, Pinkham laid the telephone down and said, "I'm an English major from Yale, what the hell am I doing even listening to this conversation?"

Managing somehow to set Perkins' fear of worms to rest, Pinkham sent Muggs on his way. J. Fred had a wonderful time in Chicago—demolishing the birthday cake by thrusting his face into the middle of it. That was just innocent fun—nothing like the sort of thing Muggs was building up to as he became more and more disruptive on the set.

When Muggs misbehaved, co-owners Buddy Menella and Roy Waldron were said to have used an electric prod to persuade him to shape up. No one questioned that the owners loved Muggs, but Garroway and others thought them insensitive amateurs. Some insiders insist that Muggs was regularly punished in a room below the studio and recall that Fred's screams during those sessions were sometimes audible upstairs. French comedienne Genevieve, who heard the screams on one occasion, reported it to the American Society for the Prevention of Cruelty to Animals, which then began monitoring the show.

Menella has denied these charges and insists that Fred never bit anybody. People *were* injured, he admits, but only because they "jerked their hands away when Muggs had his teeth around them." Menella explains: "This isn't a bite," but rather a gesture of affection that people misinterpret. "They hurt themselves," he added.

Buddy and Roy were never able to convince Garroway that it was possible to extricate flesh from Muggs' teeth without injury. Garroway recalls that Muggs once clamped down on his cheek while the camera was on and the cameraman was "gazing out the window." Since the chimp's image as a charming, harmless tyke was crucial to the show, Garroway had to "sit there with my hand over my cheek, blood running down my neck, hugging him and saying what a cute little chimp he was" until the cameraman woke up and focused elsewhere.

Garroway insists that once Muggs reached the age of about three he changed from a delightful infant to a "strong and not very pleasant animal. Toward the end, he was acting up so badly that it was a constant concern. He knocked a girl off a desk, injuring her, and he bit me not once but many times. I made numerous visits to the NBC infirmary for a tetanus shot."

At last NBC decided that Muggs could be tolerated no longer, and he was eased off the show—four and a half years after that happy, eminently successful debut. It was obvious from the press release that this was a delicate matter. The announcement was terse, barely a page long in double-spaced typing, and there was no mention of Buddy Menella or Roy Waldron. The release began by saying that J. Fred Muggs "has decided to terminate" his association with the show in order to "extend his personal horizons." A bit of rancor may have crept in with the characterization of Muggs as both "mirthful and Machiavellian," but it was all sweetness and light apart from that. For those who knew the circumstances, there was a note of relief in the final paragraph. "Boss man" Dave Garroway was quoted as observing, "It will be a different world around the set without him."

The firing went off without a hitch, though the network people knew that Menella and Waldron were mulling a lawsuit. In time they did sue Garroway and the network, charging that Muggs' image had been injured and that this had reduced his value as a performer. By the time he was terminated by the network, Muggs' wage had risen to $1,275 a week, which was padded out with "sizable" income from products such as shoes and toys—all using his name. The owners alleged damages of half a million dollars.

Garroway recalls that the lawsuit dragged on for six years. Late in that period, Garroway was asked to go to the lawyers' offices to identify Muggs. NBC had raised the question as to whether the anthropoid Menella and Waldron were billing as J. Fred Muggs was the original animal. When Garroway arrived, he found a dozen lawyers grouped in an anteroom.

"One lawyer read something to me that went something like this: 'Now, Mr. Garroway, open the door, find said chimpanzee within, examine him and tell us if that is the chimpanzee known as J. Fred Muggs,'" Garroway recounts.

What followed was "classic" in Garroway's mind. He carefully opened the door into a room more than forty feet long to find a stern-looking, full-grown chimpanzee sitting at the end of a conference table. "He was a great big guy. He looked as big as a man—maybe not quite that big, but *awful* big." Fearless Dave walked all the way in. He didn't move a muscle.

"He glared at me and I glared at him. I should have been scared, but I wasn't, somehow. I looked very carefully for two little whitish marks on his chest. I was close enough to see them and would have if they had been there, but they weren't. Finally, I backed out cautiously and told the lawyers that it wasn't he—I didn't say how I knew."

Menella and Waldron later settled for a sum described as "moderate," a neutral word for both sides. Garroway says the sum was $6,000. NBC still won't say.

In a story written about the chimp in 1971, W. Stewart Pinkerton, Jr., of the *Wall Street Journal* visited Menella in Mahwah, New Jersey, and found an ape called J. Fred Muggs, "middle-aged, paunchy, and balding . . . weighing 175 pounds, or 40 pounds more than Menella." To Pinkerton, he looked "something like a junior-sized King Kong."

Pinkerton was doing a follow-up on a *Today Show* article in which Garroway told his bloody-cheek story and Frank Blair called Fred a "real pain who threw the furniture around." The reporter got denials on all of this and more from Menella. Passing to the basement of the ranch-style house the two men then shared with Muggs, Pinkerton found a large enclosure: "Upon noticing the visitor, Muggs screeches loudly, and shakes the heavy iron bars of his cage. As Muggs jumps up and down, his thumping feet spray the visitor's shoes with cage floor residue."

Pinkerton then quoted Menella as saying: "Don't worry, he's just doing his routine." Menella offered Pinkerton a towel and added, "Besides, he doesn't know you."

Menella and Waldron have since moved to Florida, where at last report the chimp they call J. Fred Muggs entertains at a 300-acre Florida amusement park, performing thirty-minute shows. The chimp imitates Ed Sullivan, Jimmy Durante, Jack Benny, and Richard Nixon. He also plays an octave of bells and fingerpaints. His art has appeared on the covers of *Relax* and *Mad* magazines.

Today replaced J. Fred Muggs with a prepubescent chimp called Mr. Kokomo who was to Muggs what a tank town bum is to Muhammad Ali. During his short reign Kokomo never hit the newspapers—even those provided for his pit stops.

CHAPTER 12

The Deterioration of the Morning Monarch

There's a story about a movie actor who confided to his psychiatrist, "Let's face it, Doctor, I can't sing, I can't dance, and I can't act."

The psychiatrist pondered that for a minute and said, "Then why don't you get out of show business?"

Suddenly agitated, the actor replied, "Oh, I couldn't do that!"

"Why not?" the doctor asked.

"I'm a *star*!"

Late in Garroway's career at *Today*, some staff members forgot his accomplishments and began to feel that the increasingly erratic host was simply a mediocre talent. But Garroway had that indefinable something that sets a performer apart—a quality that knocks 'em dead. He didn't sing, dance, or even "act," but he was nevertheless so good he could read from the telephone book and hold the *Today Show* audience. On at least one occasion he did just that—reading names in a manner that was somehow effective as "good theater."

Still, a deterioration in the *Today* host had set in by the late 50s, a deterioration that led to doubts. The biggest doubter of them all was Garroway. He knew he still had something and knew when it was working. But as his confidence ebbed, he became increasingly baffled as to what it was and how to sustain it. He clearly recognized that what he projected was not Garroway the man. He was never really the soothing syrup of a man who greeted listeners in his Chicago radio days with a beguiling "Hi, old tiger." Nor was he the father figure who calmed millions of *Today* listeners with his benediction "Peace" and hand held up like God's traffic cop—the brief homily and gesture somehow not incongruous with Garroway's performing style.

Bud Lewis, later a key writer on *Today*, at first found it difficult to write radio copy for Garroway at NBC's *Monitor*. "It seemed to me that I had to find out what image Garroway wanted to project and write to that. It suddenly occurred to me that he wanted to be someone diametrically opposite to what he was. He wanted to be the old shoe. But he was the most uptight person you can imagine. He would go to parties and sit with his back to the wall and say nothing all evening. He wanted no one behind him.

"He was really an inner-oriented man and his [home] reflected this," Lewis continues. "He had a *bomb* shelter. Holy Hannah! He and Nelson Rockefeller shared the same psychiatrist. Both of them were nuts about shelters—concerned about an atomic bomb attack. Dave did spots about it on the show. One day he took me down into his basement hideaway. There was lots of food, water, and supplies. There was also a shotgun in the corner.

"I said, 'What's that for?' and he said, 'Oh, everybody's going to want to come in.'"

Another source said that Garroway's insistence on a private john in his office at NBC reflected his desire to avoid confrontation—"being buttonholed in the men's room"—more than a wish to be pampered.

Garroway's idiosyncratic tendencies increased as time wore on, reflecting marital problems, the strain of ten hours of television a week, additional hours on *Monitor*, the difficult early morning schedule, and his increasing dependency on that vitamin compound "The Doctor."

Some ambitious people associated with the show quickly discovered that they could get away with things. One associate who had a hand in picking guests said producers and others would do things that were better for their careers than for Garroway's. For instance, it could help a staffer to get a friend on the show—even if this put Garroway at a disadvantage.

"Why put two people together if there is something going on the viewers don't know about?" the Garroway associate asks. "I always felt that Garroway should be consulted on everything on the show that involved him—and so did he. In time Garroway began asking for a list of guests and would blue-pencil the ones he didn't want. I would respect that. But one producer would say, 'No, it is the show that is important and we'll use who we want.' I had more deference for what Garroway wanted to do."

Garroway often became conscious of the fact that he was being used—and was darkly suspicious even when he was not. Whoever tried to put something over on him did so at his peril, and others who didn't also were in jeopardy. One of the singular qualities of the Garroway regime was that Dave was the Boss, especially after Mort Werner moved up in the NBC hierarchy to be succeeded by producers with less power than he had enjoyed. Garroway could fire anyone he chose to, but he didn't do it personally. It is perhaps a mark of his insecurity that pink slips usually appeared when Garroway was out of town.

"It got to be a joke around the studio," John Dunn, who became *Today*'s editor, says. "Every time Garroway took a trip we'd all look around and ask, 'Who's going to get the ax this time?' "

When John Dunn was hired as a writer in June 1958, he found "confusion at best and chaos at worst." Dunn was a superb editor and a former newspaperman who collected facts and esoterica as a vacuum cleaner collects lint, and his mind was as retentive as it was broad. John was grateful to Jac Hein, then the *Today* producer, for hiring him away from a public relations job he detested. What Dunn did not know was that Hein's relationship with Garroway had soured. Within days Hein was fired, and "I felt naked in the wind," says Dunn. Fortunately, he had already submitted a few ideas to Hein indicating the kind of item he thought should be done on the *Today Show*. Garroway found it difficult to write straightforward sentences but was nevertheless a good editor; he went over the writers' copy line for line with a blue pencil.

"He saw my scripts, and that did it for me," Dunn says. "I was given the writer's job. I had an advantage. Most of the writers then on the staff were pretty bad."

If John Dunn had been aware of the seriousness of *Today*'s problems in mid-1958, he might never have applied for the job. The show's revenues had evidently been faltering for some time, and the severe recession of 1957-58 caused advertisers to leave the show by the dozen. Suddenly, an attraction that had grossed at least $10 million a year to become television's all-time box office champ was down to the $3 million-$5 million range.

NBC decided it had to grab a bigger slice of *Today*'s revenue cake if the network was to make a profit on *Today*. It was unworkable to continue giving the local stations five minutes at 25 and 55 minutes after each hour and also let them have participation in the revenues the network pulled in on the rest of the commercial breaks. That had been the price Pat Weaver was forced to pay in 1951 to get the affiliates to clear time for the show. But now, with the show in trouble, something had to be done, and the affiliates knew it.

What NBC did was masterful. Dave Adams, currently NBC vice-chairman and for a long time RCA's canny behind-the-scenes man, dreamed up the solution. The network reclaimed the five minutes before each hour but left the affiliates with their two spots five minutes before each half hour. In exchange for giving up the two five-minute spots, the affiliates would have to themselves the two one-minute commercial spots in the first half hour of each *Today* hour. The network, meanwhile, would get exclusive use of the two one-minute commercial spots in the second half of each hour.

Thus, in the first half of each hour as a commercial minute loomed, Garroway would announce, "This is *Today* on NBC" —a phrase that was long enough to give affiliates time to cue in the commercials they sold locally. Those commercials were sold at whatever the traffic would bear, and the affiliates in major markets loved this. It meant more revenue than they would get by participating in network ads. They undoubtedly used their clout to help NBC sell the idea to the smaller affiliates, which by this time were locked into *Today* and had no alternative programming on hand. What NBC was *really* thinking about, according to one source, were the five stations in major markets which NBC owned and operated itself—New York City, Chicago, Los Angeles, Cleveland, and Washington. They could sell those four exclusive-to-the-affiliates one-minute spots at high prices, even if the smaller affiliates couldn't.

At the same time that the new revenue division was made, the network announced a change that would cut costs. Beginning on October 6, 1958, the show, seen live in the East and

Midwest, would be taped for later showing on the West Coast. Until then the show had been repeated live—at considerable expense—for the Western audience. Quality video tape, which unlike film required no developing, was finally available for immediate replay.

These developments coupled with a sale to DuPont—a bell-wether advertiser—at a reported $1 million got *Today* back on the track. The NBC salesmen would tell their prospects, "If DuPont is willing to spend $1 million, won't you spend $50,000?"

"That was the rate-card contract figure," John Dunn comments. "You and I know that that had little to do with what DuPont actually paid."

In the summer of 1958, while the bottom-line men at NBC were busy restoring *Today*'s financial health, Dave Garroway's voice was usually in low gear. When Garroway was angry, he didn't raise his voice, he whined, like a heavy truck creeping up a hill. "Oh, I'm being persecuted," he would moan, and a *Today* staffer with any sense would tool along quietly behind the star without calling attention to himself. For Garroway had the authority to dismiss anyone on the show, including producers, whom he hired and fired with increasing frequency in his final years. Not only did he fire Jac Hein, he made no move to replace him. All that summer the show's general manager, John Lynch, carried the responsibility of a producer but had no real authority. Described by an associate as "a very dear man and very capable in certain ways," Lynch was nevertheless not a guy to take charge. He plugged along from one week to the next, doubtlessly hoping that Garroway would let it be known that Lynch was to have the title as well as the job.

In September, however, Garroway moved Robert Bendick into the job. Bendick had held the job briefly on a previous occasion and was completely familiar with the technical aspects of production. But he was indecisive. Someone once said that if Bendick were handed a cup of piping-hot tea and asked whether he would take lemon or milk, the tea would freeze over before Bendick rendered his decision.

Bendick was soon busy acting as a diplomatic troubleshooter —keeping Garroway happy and out of contention with the NBC management. By this time, diplomacy was a constant uphill struggle. Like Sisyphus, Bendick repeatedly got the Garroway stone to the peak only to have it thunder down again in a firing, an internecine conflict, or a row over a production mishap.

Garroway could be petty. "Where are my scripts? How can I ad-lib without my scripts?" he growled in a now-famous line that sent production assistants scrambling for the missing materials.

Garroway was capable of extended campaigns against staff members, particularly those who did not measure up to his expectations. And Garroway's expectations ran high. Clearly harassed after years of carrying the burden of the *Today Show*, Garroway was always looking for someone who could bring perfection to the show. He wanted "a Jesus Christ," as someone described it.

It wasn't that Garroway didn't have a model. Gerald Green, the news editor in the early days and then a producer, was not perfect but he came close to being perfect for Garroway. Green was a man Garroway could admire. Garroway, a highly intelligent man, possessed a little knowledge about a lot of things and a comprehensive knowledge about relatively few. Jerry Green with his Phi Beta Kappa key and a dog-eared copy of the *Journal of the American Anthropology Association* usually in evidence seemed to Garroway to be a true intellectual, and Garroway respected that.

Green respected Garroway in return. "He was a very easy guy to get along with and easy to work with, too," Green says. "And I didn't have to kiss his ass."

Green developed a genuine affection for Garroway and confidently programed the show thinking about what "the big fellow" could handle best. Even when Garroway did not like all the material, Green could usually persuade him that it was best for the show and best for Garroway.

The only trouble was that Garroway needed Green more than Green needed Garroway, and Green resigned from the show to write *The Last Angry Man*.

In his later years on the show, Garroway, hoping to find another Green, was sometimes victimized by would-be saviors. Mediocre people would cuddle up to him—but they didn't last long. He soon saw their weaknesses and then they were out. One long-time *Today Show* Kremlinologist comments: "I saw phonies crawl into and out of Garroway's lap in a hurry."

When Garroway signed with the William Morris talent agency, the agent assigned to handle the account was Les Colodny. Comments a *Today Show* writer: "Colodny looked and talked like he could have been the Three Stooges' fourth, though he claimed a master's degree in English from the University of Illinois."

Colodny's great talent was as a supersalesman of himself. He soon began moving in on the *Today Show*, believing that his future lay there. In an effort to appear helpful, he convinced Garroway that four or five of the writers should go—a small loss in any case. The idea was for Colodny to bring in four whizzes. None of Colodny's writers was any good, though one managed to hang on for a couple of years anyway.

In time, Colodny was fired by William Morris. But Garroway, hoping Colodny would be another Jerry Green, insisted that Colodny be given a job as a writer. He got the job, though it soon became apparent that Colodny's verbal skill was mostly limited to inventing nicknames. Colodny called Win Welpen —probably the most nattily dressed man at NBC—"Irving P. Neat." Usually, though, Colodny ignored names and nicknames, summoning everyone with a "Hey, cockamaimie!"

It was inevitable that Garroway would see through Colodny. When he did, Garroway began to harass him. Dave developed a meticulously precise pattern for his pencils and made it Colodny's job to set them up each morning. He once made a rather absurd demand of Colodny for directional signs. "I want signs that I can see easily from where I sit," Garroway explained. "North, south, east, and west . . . so I'll know where I am. If I refer to something in Canada, I can point to the north." Colodny dutifully secured huge white sheets of cardboard, lettered them, and placed them in appropriate spots— though Garroway never used them.

Eventually Colodny was canned, and he went to the West Coast. Five years later, the *Today Show* was in Hollywood on a remote. John Dunn recalls that the studio dining room had different levels and everyone was seated in terms of status. The *Today Show* people were ushered to the top. "Jack Benny was sitting opposite me, picking his nose at lunch. I was fascinated.

"Anyway," Dunn continues, "a guy comes in doing that typical fatuous Hollywood business with a coat over his shoulders, arms free, giving the coat a cape effect. Barrymore used to do it with great effect. It was Colodny. I said, 'Hey, cockamaimie,' and he tried to evade me, but I wouldn't let him get away. When he finally gave up, he was quite willing to brag of how well he had done."

Garroway's treatment of Colodny was a calculated and not atypical effort to drive an out-of-favor functionary up the wall. There were times, though, when Garroway's actions seemed beyond the bounds of rational behavior.

Garroway began to suspect plots. He wired the stone lions in front of his house for sound and would listen to passersby, expecting to learn of dire schemes. Once during a *Today Show* trip, he ripped apart an electric blanket in a motel, thinking he would find a "bug." Then there were Garroway's poltergeists. Dave came to the studio very upset one day to report that the tools he had cleaned and stacked so neatly in his basement garage had been shuffled and misplaced by the playful spirits. Once, during a luncheon meeting with NBC's president, Robert Kintner, Garroway excused himself to go to the bathroom. He came back complaining that the poltergeists had been fooling around again; they had turned his shorts around so that the fly was in the back. An hour later Garroway excused himself a second time and came back to tell Kintner that the poltergeists were now behaving themselves; the fly was in front again.

Bendick suggests that it was part of Garroway's charm that he "always looked at things from an angle 180 degrees away from standard." Bendick felt that, as Garroway's condition deteriorated, he moved easily into the world of spirits and the like. Garroway might have needed supernatural help to make himself feel important enough to be Dave Garroway, according to Bendick. Yet for a man who felt responsibility for informing millions of people, Garroway enjoyed little sense of accomplishment. After years of being associated with history and big events, he apparently began to feel that he had the answers to the bad things in the world. But when he offered solutions—nothing happened, no one cared. Other television personalities have experienced the same sense of frustration— Steve Allen for one. Soon the Garroways of the world realize that people don't want to be warned constantly about the apocalypse. "After all, he's only a television person," is how the public ultimately reacts. An intelligent man like Garroway senses this and begins to feel disheartened.

The poltergeist stories came out when Garroway was particularly disturbed. Bendick heard these stories often enough to realize that Garroway desperately needed relief. In a decision that Bendick now regards as a mistake, he arranged to tape the *Today Show* late in the afternoon for telecasting at the usual hours the next day. The primary motivation, according to Bendick, was to give Garroway a chance to recover his physical stamina and perhaps give him a little brighter mental attitude.

"*Today* Becomes Yesterday" was the way *The New York Times* headlined the story. At the time, NBC claimed that the new, more convenient hours were chosen so that more VIPs would want to do the show. Also, NBC explained, the taping would resolve a union problem. Portions of the show which had been taped in Paris, and were highly successful, had not met all union rules, and New York members struck the network for seventeen days. The problem had been resolved under the new taping format. Garroway's health and its role in the switch to tape was conveniently left out of the announcement.

The same week the taping decision was announced, the hazards of live broadcasts and the power of *Today* were both made abundantly clear. Canada's Joyce Davidson, a beautiful actress and television personality, was interviewed by Garroway and remarked that she was rather indifferent to the forthcoming Canadian visit of Queen Elizabeth marking the opening of the St. Lawrence Seaway. Joyce added that her attitude was shared by many Canadians. Almost before she stopped talking, Joyce was being asked to resign from her $12,000-a-year job with the Canadian Broadcasting Corporation—which she did—and Garroway found himself and *Today* embroiled in an international controversy involving freedom of speech. Weeks passed, the controversy died down, and Joyce finally got her job back.

If live shows were hazardous, taped shows could be even more so, Bendick and Garroway soon discovered. And the man who caused the problem happened to be one who Garroway, in his most extreme state of emotional insecurity, never suspected of plots or phoniness.

In 1958, Charles Van Doren, one of the hottest properties in broadcasting, became the *Today Show*'s resident wise man. A personable young teacher-scholar from a distinguished literary family, Van Doren had beguiled a nation of egghead haters while winning big money on NBC's quiz show *Twenty-One*. Pitted against Herbert Stempel, a savant whose vast knowledge was equaled only by his unpopularity with viewers, Van Doren seemed to be struggling feverishly. He'd pause before answering some parts of a question, skip and then return to tough sections later, until he had gotten the solution to brain-teasers so complex the American public could scarcely believe it. Charles went on to defeat other contestants and rake in $129,000.

Van Doren was a natural for regular appearances on *Today*. He read and discussed poetry as he might in a freshman English class and handled other cultural subjects with ease. Soon Van Doren was so popular he was the obvious choice as Garroway's summer replacement. He was serving in that capacity when Herbert Stempel charged that the *Twenty-One* show had been fixed. The public, and Van Doren's friends at *Today*, sought reassurances from the man who now represented intellectualism in the nation, and Van Doren complied, insisting on a *Today* broadcast that he knew of no irregularities. Thousands of letters flooded *Today*, many from schoolchildren, expressing confidence in the young scholar.

Today staffers sighed with relief—not only because they genuinely liked Van Doren, but because they too wanted to believe he was a bona fide American folk hero. But Stempel persisted, and a New York grand jury began to investigate. In January 1959, Van Doren again gave assurances, as did other quiz show veterans. The game, all chorused, was played straight. But discrepancies cropped up in their stories, and Congress became alarmed that the American people might have been flimflammed in a colossal charade on the sacrosanct public airwaves. A special House subcommittee commenced a full-scale investigation.

Feeling that their associate was being persecuted and having Van Doren's personal assurance of his innocence, Bendick and Garroway decided to make a public declaration of 100 percent support. In the 3 to 5 P.M. taping that day, Garroway defended Van Doren, saying he simply did not believe Charles knew anything about the matter. Garroway wept while delivering his tribute to the young man.

Meanwhile, Van Doren had been wrestling with his conscience for some time. Finally, he decided to come clean. He wrote NBC a letter admitting he was carefully coached in his answers on *Twenty-One* and that even his manner of answering—straining for bits of information, his face screwed up—had been a sham as well. The news broke, loudly, just after the *Today Show* with Garroway's defense of Van Doren had been taped.

Bendick had made a rule that the tape for the next day's show would always be shown as recorded, without editing changes. So Bendick and Garroway decided to let this show's tape run as is the next morning, believing that an unedited tape was essential for credibility. Almost no one else agreed. The newspaper critics laid into *Today*.

"It was our decision, Dave's and mine," Bendick says now. "We felt we were right at the time, but quickly realized we were not."

Today's managing editor at the time of the debacle still hasn't forgiven Van Doren. Al Smith says, "None of us felt strongly about the fact that Van Doren was getting the answers. After all, *Today* was called 'spontaneous' when in fact it was basically a scripted show. What hurt was that the man we all thought had such quality had proved himself to be a damn fool. If he had simply said, 'Look, this is a *game* show; a *controlled* show. I did it, sure, so what?' But to *lie* about it! We all felt like someone had kicked us in the gut."

Another *Today* writer of the period comments: "Remember, they didn't buy him for big money. They gave him the answer to that *first* question. He sold out for $1,000."

Bendick's mistake didn't help his already insecure position. For the past year, Bendick had officially been the show's producer, but the person who mostly ran things was the "program manager," Gene Jones. An ex-Marine, Jones was described by a colleague as "a real tough monkey," and had established a reputation for courage in Korea as an NBC cameraman.

As program manager for the *Today Show*, Jones always prefaced his orders with the words "I'm acting for Bob Bendick." But everyone knew that Jones was in effect the biggest chief this side of Garroway. Bendick was just hanging on, in a limbo. To the surprise of many, however, Jones left the show before Bendick did, because he ran afoul of Garroway.

Each year the show did something special to mark its anniversary. And in January 1960, Jones had had an idea for the anniversary show, which was approved by Bendick. They would tape the entire show in Washington, D.C. The highlight of the broadcast would be a television first—Garroway in the White House interviewing Dwight D. Eisenhower. Martin Agronsky, NBC's Washington correspondent, assured Jones that Eisenhower would appear with Garroway. Jim Hagerty, the President's press secretary, had told Agronsky that the "old man" would give his approval. Plans went ahead even though final approval hadn't come from the White House. Then, only hours before the taping, Hagerty called to report that Ike wasn't going to open the White House door.

As Garroway moaned his complaints, the staffers looked at one another with helpless "What do we do now?" expressions. About half an hour of the anniversary show had been allocated to the Eisenhower interview.

Garroway recovered enough to suggest that if he had some background material, he could "stand on the White House lawn and talk about that wonderful place."

But there was no script. The staff had an enormous suite in the Sheraton Park Hotel, and Garroway went there with Al Smith and another writer. Fortunately, Al had complete materials on the White House. But there was no time to write it, at least not in the normal way. Improvising, Al gave Garroway facts about the White House and Garroway dictated into a tape recorder. Garroway's "script" was then put on the teleprompter. The writers looked it over and were aghast. There wasn't a single complete sentence. But later on, on the White House lawn, Garroway read it in his inimitable style and it worked beautifully.

The production wasn't in the clear yet. Garroway was scheduled for another piece, this one to be taped at the Supreme Court that afternoon. Arriving quite late, Garroway stood around morosely waiting to start. Gene Jones' twin brother, Charles, a lighting man assigned to the show, ran into a problem. It was the writer's responsibility to stick at Garroway's elbow to answer his questions, but when Gene spied John Dunn standing near the star, he told Dunn to help move a lighting table. Dunn knew Garroway's moods well and realized how angry Garroway was then. Apprehensively, Dunn replied, "Well, listen, I'm supposed to stay by Garroway." With that Gene Jones yelled, with Garroway just thirty feet away, "Fuck Garroway!"

Says Dunn, "I was stunned . . . the bell was tolling for Gene Jones. But it was also tinkling for Bendick because Garroway would hold the producer responsible in the last analysis."

Jones was gone within weeks—to an NBC historical documentary unit.

The bell tolled for Bob Bendick in the Forum in Rome. Elated by the success of the Paris remote, *Today* planned subsequent week-long visits overseas, beginning with the Italian capital in April 1960. Dealing with Garroway in Rome proved to be difficult. His general condition was quite poor by then, and his moods were occasionally severe enough to interfere with the show.

The company was taping a complicated segment at the Forum, and things had gone wrong all day—one technical problem followed by another. Garroway was standing in front of Caesar's tomb, doing Marc Antony's funeral oration.

"Garroway was a master nit-picker," John Dunn recalls, "and he was nit-picking me. Bendick was sitting in a truck fifty yards away and could hear us on the sound equipment. Finally, I got fed up. I turned to Dave and said, 'I've had it, Dave. If you want me sent back to New York, I'm ready to go.' "

Dunn turned and began walking away. Then he saw Bendick bounding up to Garroway. Though a very quiet, polished man, Bendick looked furious. Like any writer with a sense of the dramatic, Dunn was unwilling to miss what promised to be a choice moment, and he slowed down. For once, Bendick was in full voice.

"He let loose on Garroway," Dunn recalls, "and gave him a tongue-lashing such as I never heard and justified it by the fact that we were just about to lose the sun, which was dipping behind the Palatine Hills on the west side of the Forum. If we lost it, it would mean another day of shooting.

"Garroway just stood there—shocked to get a public tongue-lashing. Finally, he said, 'Let's get on with it.' He got down to business and finished in a couple of minutes. But he also finished Bendick. At least, from there on in everybody knew Bob wouldn't last much longer."

Like so many others on *Today*, Bendick was dropped while the show was out of town. It happened a few months after the Rome visit when the show was covering the Democratic Convention in Los Angeles. Quite by chance, NBC president Bob Kintner and Dave Garroway met in the L.A. airport and discovered that they had an hour-and-a-half delay before their flight to New York. It was the perfect opportunity for Garroway to speak his mind and he did so, listing all the reasons why Bendick had to be fired. "It was a lot of bull," says one source, but Garroway convinced Kintner. A man given to immediate action, Kintner strode to a pay phone, called someone in New York, and said to tell Bendick he wasn't producer any more.

Thirteen years later, in May 1973, John Dunn retired from the *Today Show* and invited his old friend Bob Bendick to his farewell party. Dunn remembers, "I hadn't seen Bendick in a number of years. I said, 'I guess neither of us will ever forget the Roman Forum,' recalling that fatal moment."

Dunn was startled when Bendick grinned and said, "Yeah, wasn't it great riding those horses," recalling a horse race down the Via Sacre that the two of them had staged.

"*He* remembered the happy time and I remembered the incident that led to his dismissal," Dunn says. "I told him how I admired his courage because he was supporting me, really. And he said, 'That!' and wiped it away with a wave of his hand."

After the Roman Forum incident there were a few more firings, and one tragic death, before the Garroway era of *Today* ended.

CHAPTER 13

Garroway's Final Curtain

Gerald Green saw Dave Garroway as "pleasantly eccentric." But one Garroway eccentricity that struck many as less than pleasant was his tightness with a dollar. It was probably a measure of the personal insecurity he felt that he concerned himself so much with saving small change toward the end of his *Today* career.

Seemingly Garroway was made wealthy by *Today*. By 1960, NBC was paying him about a quarter of a million dollars a year to do the show. He often talked about oil well investments and was known to pour thousands of dollars into vintage car restoration. And yet Garroway's small tips left waitresses fuming, and the souvenir-quality gifts to *Today* staffers at Christmas often as not wound up in waste baskets. In a business in which presents costing $50 to $100 were common, one *Today* person says that two-dollar "reflecting cuff links" and key chains and timers to monitor parking meters were typical of Garroway's largesse. Anxious even about the money he carried on his person, Garroway was the first man Al Smith ever knew to chain his wallet to his belt.

In much better health and emotional condition today, Garroway remains careful. A recent Garroway Christmas card was an elaborate money-related gag. It contained a lengthy handwritten "formula" which he called a "quork" and said was derived from readings of Einstein and Newton. The card went on to say that the quork was designed to measure affection and loyalty factors on both sides. The available gift money was then divided among all recipients according to quork score. Charles Andrews, Garroway's best friend, opened his card and a personal check for $4.45 dropped out. Since Andrews was so close to Garroway, just how much money was in the Garroway Christmas fund? Not much, obviously. At least it was a *funny* valentine.

Today writer Bud Lewis was bothered by another manifestation of Garroway's insecurity—his extreme dependence on others. Lewis is the least charitable of Garroway's critics, which may reflect the fact that for the bulk of the time Lewis wrote for the show Garroway was too far into his decline to allow normal relationships with his co-workers. Others believed that Garroway in his prime was a good editor and thoughtful counselor as well as a performer, but Lewis saw him only as the latter. He believed Garroway to have a "paper thin" mind, based on the degree to which Garroway relied on the scripts Lewis prepared for him. Lewis scoffed at Garroway's efforts to convince the public of his encyclopedic knowledge, and comments that Garroway could ask "three questions on almost anything" and then there was nothing more.

"He liked people to think him really deep," Lewis says. "He wanted to be thought clever, when as a matter of fact he couldn't even manage a joke. He could manage an amusing feeling, but not a joke. I did a warm, amusing 'Talk of the Town' kind of writing for him and he could handle that.

"I had a theory about David. He came to this kind of superstardom at a time when there were no established criteria for a TV star. If you were a stage personality and I were to say to you that you had star quality, you would know what I meant. But there were no such concepts on TV. The fact is, Dave didn't know *what* he had. I thought I knew. He had a quality. You could see him happening on the air, and he was happening all the time—he was fascinating to watch. It was as though you were observing him through a keyhole.

"Not knowing what he had, Garroway seemed to feel that the reason he had gotten ahead was because he had surrounded himself with terribly clever people. He found them and then depended on them entirely."

As the *Today* host turned more and more to Lewis—telling the other writers, for instance, that he wouldn't speak any lines unless Lewis approved them—Lewis became apprehensive over his role. "I almost had a feeling of what it was like to be a woman," he says. "I can tell you that I felt uneasy in this kind of relationship."

This feeling, Lewis indicates, reflected what was by now "a terrible insecurity" that led to unreasonable demands. Garroway began to lose his confidence to a degree that can only be described as bizarre.

"Garroway was involved in some charity, and the President invited him to the White House," Lewis recounts. "He was to go down there and receive an award. Jack Kennedy would shake his hand and there would be pictures. Nothing more. Garroway called me in and told me about the award, and I said, 'Fine.' Then he said, 'I want a script.'"

Lewis was baffled, and Garroway told him that what he wanted were "ad-libs" in case he and the President got involved in a conversation. There could be no way for Lewis to anticipate what might be discussed between the two men, and he asked Garroway, "How?" Finally, when Garroway persisted, Lewis compiled a set of 3 by 5 inch cards with "interesting comments" Garroway could drop in if the occasion demanded.

Still not confident about going to Washington and facing the President alone—though he had interviewed many world figures on the show—Garroway insisted that Lewis make the trip with him. "I was actually there when he met the President," Lewis says. "They had maybe fourteen words together, and then we came back. Garroway wasn't clever; he had no sharp turns of phrases, but he wanted to project all that."

Another trying occasion occurred when Bud Lewis and his wife were attending an opening night at the theater. A note was brought to Lewis from Garroway, who wanted to see him at once. When Lewis telephoned him, Garroway demanded that Lewis come over immediately. Lewis recalls: "I said, 'Can't it wait until after the show?' He said, 'If you don't come right now I'll jump out the window.' My wife was furious, but I went over and it was absolutely trivial."

By this time Garroway's erratic behavior was affecting his on-air performances. Always concerned about attack from Communist countries, Garroway during one show said that the United Press was treasonous because of a story they ran. The show had gone back to live broadcasts sometime after the Van Doren defense, and after the Garroway remark about the U.P., Lewis said, "The place was crawling with lawyers."

Lewis' relationship with Garroway started on its predestined decline. Garroway began to feel abandoned in front of the cameras, as he always did, thinking that those he had trusted were pursuing their own selfish ends at his expense. First, Garroway decided to get rid of his producer, Robert "Shad" Northshield, who had succeeded Bob Bendick.

Earlier Garroway had asked Northshield to produce a one-hour Garroway evening special. Garroway knew that his hold on *Today* was shaky, and he perhaps hoped that the special would lead to a fall-back position—a regular show in NBC prime time. To write the script Shad hired Andy Rooney, a well-known television writer who had worked for Arthur Godfrey and was the only writer Godfrey never fired. But when Rooney turned in his material, Garroway read it and hated it. He then turned to Bud Lewis and another writer. The effort, according to Lewis himself, was "slap-dash." *Dave's Place* was "all about Rockefeller Center and not a particularly good show."

But that was a small matter. Shad spent heavily on the production, and the show went way over budget. It turned out that Garroway, who never so much as bought lunch for Bud Lewis, had backed the show with his own money.

The firing of Northshield followed the standard pattern. Garroway was out of town the day Shad got the sack. Garroway then brought in Fred Freed as producer, and he was "hired to fire," says Lewis. He did so. Lewis and others were axed—just a month or so before Garroway himself left the show in the wake of a tragedy in his personal life.

Pamela Wilde de Coninck, Dave Garroway's second wife, was born in Los Angeles but grew up in Paris, where her father was a movie company executive. In Paris she had been successively a ballet dancer, actress, radio commentator, movie and TV producer. Back in New York with two children and divorced from the Marquis de Coninck, Pamela had a speaking part in *Lute Song* with Yul Brynner on Broadway. She and Dave met at a weekend party at producer Billy Rose's house in Mount Kisco, New York, when Pamela was twenty-six and Dave forty-one. Though she sat opposite Garroway at dinner, he didn't speak a word to her. But he called later and professed to have been fascinated. They dated. She found him to be gracious and courteous, always lighting her cigarettes, looking to her comfort. Pamela was a good cook, and after Dave cindered some steaks on an early date, she took to the kitchen. Dave had told her that his seven years of living alone since his divorce had been neither happy nor unhappy, but he was obviously impressed with Pamela's domesticity.

When he finally proposed, he was both offhanded and firm: "I bought you a ring. Would you like to wear it? . . . You had better tell your bosses that you are going to quit your job this summer."

They were married on August 7, 1956. In time, Pamela and Dave had a son, David Cunningham Garroway, Jr. While Pamela was giving birth, Garroway spent the hours with his stepson Michael, watching TV and working with him in the basement garage.

Pamela painted a favorable portrait of their marriage in a March 8, 1959, article entitled "I Married Dave Garroway" in the *American Weekly*. She said that the word that best characterized her husband was "wise." She spoke of arguments— but no shouting matches. Even in domestic disputes Dave's words were understated, she indicated. "I would prefer things *not* to be this way," he would say. If that was a true picture of the marriage, it changed for the worse thereafter.

Charlie Andrews had a far less charitable view. He saw Pamela as "beautiful, but mixed up." He adds: "Garroway should have married a milkmaid and she a dentist. Instead they found each other."

By early 1961, Dave and Pam were strangers in the narrow brownstone they occupied on the fashionable East Side of Manhattan on East 63rd Street near Madison Avenue. Dave used The Doctor so often those days that it was difficult for him to get to sleep. He began spending more and more of his off-hours in the basement, working on his Jaguar and his vintage Rolls-Royce. Bud Lewis was aware of Pamela's growing unhappiness. "She once told me that he would go to the cellar and work on his cars for ten to twelve hours before coming to bed," he says.

On April 28, 1961, Dave Garroway was in their summer place in Westhampton, Long Island. (It was his second home on the Island. The first one was sold at a huge profit. The day after the buyer took title, a hurricane struck the site and totally destroyed the house.) Pamela on this spring day was in New York City at the Garroway brownstone.

Mrs. Garroway had been under treatment for a nervous disorder, and telephoned her doctor, Henry Horn. After she hung up, the doctor reflected on her nervous manner and put in a call to the Garroway housekeeper, asking the woman to look in on Pamela. The housekeeper and Pamela's daughter went to her room and found her dead. She had taken an overdose of barbiturates. Pam's son Michael was also at home. David Garroway, Jr., was just three years old.

Garroway was obviously shaken but he didn't leave the *Today Show* immediately. He had been seeking a new contract and continued to press for it after Pamela's death. One day, just before the show was to go on the air, he lay down on the floor and wouldn't get up. Garroway had warned that he would quit if he did not get the conditions he demanded. The floor caper was the last straw. NBC called his bluff and said goodbye to its flickering star. Garroway was at liberty for the first time in years.

The newspapers carried the story as presented to them, and the rupture got the obligatory powder-puff treatment. Dave was quoted as saying that he regretted the need for resigning, "But I've become increasingly aware lately that for the past ten years, I've been on the air doing a great deal of talking. I want to start looking, thinking and listening to people."

He then alluded to the death of Pamela, saying: "Even more

important to me, I want to be the best father I can be to three beautiful and exciting children during a critical period in their lives. Our family needs each other now more than ever."

The *Today Show* was a fixture by then. It was respected and even loved. Busy men who saw little other television during the week watched *Today*. Newton N. Minow, chairman of the Federal Communications Commission, named the program first as an example of TV programing that did not fall into the "vast wasteland" which Minow had said characterized TV.

But Dave Garroway was finished on television. He never really managed a comeback, though he tried several times.

Six years after Garroway left *Today*, the show approached its fifteenth anniversary. Al Morgan, then the producer, had arranged for film clips of early shows to be put together and for the three men who had occupied the host's chair to make an appearance. Hugh Downs, the current host, would preside, assisted by his immediate predecessor John Chancellor and by Garroway.

Downs and Chancellor were bright-eyed and bushy-tailed for the occasion. But Garroway arrived in a fog, barely able, it seemed, to stay awake. He entered the studio shortly before 7 A.M. and slumped into his chair.

Morgan was so apprehensive that he considered a last-minute substitution of a full-sized cardboard figure of Garroway, a sales aid during the Garroway years for drugstore and supermarket promotions. Instead, Morgan took a chance with Garroway live. As the cameras focused on Downs—ready to switch to Chancellor and then to the inanimate form of Garroway—Morgan realized that he had taken a wild chance and apparently lost. The countdown began. When the *Today* clock said 7 A.M., the camera focused on Hugh Downs, who said,

"Good morning, this is *Today* in New York." The camera then focused on Chancellor, who also said, "Good morning, this is *Today* in New York." Then the camera focused on Garroway, who at the last possible moment had perked up, assuming his familiar relaxed pose to say, "Hi. How are you? I've *missed* you."

Fairly recently, Garroway had a radio talk and music show out of KFI Los Angeles, not far from his present home on top of the Hollywood Hills. But the show is now off the air.

Garroway hasn't had a network show in fifteen years—with one exception. His agent had scheduled another client to do a summer replacement. But, comments Garroway, "CBS's Fred Silverman, bless his heart, said, 'I don't want an unknown. Isn't Garroway out there? Have him do it.' "

Garroway explains that either his show or another CBS summer replacement would make the CBS fall schedule, the outcome to be determined by the ratings. Unfortunately for Garroway, the other show was *Sonny & Cher*.

Recently Garroway attempted to sell a network on an afternoon show not unlike *Today* but aimed at viewers forty and older, including those preparing to retire. When Garroway approached Freddy Silverman, who had switched to ABC, the network's president of entertainment lifted Garroway's spirits but turned the idea down. Garroway quotes Silverman as saying: "Dave, this is a bomber, I'll tell you. Come back in three or four years and I'll be a hero. But if I went in this afternoon with it, I'd get thrown out on my ass."

Not long afterward, a *Daily News* gossip column carried an item that appeared to blow Freddy's cover. The columnist reported that Silverman's tactful way of letting "has beens" down gently was to tell them their ideas were just great, but too far ahead of their time to be usable: "The old-timers go away without a sale, but with their egos glowing," explained the columnist.

Too bad. To the author the idea seemed workable. What's more, Garroway seemed in excellent health and in good spirits when he spent hours with the author and his wife, captivating them both some months ago in Swarthmore, Pennsylvania, at the home of a Garroway friend. He seemed very much the Dave Garroway who had millions of fans two decades earlier. He was charming, overflowing with anecdotes as he phrased his tales like an experienced writer, editing his remarks for full dramatic effect. And not a script or teleprompter in sight. He even bought us lunch.

CHAPTER 14

The Evening News at 7 A.M.

Garroway's departure from *Today* was so sudden that there was little time for NBC to analyze his extraordinary accomplishment. For without a doubt, Garroway's curious blend of magnetism and intelligent curiosity was critical to *Today*'s success in its first decade. Personal problems aside, Garroway was emphatically the communicator Pat Weaver had in mind when he dreamed up *Today*, and Garroway remained the master of the method to the end.

Few viewers, it seems, were aware of Garroway's disintegration, though *Today* staffer Win Welpen remembers being annoyed when his mother said, "I'm sorry, but I don't understand what he's saying," only to discover on careful analysis that *he* didn't always understand what Garroway was saying either.

Perhaps NBC can be forgiven its failure to appreciate Garroway, for in 1961 they were dealing primarily with his intractability and not his talent. The network itself had no clear plan for the show, so it is understandable that the news department, which had always hated the independence enjoyed by *Today*, quickly moved to take control of the production. Without the least notion of the critical importance of the Garroway style and skill at delivering commercials, News moved to find a successor.

The race was restricted, naturally, to electronic journalists —three NBC correspondents, all solid citizens with little discernible humor and not an ounce of show business savvy in the lot. They shared a common restraint: they were *newsmen*, not hucksters, and the commercials, regardless of who won, would have to be done by someone else. The network decided to let the public in on the competition and announced that contenders would be Edwin Newman, recently back from Europe; Ray Scherer, correspondent in Washington, D.C.; and John Chancellor, who was returning from Moscow.

It was an odd race. Only one stallion left the standing gate. While the plan had been to allow each man two weeks as trial host, one week into the kick-off performance by John Chancellor and News had seen enough. Chancellor got his working papers. Frank Blair, the man then widely regarded as the best news reader in the business, was succeeded by Edwin Newman, and Blair became resident purveyor of light features. That had been Jack Lescoulie's job, but Lescoulie was off the show—and mad as hell about it.

Producer Fred Freed, brought in from CBS to sweep Garroway's final team out of the shop, was experiencing one of the shortest reigns ever. Shortly after passing out the pink slips, Freed took to his bed for six weeks, seriously ill with a disease that normally affects children—chickenpox. An able executive, Freed had begun to bring some order to the show, but Chancellor, who had known Shad Northshield in salad days in Chicago, wanted his old friend back as producer. Northshield had been off the show less than six months when he returned to do his second stint as producer. Shad was the show's eighth and tenth producer; Bob Bendick had been its fourth and seventh.

Chancellor hadn't really wanted to hang up his trench coat and slip behind the Garroway desk. But, he explained: "I couldn't resist the overnight differential." His pay was hiked from a middle-class neighborhood of $20,000-$25,000 to a Park Avenue $100,000 a year.

It was certainly a change from a couple of years earlier when Chancellor was number-two man for NBC in the British capital and the frosty Joseph C. Harsch was number one. John once drew a fellow London newsman aside in a bar frequented by journalists to ask why they were all calling him "boy." Chancellor learned that whenever anything official came up that Harsch didn't want to attend, he would say, "I can't come, but I'll send my boy."

Though by all accounts Chancellor can be very amusing, it quickly became apparent that *Today* viewers were being served bland Chancellor. Somehow it was Chancellor's dignity, not his wit, that viewers experienced. He wasn't able to turn on the charm.

Two months into the *Today* run, the Chancellors had dinner with NBC president Robert Kintner and his wife. John regaled the foursome with stories so amusing that Kintner felt compelled to ask Chancellor why he didn't use humor on the show. Chancellor replied, "I never know when I say a funny thing until somebody laughs."

Perhaps canned laughter would have helped loosen him up. The new team certainly needed something. Newman, who had a reputation for dry humor which he still revels in today, was just plain dry. Frank Blair's Irish wit was mostly too black and bawdy for television, and besides, he too liked to project dignity. Within months the grim two-hour show resembled nothing so much as a morning edition of the evening news, at a time when nobody was ready for that except Edwin, John, and

Frank. Everyone was desperate for comic relief. The show turned to skits—an old standby. But the writers on the show were not professional comedy writers, and the cast members were certainly not actors.

Today writers were forever leafing through almanacs looking for light feature ideas, and one day someone discovered that it was the fiftieth anniversary of an obscure anti-saloon melodrama. *Today* decided to do a condensed version with Frank Blair as a drunken father and Newman as an evil saloon keeper. To Newman, the whole thing was a lark. To viewers, it was a disaster.

Occasionally, the light stuff did come off—silent film star Harold Lloyd describing his funny cliff-hangers, humorist-poet Ogden Nash reading from his *Golden Trashery of Ogden Nashery*. And the content of the show in general was certainly superior to most television fare. But the overall effect was just too heavy for morning viewing. And skits were obviously not the answer with the Newman-Blair duo.

Frank Blair was supposed to provide the humor that used to come from Lescoulie. Lescoulie was a sort of Peck's Bad Boy who could be relied on to accidentally fall into the Trevi fountain in Rome, deliberately dive into an open tank truck filled with water, make corny but amusing ad-lib comments, and even ape an ape in the J. Fred Muggs years.

But Blair in that role? With his sense of dignity, giving Blair comedy material was a little like casting Robert Young as the Fonz. It was nonsense like this and a tentative quality about the show that turned off viewers, who turned off sets. They began looking for alternative wake-ups—other TV, the radio—by the millions.

Advertisers became restless, even DuPont. During the final Garroway period, DuPont had been *Today*'s mainstay. Northshield says the giant chemical company once bought close to half the advertising time on the show. But shortly after the switch to Chancellor, DuPont advertising chiefs began edging toward the door and then walked out.

The sales department, meanwhile, vainly beseeched Chancellor to do commercials. The pressures mounted, but Chancellor was adamant. Comments an associate of those years, "I don't think he could have gotten a commercial out of his mouth. He simply didn't have the temperament for it."

For some reason, Sales never approached Newman. The head of the news department, Bill McAndrew, once asked Edwin wistfully, "You wouldn't do commercials, would you?" His tentative question revealed his own misgivings about the never-never, and provided Newman with the expected answer. Newman and Chancellor kept their virginity.

Naturally, things got worse. Northshield comments: "We began to lose sponsors like nothing you ever saw. Oh *boy*, did we lose sponsors!" Less than a year after the new cast took over, Northshield adds, "We were certainly not making any money."

The solution was all too obvious. In May 1962, Newman was canned. That summer Chancellor, who insists he resigned, was actually fired. In keeping with *Today* tradition, Chancellor and Northshield were both out of town, on a remote broadcast in Hollywood, when NBC swung the ax lopping off both heads.

In deference to Chancellor—still regarded as a comer—the official word given out was that he left voluntarily. He remained in the host's chair until October 1, when his successor, Hugh Downs, arrived after finally having worked out his prior contract. In time, of course, Chancellor became anchorman for NBC *Evening News*, the job he had been aiming at all along.

Newman, NBC's utility infielder, does occasional by-lined pieces on *Today*, instant specials for the network, and writes books about English usage. *Plain Speaking* was Newman's bestseller. Like most of those who care so very much about the sanctity of language, Newman cannot resist correcting those who make mistakes in grammar and pronunciation. The author visited Newman shortly after Tom Brokaw was named *Today* host and mentioned the name. As a midsentence aside, Newman said, "And by the way, it's pronounced 'Bro-caw.' " The author had been forewarned. A hand-lettered sign in Newman's office says, "Abandon all hopefullys ye who enter these gates."

Newman, who has probably served as substitute host on *Today* more than anyone else, apparently still believes that he might have made a good permanent host. During a lull in the conversation, Newman said, "I expected you to ask why I never became host of *Today*."

Newman had remarked earlier that the questioner who doesn't rush in with the next question often discovers that the interviewee feels obliged to fill the gap—often telling more than he intended.

"Why didn't you become host of *Today*?" asked the author.

"I never did because I was never asked," Newman said.

CHAPTER 15

A New Star, a New Producer, and an Old Smile

When Hugh Downs arrived to host *Today*, his new producer, Al Morgan, was already on the set. The two men had worked together on Pat Weaver's *Home Show*, the third star in Weaver's galaxy with *Today* and *Tonight*. An army of homemakers thought *Home* marvelous, but Bobby Sarnoff canceled it in favor of a string of soap operas after Weaver left NBC. Downs and Morgan were both hired to do *Today* by Carl Lindemann, a former unit manager at *Home* who was now the executive in charge of *Today* as special projects director for NBC News, which still had final authority over the show. Everyone, including probably Lindemann, assumed that the new producer and his star, as old *Home* folks, had a close rapport. Everyone assumed wrong.

Morgan arrived in the summer of 1961, while Chancellor was running out his string. Jack Lescoulie returned to the show at the same time, to help provide comic relief. Downs came at the end of September, after completing his contract to the *Jack Paar Show*.

145

In 1961, Jack Paar, with Hugh Downs as his announcer, was almost as successful with the old *Tonight* format—renamed in Jack's honor—as Johnny Carson is today. Those who worked on the show were always being asked, "What is Jack Paar *really* like?" People seemed to suspect that the mercurial host might be pretty mean. For nice guy though he usually appeared, Paar did have a quiet, sinister aspect and on occasion was quite rough and abrasive. Downs, by contrast, was always the cool, unflappable gentleman. Paar's usual shtick with Downs was to suggest that his announcer was one of the world's brilliant men. Downs would then rattle off facts on esoteric subjects, thus furthering the impression.

Downs had been to college—at Bluffton (Ohio) and Wayne State University in Detroit—and was unquestionably intelligent, with a wide-ranging mind. His light symphonic piece, using a self-taught scoring system, was once offered in concert by a major orchestra, and he was as interested in polishing and looking through telescopes as his old friend Garroway.

Downs had started announcing at the age of nineteen in Lima, Ohio, in 1930. By coincidence, he was discovered by the same canny NBC Central Division executive, Jules Herbuveaux, who also discovered Garroway and Chancellor. Hugh joined NBC in Chicago in 1943 after serving in the Army. He was brought to New York in 1954 to be the "young man" opposite Arlene Francis on the *Home Show*. Downs often did "gee whiz" pieces. He might say, "Isn't man strange? He builds a house to get out of the cold, but it's too hot for his food, so he builds a refrigerator, which is too cold for the butter, so he makes a little box within the box within the box for it." Hugh was good at that kind of fresh look at things.

Downs loved nothing more than the opportunity to sound authoritative. Once on a remote in Quebec, Hugh, Joe Garagiola, and their wives were sightseeing when Joe noticed that the cathedral they were touring had not been completed. It seemed to Joe that every cathedral he had ever seen was still unfinished, and he wondered aloud if there was a completed cathedral anywhere in the world. Ruth Downs said, "Hugh will know," and when Hugh joined them, Ruth asked. Hugh said cautiously, "Don't any of you know?" All said, "No." With that, Hugh began confidently, "Well, then . . ." and spoke with authority on the finishing of cathedrals.

Judith Crist, a *Today* movie reviewer during the Downs years, says that the two questions she was asked most on lecture tours were: "Is Hugh Downs as intelligent as he seems?" and "Is that Barbara Walters' own hair?"

In answering the first question, Judy says Downs is "surprisingly broad" without being an intellectual. "And he did know a lot about a hell of a lot of things," she says. "You would discover him to be a musicologist and great at needlepoint. He and his wife did squares on the plane. He did motorcycles and deep sea diving—so many things men his age wouldn't do. I happen to like Hugh Downs very much." According to a less charitable *Today* staffer, "Downs is a mile wide and an inch deep."

Downs was once made to appear stupid by a man who apparently knew nothing of Downs' reputation for intelligence. Ian Fleming, author of the James Bond stories, had perhaps become bored by repeated television appearances before he did *Today*. In any event, just before the two men went on the air, he whispered to Hugh, "Ask me why I bought a Mercedes." Hugh said okay, and when they went on dutifully asked, "Tell me, Mr. Fleming, why did you buy a Mercedes?" Fleming retorted hotly, "Huh? Who told you that? What kind of nonsense is this?" Simple perversity, it seems, but Downs was badly shaken.

Though Downs usually managed to appear well informed, a scholar he was not. Rather, he was a quick study. Hugh could commit to mind surprising amounts of information in a jiffy.

He once spent two minutes studying twenty-five questions to be asked on *Today*, then handed the list to a *Today* associate and recited each question back word for word as the associate called out the question numbers at random.

It was memory more than brilliance that had enabled Downs to appear so erudite on the *Jack Paar Show*. "Jack Paar *invented* Hugh Downs," one *Today* writer says. "Downs began to believe Jack Paar was right—that he was that bright . . . Downs is the only guy I know who read the Great Books alphabetically."

Not long after Downs joined *Today*, someone remarked that Downs had been the intellectual of the *Jack Paar Show*, and Al Morgan quipped, "J. Fred Muggs could be that." It was the opening gun in the longest war in *Today* history.

Morgan began his broadcast career before World War II. As a student of radio at New York University, Morgan found Long Island's smallest radio station and offered them free half-hour dramas weekly. In the next three years he wrote 150 scripts, acted in many of them, and subsequently sold most of them to the radio networks. He then wrote scripts for *The Lone Ranger, The Thin Man, The Falcon,* and *Columbia Workshop*. During the war, he served with the Army in Europe, collecting a bullet in the leg and a case of malaria. He kept the malaria in check with doses of atabrine. When the war ended, he skipped his regular atabrine doses and keeled over in the vicinity of Munich, Germany. When he woke up, his money and dog tags were gone and the MPs were looking for an AWOL soldier named Al Morgan. He squared that away, and then served briefly as drama director of the Armed Forces radio network in Paris. Four days after returning to the States, he married his girl back home, Martha Falconer, an Army colonel's daughter and an actress with successes on Broadway and in radio.

Morgan worked for CBS for ten years before joining NBC

and the *Home Show*. He also squeezed in a moderately successful Broadway musical, *Oh, Captain,* which he wrote with José
Ferrer. Morgan wrote his way out of the *Home Show* by hit-
ting the jackpot with a novel about a broadcast personality
called *The Great Man*. When asked by Lindemann how he
would like to produce *Today*, Morgan responded, "Are you
nuts?" Lindemann asked why not, and Morgan explained that
NBC would never meet his outrageous demands for salary and
working conditions. Lindemann, however, said yes to everything, and Morgan found that he had hired himself out.

Morgan, a man with Pat Weaver's instincts for the show,
was well qualified to save *Today*, which was experiencing an
alarming slump. Viewers had been abandoning ship, with the
advertisers following them into the life rafts. Morgan thought
the show deadly with Chancellor's "trenchcoatitis" and ambition to "go cover a war somewhere."

Morgan as producer had more clout than any of those who
preceded him. NBC's management had had enough of Garroway's erratic behavior and had decreed that the star would *not*
run the show, though it is not entirely clear that the word
reached Hugh Downs. Management was represented by Lindemann and William McAndrew. Despite being head of NBC
News, McAndrew agreed that the show should be entertainment oriented, and he gave Morgan his head. Al loved power
and "had the balls to use it," according to an admirer.

But Morgan wasn't a megalomaniac. He realized that his role
called for making deals with his star and mediating between
warring members of the cast. Morgan came aboard while John
Chancellor was wrapping it up and found himself in the middle
of a sticky situation right away. Chancellor, who had seemed
to like *Today* Girl Louise King more than she liked him, became annoyed with her off-camera slights. He began to make
fun, on the air, of her limited vocabulary and her mistakes in
pronunciation. Louise, an actress, had complained to Chancel-

lor's buddy, producer Shad Northshield, to no avail. Al tried to negotiate a truce between the harassed Miss King and an uncooperative Chancellor long enough to bridge the gap until Hugh Downs arrived.

Morgan not only thought Chancellor a "lousy host" who "wanted to be Richard Harding Davis," referring to a famous news correspondent, but he was unimpressed with the entire cast. Ed Newman, Morgan says, was "at his most elephantine." Morgan explains that there are men in television news who are known as "the uglies." They run to fat or are just too plain and uninteresting to look at. Usually the unlovelies are transferred to radio or they bust out of broadcasting entirely. Newman, says Morgan, was almost an ugly because of a weight problem. As the pounds mounted, Newman would begin to diet, just short of exile. On *Today*, Newman "was the fat lady at the party being terribly, terribly cute." Meanwhile, Frank Blair's suave, dignified manner struck Morgan as a poor imitation of Maurice Chevalier, "the most horrible thing I ever saw," says Morgan. "The show was absolutely dead. My problem was to liven it up and keep it on the air for two months so that I would have the chance to rebuild it."

Finally, Hugh Downs arrived to put his unique stamp on the show. To the nation's mothers, Hugh was the ideal young man, a marvelous, well-informed peach of a guy who would make daughter a perfect husband. To some associates—including Al Morgan—Downs was an advertiser's dream, a supersalesman viewers trusted implicitly. At best, though, he was a barely adequate interviewer. He was a "six foot toe in the sand," a "race track in Ohio," or a "mashed potato sandwich" to *Today* writers who envied his $500,000 network salary and his easy schedule.

Downs would arrive on the set in time to interview an author, brag that he hadn't read the book, and ask the author to tell viewers the plot. The ensuing performance could be embarrassing to everyone. Downs took the position that the viewers knew little or nothing about the subject of almost any interview he undertook, and it would therefore be unfair were he to cram in advance and ask questions they wouldn't understand.

Sometimes in acting as a surrogate for the uninformed, Downs would ask four of the five "W's" newspaper editors tell cub reporters to answer in the beginning of their stories—what, why, when, and where. ("We already *know* who," explained Downs, "it's the person being interviewed.")

Usually Downs relied heavily on the scripted questions prepared by the writers, and he was nonplussed when an interviewee changed the subject or opened a new line of thought by an answer. In such cases, Downs was likely to say, "er, uh . . ." and ask the next question on the list. He certainly didn't leave any "dead air." Like many radio men, Downs feared silence and was always able to ramble when the camera was on and there was nothing to say. The writers loved to analyze such moments which "worked" but didn't make a lot of sense. It was a technique that went something like this: "Well, now, that's . . . how we do it . . . Coming up we'll have more . . . and Barbara will be back . . . and the time is twenty minutes after the hour."

Downs hated Video-Cue, the *Today Show*'s prompting device, and liked to memorize introductions. Once, growing confidence prompted him to suggest that the writers simply give him "the facts" about a subject and he would ad-lib around them. The writers smirked when Downs attempted to execute this one. He wound up simply reading the facts, word for word, as listed by the writers.

Today editor John Dunn says he knew other young men like Downs when he worked in Ohio—young men who were convinced that a "pleasing personality was a sure way to win friends and influence people." Dunn adds, "This conviction was strengthened, of course, by his experience as a radio announcer and, later, as one of the great salesmen on TV." Dunn, who is half Irish, says that Downs is what the Irish call a "chancer"—someone always looking for the main chance.

It was Al Morgan who said, "Success on *Today* goes to the bladder as well as the head." He made the remark after Hugh Downs discovered that Johnny Carson had his own john, then asked for a private john too. Though there was no place to put a toilet in his office and no plumbing, Downs was as persistent as Montezuma's Revenge. Finally, NBC sent engineers who took a long look at a wall in Hugh's office. The carpenters came and knocked down the wall. The plasterers arrived and then the plumbers. Soon, Hugh Downs had instant scato-status. He had been elevated to Johnny Carson's level, toiletwise. Meanwhile, the office adjacent to Downs' had shrunk and featured a strange "blister." One day Al Morgan and a writer slipped into Downs' bathroom for a quick wash-up and noticed tiny bars of soap in all colors. Morgan picked up a bar and said, "Hmmm, peacock droppings!"

Each morning as Downs finished his *Today* broadcast he would split to host NBC's daytime game show *Concentration*, after which he scrammed. He didn't spend time huddling with *Today* writers or preparing for the next show. Morgan was appalled at Downs' indifference and regarded him as the world's laziest man. There wasn't a man anywhere better qualified to judge a lazy man than Morgan. He was so superbly organized that, according to one *Today* writer, he could have accomplished the world's most difficult task without rolling out of bed.

Morgan rarely *did* get out of the sack for *Today*. Instead, he watched it at home in Bronxville, New York. While his wife served him breakfast in bed, he occasionally telephoned the show's directors to make suggestions or comment on timing.

Morgan was the first *Today* producer who arrived at NBC after the show's sign-off, usually around 10 A.M.

An able executive, Morgan believed in delegating authority. He would throw the ball to the writers, and the good ones would catch the ball and run with it, usually with excellent results. At times, though, they found themselves over their heads. Al Smith remembers cursing himself out over a "disastrous" film piece he did in Amsterdam. When he met Morgan, the producer said he wasn't going to say anything because he knew he wouldn't be able to top what Smith was saying to himself and to forget about it.

Morgan would give the responsibility for each day's show to a different writer—making each "Producer for a Day," as one explained it. The writer would schedule and script the forthcoming show, sometimes with insistent suggestions from Morgan. Morgan would then look over the plans, perhaps making a change or two, and lock them up, writing the syllabus of the show into a massive diary.

A full week's forthcoming shows were put in the book no later than Friday. Some complained that this advance-booking technique reduced spontaneity, but there were never alarming holes at the last minute as there had been in prior years. Something could always be scratched—often it was an author's coveted *Today* shot, for which he wouldn't be rebooked. If there was an important late-breaking news development that demanded attention, the whole show went by the boards. When that happened, the entire *Today* staff, which was very loyal to Morgan, responded as a team.

"You sort of expected to be able to reach anyone any time of the day or night," managing editor Al Smith comments. "Occasionally, I would feel a flash of resentment if I called someone at 3 A.M. and couldn't get an answer. 'How dare he lead a normal life' flashed by. It was kind of stupid, I know."

Without even thinking, following a news break, Smith would call Al Morgan—"even at 2 A.M."—and say, "Hey, I'm headed in, I'll pick you up.

"By the time we got to the office and without having made other calls, I would find that others were coming in early and that half the work was already done," Smith remembers. "I never traveled without a pocket telephone directory, which had every staffer's name, address and telephone number."

Most of the time, however, the *Today Show* was on automatic—schedules set and ready to go days in advance—and the only things to disturb the comfort of Al Morgan's bed in Bronxville were problems with either Hugh Downs or Jack Lescoulie.

When Lescoulie returned to the *Today Show* in July 1961, he had somehow gotten the idea that *he* was the star of the show, not Downs. His manager encouraged him in that dangerous belief, and Lescoulie became dissatisfied as Downs' importance proved to be paramount to the show. He continually complained about his second-banana role and about not getting enough air time.

He was a constant problem for Al Morgan, especially after he began to emphasize his beef by doing the unforgivable. Lescoulie was hired to help Downs keep the broadcast ball rolling, but, according to an associate, Downs would "pass some pleasantry" and Lescoulie would "cold-cock him." For example, Downs might say, "Well, Jack, it certainly is warm for March, isn't it," and Lescoulie would "just sit there and stare at him."

Says a *Today* writer of the era: "I'm fond of Jack but if I had been Al Morgan, I would have taken a baseball bat to him." With Lescoulie acting like that, something was bound to happen, sooner or later. Lescoulie set himself up for the inevitable by clashing with *Today*'s unit manager, Tom Sternberg.

The unit manager is the watchdog of the show's treasury. He doesn't work for the producer, but rather for the network's business affairs department. He is supposed to see that the show stays within its budget.

"Some of them you love," John Dunn explains. "I'd have walked across broken glass for a couple of them. When I had need of facilities in Chicago, Boston, or a line into Little Rock, the unit manager had the responsibility over it. He could say, 'If you want to go to Little Rock, it will cost you $1,000 over budget' and then either say okay or no. He can be decent or he can be a bastard.

"Sternberg went to Princeton. In my experience, Princeton men sometimes think they should be president of the network at age twenty-five. Some wind up as unit managers and find it hard to deal with the frustration. Sternberg is the only unit manager who ever questioned a voucher of mine."

Lescoulie had been on a remote in the Virgin Islands for a day and a half when he decided he needed more money. Most unit managers faced with such a request would take the position "Here it is, but you'll have to pay it back." You just didn't argue with the talent. But Sternberg listened imperiously to Lescoulie's request and said, "You don't need more money." Lescoulie could hardly believe his ears. He apparently didn't know that neither Downs nor anybody else liked Sternberg. Instead of going to Al Morgan and telling the producer, "Keep that unit manager out of my way," Lescoulie wrote a memo stating, "If I come on the set any morning and Sternberg is there I will not go on the air." Were he to follow through on *that* threat, he would be in direct violation of his contract.

Not long after this, the *Today* Girl was indisposed, and Downs was going to have to take his chances with Lescoulie's dark stares during a special three-hour *Today* broadcast. Lescoulie walked into the studio, saw Sternberg, put on his hat again and walked out. That left Downs with the murderous show to do himself. Downs needed somebody to talk at—even if his words were met with Lescoulie's silence.

Today's second banana had slipped on his own peel. He was fired forthwith.

That left Hugh Downs and Al Morgan to work out their feud without the distraction of a mutual enemy.

CHAPTER 16

On the Road

Some felt it more than others, but everyone associated with the *Today Show* knew that theirs was a world apart. Working in the pre-dawn hours and sleeping during the day meant that, except for the people they knew on the show, almost everyone else in their lives, including family, existed on a different planet.

Most of the staff adjusted their internal clocks by going to bed early. As Mort Werner, the first producer, told an interviewer: "When my wife says, 'Okay, kids, time for bed,' I go too." That hour came at 8 or 9 P.M. for most members of the staff; otherwise 4 A.M. is a cruel hour to awake. Apart from Dave Garroway's bottle of instant vigor, the best eye-opener was coffee. Down the winding staircase at the RCA Exhibition Hall a dignified black gentleman called "Major" presided over the coffee urn and the danish. The staff would mingle there with the advertising agency people and with the guests, all gulping down their wake-up java. The coffee bill ran to $800 a month.

In the early years of the show especially, *Today* staffers strongly felt an esprit de corps. In that they functioned in such a self-contained world, this bond sometimes resembled that of soldiers engaged in a foreign war. Most, though, preferred to think of the staff as an extended family.

"All of us knew a great deal about the others' personal lives," managing editor Al Smith says. "We all knew if someone was having a problem with a wife or a child. We wouldn't send a man out of town if he had a problem at home. Or, if he had to go, we would send him back early if we could. We were a family in almost every sense. We ate our meals together, lived together on the road, spent most of our waking hours when not on the road together in the office.

"There were, of course, little cliques, like in any office. But I cannot recall instances of wars, of anyone not speaking to someone else. There were damn few personality clashes. People would get uptight periodically and blow, as in any family. But then it would be forgotten. If someone screwed up—and this happened infrequently—the family might know about it, but the outside world, including others at NBC, would not."

At least that's the way Al Smith remembers things. There were a few spectacular flaps—one involving Al himself. During the rehearsal for a filmed feature of stock car races at the Daytona 500, the splicing of the film with the taped audio portion kept coming apart.

"It was not my fault," Al explains. "Splices did open up. It happened a lot in those days. But I did have the overall production responsibility for this piece, so in a sense I was responsible. And Garroway blew up. He chewed me up one side and down the other and back up again—in front of everyone in the studio. I was so tired, I said to myself, 'Screw this, I don't need it.' I turned and walked out, crying. I had quit as far as I was concerned. It took me three-quarters of an hour to get home to Kew Gardens. Just as I climbed into bed, the phone rang, my wife answered it, and it was David. He told me they had just run a piece on the air—the old story, terrible rehearsal, great show. He said, 'I must have been coo-coo. I was wrong . . . I want to apologize.' I learned later that he made that call from the studio floor—within earshot of everyone. I loved that son-of-a-bitch."

Bud Lewis, who joined the show as a writer about the time Al Smith did, believes it is easy to make too much of the "family" idea. His recollections, more oriented to his own family—"I had a couple of kids then"—were less pleasant. He remembers being on the set at 4 A.M. on Christmas Day. By the time he got home, he was "dead" and Christmas was over. "My Christmas was the *Today Show* Christmas party," he says, unhappily.

Self-contained as the *Today* world was at home, the family ties and tensions, the good times and bad, were accentuated when the show went on the road. Some of the happiest and wildest times for the *Today* staff happened on remotes, but these trips could also spark resentments and disharmony. Those out of favor were sometimes left off the roster of a trip every staffer wanted to make. Whatever the advantages or disadvantages to *Today* staffers, however, remotes eventually became very important to the *Today* format. "We think remotes made *Today* exciting, and you could see this in the ratings," one staffer explains.

Two years into its run, *Today* was still under tight budgetary rein and had not been able to show its viewers the vast world Pat Weaver had planned, except through film dispatches from NBC correspondents. So when Miami Beach publicist Hank Meyer called NBC late in 1954 to ask, "Why not bring *Today*, *Tonight* and *Home* down here for two weeks in mid-January?" Mort Werner expressed interest. Such a move could open up important possibilities for *Today*.

"We negotiated," says Hank, "and finally agreed that Miami

Beach would pay a total of $25,000 to bring these three attractions to town." Thus began a pioneer television technique and the first of scores of remote broadcasts for *Today*—most of which were bankrolled by local interests.

The *Today* and *Tonight* staffs both stayed at the Sea Isle Hotel on Collins Avenue in Miami Beach that January. Bob Bendick, who succeeded Mort Werner as producer, described what resulted as literally a "hot-bed situation."

"We'd get up at 3 A.M. to get our show organized and on the air," he explained, "and as we went back to the hotel and to bed thereafter, the staff of the *Tonight Show* would be rolling out of the same beds to do their show."

On the first telecast from Florida director Jac Hein scheduled a Seminole Indian who would wrestle an alligator in the Sea Isle swimming pool. Then, Jack Lescoulie would follow that act with a little wrestling of his own, against a man in an alligator suit. The decision to put Jack into the water was a late inspiration, and Bendick's assistant Lou Ames called New York City to order an alligator suit from a costume house. Later, the costumer called to say that the alligator suit would be aboard a plane landing in Miami at 3 A.M. the next day. Ames decided to go to the airport in a rented car.

At four o'clock that morning Bendick received a call from Ames, who said he was at the police station with no money and no alligator suit. He would be back shortly. He arrived at the hotel, very shaken, and explained that he had picked up the suit at the airport and was driving across Miami Beach when three guys jumped in the car. They took the wheel and drove Ames to the boondocks. Ames was "scared to death and gave them everything," Bendick recalls. "As they were about to turn him loose he said, 'Look, I've got an alligator suit in the back and it's got to be on the *Today Show* at 7 A.M.' They told him to get lost and drove off with the alligator suit in the trunk."

At about 6:30 A.M., while Ames was explaining all this, the telephone rang and a rough voice told Bendick, "You'll find your goddamn alligator suit in the car—it's at the corner of Chestnut and Hill."

Lescoulie got to wrestle with an alligator after all, and Bendick recalls there was a sequel to the story. A couple of years later in a Boston bar, a man told a story to some strangers about how he and two friends had held up a fellow in Miami and the only thing the man wanted to keep was his alligator suit. One of the strangers happened to be an off-duty policeman, who arrested him. After the policeman checked the story with *Today*, the robber wound up in jail.

On the Florida remote, Jac Hein also contracted with a balloonist who would go up in a gondola lifted by one large balloon and many smaller ones. The balloonist had a gun and planned to shoot the smaller balloons one at a time, then put a bullet through the large one and float back to earth. Early one morning he pulled into a gas station, the attendant saw the gun on the front seat of his car, and Bendick heard from the police again. That too was straightened out, and the *Today* audience caught the exploding-balloon act.

Dave Garroway also put his stamp on the Florida festivities. While on Key Biscayne shooting a General Motors commercial which emphasized safety, Dave pulled out of a stop-sign street abruptly and was hit by another car.

Allowing the remotes to be subsidized by local interests offered problems as well as advantages. The local Chamber of Commerce was usually the organization approached for a subsidy. But individual members of the Chamber often wanted to grind their own axes. A hotel might, for instance, insist that one *Today* spot be shot at its facilities. When Al Morgan became producer, he insisted that *Today* deal only with C. of C.

executives, and that the Chamber couldn't even tell *Today* which member companies had contributed to the subsidy money.

Even this arrangement had to end. *Today* went to New Orleans in the mid-1960s and broadcast some amateur white jazz musicians in an early brief spot. The show then employed some black jazzmen from Preservation Hall and loaded them aboard a Mississippi riverboat. The show had planned a two-hour trip down the river, the camera lingering over the picturesque Mississippi scenery, with jazz playing in the background. However, it rained, and with the scenery obscured, the cameras of necessity focused almost exclusively on the musicians. Many New Orleans residents complained about that "Yankee production company" featuring so many blacks, and the newspapers picked up on the fracas. At the time the head of the local NBC station was also serving as president of the NBC affiliates. "He screamed because he had to live there, and besides he was a big wheel in the Boston Club, an exclusive retreat," says a source.

The repercussions back at Rockefeller Plaza were so severe that the network banned the Chamber of Commerce subsidies and other such freebies in the United States. By this time, however, *Today* was also doing many shows abroad, and these remotes continued to be subsidized by foreign governments' official tourist agencies. The subsidy would amount to the difference in cost between a *Today* broadcast from New York, which ran about $100,000 per week by the late 1960s, and a foreign show, which cost about double that. Many of the newsmen on the show hated the idea of foreign subsidies, but most accepted them as a necessary evil.

And foreign locales did provide interesting moments for the *Today* audience as well as the *Today* staff. Once when the show was being taped in Paris, the head chef of La Tour d'Argent lovingly demonstrated how he prepared his pressed duck. The world-famous specialty was described in ardent French by the chef and translated into English. After he finished, Garroway came on with a pot of boiling water and a carpet swatch. The chef watched uncomprehendingly as Garroway dramatically pitched his sponsor's carpet, thrusting the swatch into the boiling water to demonstrate its indestructibility. Horrified by the apparent parody of his culinary art, the chef stormed away muttering about the blasphemers of his *haute cuisine*.

Sometimes, though, the locals could be very helpful when the *Today Show* went abroad. Al Morgan remembers one such incident in London. The *Today* producer wanted to broadcast live by Early Bird Satellite the changing of the guard at Buckingham Palace, but he had a timing problem. A live broadcast of the Pope in Rome would not end until two and a half minutes after the guard ceremony was scheduled to begin.

Everyone from the guard commandant to the Queen's aides refused Morgan's request for a late start to the entire ceremony. Not wanting to broadcast a truncated version, Morgan was planning to scrap the Buckingham segment when he ran into one of the Guardsmen in a pub. The Guardsman, who had an aunt in Omaha, urged the producer not to drop the segment. "Keep it in, mate," he said with such assurance that Morgan obeyed. As the Pope spoke, Morgan watched the goings-on at Buckingham with half an eye, and was stunned to see a Guardsman, his drinking buddy, drop his rifle. By the time the officer finished chewing the Guardsman out, Morgan had said goodbye to Rome and was ready for a quick switch to Buckingham and the changing-of-the-guard ceremony in its entirety. The Guardsman's aunt in Omaha was thrilled to see him live on TV.

Such uncertainties were enough to cause considerable stomach distress. It was much easier to do the advance work prior to a *Today* visit—and much more pleasant. Al Morgan and writer Bob Cunniff thoroughly enjoyed Portugal on one such pre-program occasion—traveling hither and yon, eating and drinking at NBC's expense while planning production numbers in no great haste. Finally, as they sat drinking wine on a lazy afternoon, Morgan was handed a telegram reporting the imminent arrival of Hugh Downs and Barbara Walters. With a sigh, Morgan remarked, "Now we've got to do the fucking show!"

Mackinac Island, off Michigan's Upper Peninsula, was the setting for a *Today* remote that ranks as the staff's least enjoyable trip. Anyone who is not a fisherman, hunter, or trapper is likely to find the area desolate. There is little to do on the island but sit on the longest porch in the world—the hotel's only distinctive feature—and rock yourself silly.

A site of great importance in pioneer times, Mackinac Island had slid into the ooze of history, but that fact had somehow eluded the *Today Show* production company. They had been more impressed that Queen Elizabeth had visited the island than they should have been. (Cracked one *Today* staffer later, "*I* know why she never came back.") In part, the show had flown to Mackinac for a three-week remote telecast to visit with the jolly folks at Moral Rearmament, a semi-religious anti-Communist group that made the island their headquarters. The intimacy so characteristic of the *Today* staff on remotes was tested to the utmost at Mackinac.

Upon arrival Al Morgan checked out the hotel and immediately realized that Hugh Downs' wife, Ruth, would object to their accommodations. Ruth routinely insisted on a double bed—some called this Ruth's "We're *very* married" statement —and a fine suite of rooms. Comments a writer who made the trip:

"I was amused at the way Morgan got Ruth to accept her room. He brought her to my room and, like those of the other writers, it was so small that I had to stand to type scripts, putting my typewriter on a chest of drawers. He had told Ruth that her room wasn't ready yet. After saying in mock shock, 'Look at the way the writers have to live and work!' he then ushered her to her room, which must have looked gigantic after mine. She didn't complain. Ruth could be very nice if she liked you. She kept consoling me all during the remote with a 'How can you stand it in that cell of yours?' "

Ruth Downs, a Lebanese woman sometimes called the "Dragon Lady" by *Today* staffers, was the one exception to Morgan's strictly enforced rule that no spouses could go on remote trips. The no-spouse rule was justified as being necessary to keep husbands and wives of staffers from trying to turn a work situation into a vacation. It also kept spouses from causing morale problems by interfering with or gossiping about any hanky-panky among the staffers. (Not all *Today* affairs were secrets, however. One key figure carried on with his young protégée so openly that his wife retaliated by showing up at a *Today* Christmas party with a "young stud.")

The barring of spouses led to some problems. One prominent member of the *Today* company was arrested for peeping into motel windows. One writer who broke the rule, sneaking back to his wife at a nearby hotel, was fired after it was discovered that she came along not to vacation but to rewrite his hopelessly inadequate scripts.

As for the show's host, Hugh Downs insisted that it was absolutely necessary for Ruth to accompany him. After all, he was totally color blind and couldn't dress without her. Maybe so, growls Al Morgan, but the broadcasts at the beginning of the Downs period were in black and white. Besides, Ruth's presence caused resentments. "We all wondered why it was that Hugh needed a certain kind of loving care we didn't," says one veteran.

Another suggests that Ruth performed an important function for Hugh. "Hugh would be the nice guy and Ruth would be the bitch who got him what he wanted," the staffer explains. "But if you ever spent any time around them when they were together, it was soon clear that Hugh—without ever raising his voice—was the boss. He had the coldest eyes I ever saw in a man when he was angry."

Al Morgan had his own room problem on Mackinac Island. After driving six hours through a "blinding rainstorm" he had arrived at the hotel to discover he was sharing his quarters with an Indian wearing buckskin and full war bonnet.

"He was chopping at a log," Morgan says. "There was a foot and a half of shavings on the floor. Writer Ric Ballad explained that it was one of the penalties of command. 'He has to carve a totem pole for the opening of the show,' he explained. 'Since you're the producer, you have the biggest room. Actually, you have the only room big enough for the pole to fit into.' For once, it wasn't lonely at the top."

After a few days on the island, the after-show routine degenerated into marathon poker games and desultory discussions of Moral Rearmament and the quality of the fudge the sect was always turning out. Meanwhile, says Morgan, Hugh Downs provided an unlikely counterpoint, his voice reverberating through the lobby from the hotel loudspeakers as he shilled for Parker Brothers' new game, Concentration.

Even long walks were dreary—and worse. It was advisable to walk in the middle of the streets to avoid the large bats which infested the island and tended to hug the building walls. Many were petrified that a bat with faulty sonar would fly into their faces.

One evening as the staff settled into a poker game—badminton rackets at the ready to knock down any stray bats that passed within range, Hugh Downs' spiel in the background—there was a terrible, piercing shriek. The men raced to Barbara Walters' room, where a bat had somehow flown into the toilet. Between screams, Barbara had been trying to flush it. When the men saw that it was a bat, they dealt with it manfully. Then, as one woman who made the trip recalls, "We all sat with Barbara and calmed her down."

At least it was a diversion. The rest of the excitement on that trip was invented by a staff driven dotty by non-events. Silly after two weeks of this isolation, some of the staff began to take an interest in a grotesque five-foot terra-cotta ape in the souvenir shop window. Why anybody would want such a thing was unclear—even to the staff. Nevertheless, Morgan and his poker-playing troops put a kitty in the game to raise enough money to buy the ape. Once they had it, Bernie Florman, the prop man, built a cage for it.

It wasn't until the show had returned to New York and Railway Express dropped off a huge carton that anyone remembered the ape. With scarcely any enthusiasm, Al Morgan installed it in his office. As a sort of memorial to the Mackinac remote, the staff invented the Ape Award for the individual who was regarded as having gone ape on each succeeding remote. Ballots were kept secret, of course. There was an added fillip: Get the Ape Award three times and you've retired it.

In no time at all, two *Today* staffers had two "wins" each and the staff was about to vote again when, Morgan recalls, one candidate's "psychiatrist called to say his patient was terrified that he would win a third time." The psychiatrist pleaded with Morgan to drop the whole idea. The two-time winner's apprehension over his all-too-rosy prospects of retiring the ape was contributing to his nervous breakdown. Morgan responded to the psychiatrist's plea. The Ape Award was quietly retired without further balloting.

CHAPTER 17

A Window on Manhattan

The *Today Show* has provided viewers with a figurative window on the world. During two periods of its existence, it also provided them with a literal window on the streets of New York. For the first six and a half years of its existence, when it broadcast from the RCA Exhibition Hall, the camera and the TV audience could look through the studio window on 49th Street in midtown Manhattan. Looking back was a decidedly varied crew of sidewalk observers.

They were there from that very first morning in January 1952, and, according to Dave Garroway, their applause at the end of the maiden show more than compensated for the barbs of the critics. After the show picked up a national following, the sidewalk crowd became a microcosm of the American public. They weren't all New Yorkers. Many out-of-town tourists rose early to press their noses against the *Today Show*'s window and wave to relatives back home.

As the camera panned the crowd's smiling faces, it would pick up a southern businessman who detoured to New York on his way back from Rome simply to wave to friends back home . . . a young bride living in New York who stood broad-side to the camera to display the progress of her pregnancy to her mother in Wisconsin . . . a couple who held an infant to the camera so that a couple in Sioux City, Iowa, could see their grandchild.

The folks watching their TVs in middle America responded to this homey feature with delight. Sometimes they were treated to a view of the seamier side of life, too. Pickpockets appeared on the *Today* cameras. Flashers exposed themselves from time to time. Once a demented woman, who identified herself as "Mrs. Dave Garroway," stood patiently in front of the window waiting for her "husband" to join her. Another time the crowd included a man in an ape suit with a sign that read "I am J. Fred Muggs' long-lost brother." When the *Today* cameras focused on his message, the man flipped the card-board quickly to reveal a bold-lettered "Watch *King Kong* on Channel 9 tonight!" That channel was a local rival of NBC.

Today's window on Manhattan made viewers feel they were physically a part of the same world as *Today*. Garroway would say it was raining in New York, and the audience could see the rain splattering against the studio window. Often people came to regard Garroway as a member of the family who could keep them in touch with relatives coming to the wicked city. He would get letters beginning, "My daughter, who is fifteen, is coming to New York to visit and has to get to Mother's place. Please tell her how to get to Atlantic Avenue and Court Street in Brooklyn." Sometimes Dave would read such a letter on the broadcast and let the whole world in on an unfolding family drama.

In 1958, Philco, a rival television maker, charged that NBC's use of the RCA Exhibition Hall constituted unfair competi-tion because *Today*'s TV audience could see RCA television sets in the background. *Today* pulled out of the hall, moving to a windowless NBC studio.

There was no ratings slump when *Today* moved to Studio 3-K, and a succession of other windowless studios thereafter. The audience for the show held, but the *Today* company missed the show's connection to the outside world. Everyone felt a certain loss of spontaneity by the move to the interior, and a continuing effort was made to find a new windowed studio.

Within a year or so of the move inside, the new Time-Life Building neared completion on Sixth Avenue between 50th and 51st Streets. The NBC people noticed a marvelous, spacious room at ground level taking form behind what was to be a spectacular window on the plaza. The room was two stories high and featured a photogenic spiral staircase. The location was a stone's throw from *Today*'s former showcase but larger by far—as large as any studio at NBC.

Network officials began negotiating for what promised to be an ideal show headquarters. But at the last minute—while star, cameraman, directors, and producer all salivated in anticipation—something happened. Apparently, top network officials began to worry about the incidental value of the show to *Time* more than they worried about the boon to *Today*. One story is that NBC demanded that *Time* pay $400,000 a year for the indirect benefits *Time* would receive. That figure seems excessive even to those who report it, but one source believes the price was set by someone at NBC who became angry with the reigning monarch of *Time*, Henry Luce. Whatever the price, *Time* told NBC to forget the whole business.

Another story is that the negotiations broke down over something even sillier: "They fought over a closet *Time* wanted to retain and when NBC was adamant, *Time* said, 'Screw you, Charlie' and that was it." In any event, the *Today Show* remained inside—until Al Morgan came along.

The first thing Al Morgan did when he became producer in July 1962 was to end the practice of pre-taping the show the previous afternoon. *Today* again became a live show. Next he returned it to a "fishbowl" setting. Morgan was a great believer in the old saw that New York City was a great place to visit—even by TV camera. He believed that the folks in middle America were fascinated by the human electricity that pulsed on any Manhattan thoroughfare, and he was determined to take the show "outside" again. His search for studio space behind a big plate-glass window eventually led right back to Rockefeller Center. The State of Florida had a showcase across 49th Street from the Exhibition Hall—and it was available. The Florida Development Commission invited *Today* to use the space beginning on July 9, 1962. There was no quibble over money this time.

Everyone was refreshed by the return to a studio with a window on the street, even though the studio was small. The Duke Ellington Orchestra and other big musical groups had to be crammed into the restricted space. There were other problems, too. Florida had a connected display window with thatched cabana, sand, umbrellas, and a myna bird in a cage. The bird sometimes squawked during broadcasts. Idle members of the *Today* company began to whisper to the bird, which cocked an ear to blunt four-letter words. Soon the talking bird was screeching an occasional obscenity on the air, and had to be dumped from the show.

Outside, tourists and New Yorkers, regulars and irregulars, once again viewed *Today*'s live, through-the-looking-glass productions. Al Barney, a dapper Latin type whose pencil-thin mustache and horn-rimmed glasses made him look like an aging gigolo, was typical of those who peered through the glass. He wanted to keep in touch with widely scattered grandchildren—modeling a new suit or hat for them, and waving, a vague smile lighting his features as though he only half-believed his electronic letter was reaching its destination.

A cashier at the Ham 'n Egg restaurant on Broadway and,

172

on weekends, a 10 A.M.-to-midnight waiter at an oyster bar, Barney became the *Today Show*'s most persistent sidewalk observer. He eventually bought a portable TV set so he could hear the sound portion, which *Today* could not legally pipe outside for its live audience. Arriving at 5 A.M. so that he could be "exactly in the center" when the show started, Al remained until 8:30, when the *Today* camera focused on the window for the last time and he left for the Ham 'n Egg.

Barney received scores of cards addressed to him in care of the show. A typical note from a Springfield, Missouri, viewer during the Christmas season read, "May you have a healthy happy prosperous New Year. Will, as usual, be looking for your smiling face daily." An Ontario, Canada, viewer shipped Al a folding chair so he could watch in comfort—useful on all but cold days, when he had to hop from foot to foot to avoid frostbite.

Late in his years'-long vigil, Hugh Downs invited Barney on the show. Thereafter Barney began signing autographs "Albert Barney, *Today Show*." Barney, divorced and living in a lonely midtown hotel, had few outside interests. He told an interviewer at the time: "I never watch TV. I haven't the time. I get finished on the job at 9 P.M. and have to go to bed at 10 sharp. After all, I do have to be up at 4 A.M."

It wasn't a completely thankless vigil. When the *Today Show* went on a remote in the Pennsylvania Dutch country, the staff was surprised and amused to find that Al Barney was already on the scene, his trip paid by the promoters, who had named him Grand Master of an annual parade.

Today was eventually forced to return inside, to the windowless Johnny Carson studio, in September 1965. "We gave up the Florida showcase because NBC went to colorcasts," Al Morgan explains. "We would have had to isolate four color cameras to stay there, and RCA couldn't afford to have four of the scarce cameras out of service for the remaining twenty-two hours of the day."

Several years later, another effort was made to take the show outside. Singer Sewing Machines had an exhibit hall off the promenade in Rockefeller Plaza, by the skating rink and in view of St. Patrick's Cathedral. It was a marvelous location. The hall was bigger by far than any NBC studio, and Singer was pleased when approached about making its facility available for daily exposure on the widely watched morning program. Everything was set—except for approval from Rockefeller Center, Inc., the organization that leased the complex on a 99-year basis from Columbia University. It was in the late 1960s, at the height of the student demonstrations, and RCI said nothing doing. American society had been radicalized by then.

"RCI was afraid demonstrators would be attracted to the plaza for destructive happenings," one source says. "They were probably right. RCI wasn't going to serve as a magnet for dissidents—no way." The last serious effort to bring *Today* back to the picture window died a-borning.

January 7, 1952: T-Day. Critics verdict: "Electronic mishmash." (NBC PHOTO)

The Garroway benediction: "Peace." (RAIMONDO BOREA ©)

Muggs conquers Mount Angel Food. (NBC PHOTO)

Garroway taming the Jaguar. (RAIMONDO BOREA ©)

Harry Truman looks at Today, *and vice versa.* (NBC PHOTO)

Dave and Rocky sharing their obsession: A bomb shelter. (RAIMONDO BOREA ©)

A typical Today *stunt.*
(RAIMONDO BOREA ©)

Lescoulie takes a dive in Rome. (NBC PHOTO)

A "spontaneous" Garroway interview with RCA's General Sarnoff. (NBC PHOTO)

Eleanor, Adlai and Dave. (RAIMONDO BOREA ©)

The late Pamela Wilde de Coninck Garroway. (RAIMONDO BOREA ©)

John Chancellor and Frank Blair—with Louise King in the middle. (NBC PHOTO)

The plain-speaking Edwin Newman.
(NBC PHOTO)

John Chancellor, as Today *host.*
(RAIMONDO BOREA ©)

Hugh Downs rides the killer whale. (NBC PHOTO)

Ruth and Hugh Downs. (RAIMONDO BOREA ©

Uneasy alliance: Maureen O'Sullivan and Hugh Downs.
(NBC PHOTO)

Producer Al Morgan in charge. (NBC PHOTO)

he changing order: Hugh Downs to Frank McGee and Joe Garagi-
a. (RAIMONDO BOREA ©)

Barbara Walters interviews an old friend, Henry Kissinger. (NBC PHOTO)

Bearded producer Stuart Schulberg with staff and Today *guest Isaac Stern,*
left. (RAIMONDO BOREA ©)

John Dunn, writer and conscience of Today. (NBC PHOTO)

Twenty-five years of Today: *Garroway remembers yesterday with Lescoulie and Blair.* (RAIMONDO BOREA ©)

Today, *today—with Barbara Hunter, Brokaw, Kalber, Shalit, Pauley and Wood.* (RAIMONDO BOREA ©)

CHAPTER 18

A Woman's Place

At the end of 1963, producer Al Morgan was looking for a new *Today* Girl. After a year and a half, Pat Fontaine, a former weather girl from St. Louis, had not effervesced in the role and was on her way back home.

At the time Barbara Walters was a *Today* writer who sometimes appeared on camera. She had wanted the job before Pat Fontaine was hired, but Morgan didn't think her ready for it. With Pat leaving, Barbara again put in her bid, and was again turned down.

Before making his selection, Morgan decided to extend the family of on-camera personalities. So that the writers would not have to bone up on subjects outside their experience—and beyond the ken of Hugh Downs and Jack Lescoulie as well—Morgan looked for bright people with specialties. They would be "salami" between two slices of white bread, Downs and Lescoulie. Morgan chose Judith Crist and Aline Saarinen.

Herald Tribune movie critic Crist had recently panned *Cleopatra*, calling the over-long production three of the worst movies ever made. She had been one of the few critics with the courage to buck the Hollywood establishment on so important a production, the most expensive movie till that time. Morgan invited Judy to deliver hard-nosed movie reviews on TV, in an era when network television was famous for doing puff pieces on movies. Crist was a refreshing change and soon became a national celebrity, "getting rich on the lecture circuit," according to Morgan. Crist remembers "practically falling off my chair" when she got a fan letter from poet Archibald MacLeish, "an idol of my girlhood."

Aline Saarinen was the highly cultivated and intelligent wife of architect Eero Saarinen, whose brooding granite edifice on Sixth Avenue housed CBS. For her first assignment, Morgan asked Aline to pick the most horrible examples of American taste in art. Among other things, she picked a Steuben glass bowl Jackie Kennedy had given to a reigning monarch. She also picked Mount Rushmore. Morgan reports, "Every American Legion post in the country screamed."

When he finally selected a new *Today* Girl, Morgan added the flavor of Broadway. After considerable persuasion, he got Maureen O'Sullivan, then playing on Broadway in the comedy *Never Too Late*. Morgan liked the idea of a glamorous woman —not a tea pourer—in middle life whom older viewers could relate to.

According to *Today* editor John Dunn, when Downs heard about Maureen, "He said, 'No, no, no, no,' and he was right." But Al Morgan had the power to make the decision in spite of Downs. Eighteen months earlier, Morgan had let Downs say "yes" to Pat Fontaine after only a brief interview. Now he was confidently running the show his way and chose Maureen over Downs' objections.

Hugh and Maureen just weren't right for each other. Maureen, who was most attractive and an excellent actress, just didn't have Hugh's easy informal quality. They grated on each other. Both courteous, they never exploded, but rather "swallowed it all," says a staffer. "It would have taken a sharp viewer to detect that they were feuding constantly—but they were."

The feud took a toll on both. Maureen developed shingles and Hugh a bad back. Hugh would complain about his back and Maureen would say, more reproachfully than angrily, "That's what you get for being so mean," and Hugh would laugh nervously in response. Several who followed the action say that both the shingles and the bad back were probably psychosomatic. But whatever the tension was doing to their health, writer Ric Ballad will never forget what their feud did to one of his best pieces.

It was a mood feature about a small backwater town—Valley, Nebraska. Gail Rock, a production assistant who was to become a writer of fiction, was raised there and she had regaled *Today* staffers with stories of Valley and its picturesque life style. Ric decided to take a crew there for a *Today* feature.

"We spent eighteen hours a day for two days shooting Valley from every conceivable angle," says Ric. "We had a guy set fire to an old car so that the volunteer fire department could respond and put it out. There was a man who mourned a son lost in the war by raising the flag every morning, and we filmed that. The local women's club was meeting in the basement of the church, and we got footage of that. The minister's wife sang 'Trees' accompanied by a woman with the most leaden fingers this side of Peter Duchin. She was just awful, but kind of cute.

"We got back to New York and the spot ran for a full hour on *Today*—a total of thirty minutes of shooting time sandwiched between news and commercials.

"We opened with an aerial shot of a train arriving at the depot and the Girl Scouts were singing, 'Down by the station, early in the morning, see the little puffer bellies all in a row.'

"I made one mistake," Ballad continues. "Instead of having

the talent pre-tape their narrative of this beautiful film, I had them come in live. At the time, Hugh and Maureen could think of nothing but their feud. They never rehearsed the piece. There was one point where Downs goofed—lost his place. That was bad enough, but Maureen read her script as much as two and a half minutes behind the film—all through the spot. It was a disaster. I felt it not only for myself, but for my crew. To see it torn to pieces that way, that did something to me. I thought, I'll never again work this hard on something and let warring talent destroy it."

It was the eventual intrusion of the feud onto the air that convinced many that Maureen had to go, after only six months on the job.

"She was unhappy, and the audience was unhappy," Judith Crist recalls. "Al Morgan had thought here is a glamorous middle-aged woman with whom everyone will have associations. He attempted to blend maturity with glamour. I had thought her a damn good choice, being on the road to maturity myself. But it was disastrous.

"She made the terrible mistake of reading her fan mail. If she opened her mouth, they would write in and ask, 'Don't you ever shut up?' and if she didn't, they would ask why she just sat there like a lump.

"She said to me, 'Do you like this?' and I said, 'I love it—it's thrilling.' She said, 'But it's just *you* out there.' That was something I had never thought of. An actress in a movie or on stage is playing a role—another person. It is never *you*, it is the *role*. In live TV you play yourself."

The main problem, of course, was not what Maureen was, but what she was not. A *Today* writer of the period comments: "I liked Maureen very much. She was certainly an intelligent woman. Maureen was also a good interviewee—witty and outspoken. And some of her bits went well. I remember a couple of good spots with her daughter Mia Farrow, who was just getting started. But Maureen was hired to interview others, and she just didn't have the slightest idea of how to go about it. She didn't know how to handle the teleprompter, which might have helped her through. I don't think she could see the scripts, but she refused to wear glasses."

The firing followed *Today*'s usual offhand approach—it was badly bobbled. Maureen got the ax while the show was in Atlantic City in August 1964, covering the Democratic Convention. Al Morgan hadn't intended it that way, and neither had anybody else. But Jerry Madden, who replaced Carl Lindemann as NBC executive in charge of *Today*, didn't get the word. One *Today* staffer says that Jerry's "sole distinction was that he had been a successful child actor." At any rate, Jerry met Maureen for dinner in Atlantic City and listened to her talk of guests she was planning to invite to do the show. He interrupted, saying, in essence, "Uh, I wouldn't make too many plans if I were you, Maureen, because, as a matter of fact, you're leaving the show."

Maureen was furious that she didn't get the word directly from Al Morgan. So was Morgan, who had intended to take it up with Maureen later. Morgan was also disturbed because he had hoped for good publicity on the *Today* coverage of the convention, and a blast from Maureen could spoil this. Thus, Morgan and other *Today* staffers spent the day drinking with Maureen in a hotel room. As a diversionary tactic they encouraged her to talk about the exciting days at MGM—"Oh, ah, tell us about Jean Harlow again, Maureen"—hoping that she would not call the newspapers until she cooled off. But Maureen's Irish was up, and she kept threatening to find Downs and assault him physically for all the abuse she had taken at his hands.

Maureen, who seemed to know every columnist in the business, finally made the telephone calls anyway. She blasted the show and NBC, saying she felt like an intruder. "The show is simply no place for a woman," she said. "They haven't created a place for one."

Barbara Walters, winding up a long apprenticeship, was about to create that place. Due to Maureen's lacks, Barbara was rapidly becoming a fixture on the show, doing filmed features and building support both within the *Today* company and among viewers. Now she was about to begin a job that, it sometimes seemed, she had been aiming for her entire life, even from her childhood in Miami Beach.

When *Today* was in Florida for a Bicentennial visit—the show made similar visits to all the states in 1976—Barbara reminisced about her poor-little-rich-girl childhood on Palm Island in Miami Beach. Barbara's father, Lou Walters, a sometimes-rich sometimes-broke nightclub operator and gambler, moved the family there from Boston when Barbara was eight years old. Lou Walters, who is now supported in a nursing home by Barbara, opened a nightclub called the Latin Quarter on Palm Island, having already operated successful Latin Quarters in Boston and New York. On Palm Island the Walters family lived in a big house on the same property as the nightclub.

There were few children on the island, and Barbara was driven to the mainland in a limousine each day to the Iva M. Fisher School in a then-fashionable section of town. She described the school as the "most normal part of my life there."

But Barbara didn't fit in easily with the others at school. Her Boston background and a conviction that she had "skinny legs" caused her to wear skirts rather than the shorts worn by the rest of the girls in the informality of Florida. When school was over she was wafted back to the solitude of Palm Island—only rarely accompanied by an "imported friend."

Her free time was spent riding her bicycle with only her dog for company. Barbara's sister, with whom she has a warm relationship, was retarded. There was lots of grass and palm trees on the island and little else. Barbara spent the daytime hours by herself, down by the water, daydreaming and waving at the sightseeing boat.

By comparison, the evenings were filled with excitement. Barbara's mother and father would take her to the Latin Quarter, where top stars—Maurice Chevalier, Sophie Tucker, Milton Berle—played to packed houses. She met them all and discovered that they too had problems. She learned not to be overly impressed by the famous. Barbara remembers a movie maker and airplane builder named Howard Hughes, and a politician and whiskey importer named Joseph Kennedy.

"In the early evening I would often sit in the lighting booth . . . watch the festivities down below until about ten, when my parents would send me back to the big house," she recalled on that 1976 Florida visit.

There was a loneliness to young Barbara's life. Not only did Palm Island lack children for her to play with, it also had no stores, or even a place to swim: "I learned to depend on my imagination. I was very close to my parents. But sometimes, I felt rather like the little match girl on the outside trying to get in. I'd watch the water, looking at nothing much."

In later years Barbara Walters would reflect the toughness she learned as an outsider, along with a vulnerability that reflected her early insecurity.

When Barbara graduated from Sarah Lawrence College in 1951, her father introduced her to Ted Cott, who had the top job at NBC's local radio and television station in New York City. Not only was Ted Cott vice-president and general manager of the local operations, he was also a great favorite of General Sarnoff. The two got along wonderfully well. The story around NBC was that Ted clicked with almost no one else, but with the General in his corner, who was counting?

Ted took a liking to Barbara, and his affection was more

than passively returned. While Barbara has been quoted as saying "I was 'in like' with him," Cott meant a great deal more to her than that. There would be tearful moments later as she cried on the shoulder of an associate after Ted Cott showed no interest in marrying her.

Ted made the rounds with Barbara at NBC, trying to find her a niche. Says Phil Dean, a Cott employee as director of publicity, promotion, and advertising for WNBC-TV, "He didn't tell me to hire Barbara, but he said he would be happy if I could do anything for her, adding, 'Make up your own mind.'"

Phil Dean did hire Barbara, and he was never sorry. Barbara came to work during a newspaper strike in New York City. Dean's staff was helping gather news for stories to be used on the air and in a daily news round-up NBC was mimeographing and distributing to commuters at Grand Central Station. New York City was more strike-torn than usual then. The cab drivers had also left their wheels, and the head of the association would not grant interviews. Dean sent Barbara. Not only did she get a story, she also got a picture of the elusive labor leader. In Dean's eyes—and those of everyone else who learned of it—Barbara scored a "real coup." It was always that way, says Dean. "Any time she was given an assignment, she did it beautifully. She was creative in her own way. She would initiate things—go out and develop ideas."

Barbara quickly learned to do people favors by using her contacts, even her family. Dagmar, a buxom blond entertainer, was a popular fixture on the NBC network—and making $8,000 a week moonlighting at the Roxy Theater with Milton Berle—when she decided to quit the business. When some time later she wanted to make a comeback, she found that no one was willing to take a chance on her. It was Barbara who got her back into the swing. She arranged to have Dagmar's nightclub act auditioned by her father. It was a good act, and Dagmar opened to rave notices in the press. Barbara attended opening night with Ted Cott, who was getting divorced.

Cott was his usual charming self when he came to Phil Dean one day to arrange a transfer for Barbara, explaining, "She's too valuable a person to waste on publicity." He told his publicity aide that he was assigning Barbara as producer for *Ask the Camera*, an NBC-TV show. The move was a good one for Barbara's career. She didn't stay for long, though. She soon took a job at another local TV station, WPIX, a move that, perhaps, was what doomed her relationship with Cott.

From WPIX, Barbara went to CBS to work on their morning show, in competition with *Today*. She stayed five years, leaving only when the last of that series of CBS morning shows died. Barbara had been working in television for ten years at that point, but with no TV openings available, she joined Tex McCreary at Tex Com, a radio-oriented public relations agency.

Tex and his wife, Jinx, had their own popular radio show. Jinx, the first Miss Rheingold beauty queen, frequently went on foreign visits to interview the rich and famous, and her absences left a gap that hurt the *Tex and Jinx Show*. Barbara dreamed up a contest to select a "Junior Jinx," which some thought Barbara hoped to win for herself. Barbara did not, however, enter the contest. Sue Oakman, who had a doctorate in communications, won. Later, the blond Miss Oakman became the wife of Ted Cott. Cott died in 1973, and his widow now does editorials on WCBS News in New York.

Barbara stayed with her public relations job less than a year, but while she was there that she established her contact with the *Today Show*—indirectly through Fidel Castro.

Christmas in Havana was hardly peaceable. Dictator Fulgencio Batista was preparing to flee the country to escape Fidel Castro's rebel army, which was swarming out of the mountains toward the cities. Paul Cunningham, reporter-at-large for the

Today Show, was on assignment in Havana when he heard a knock at the door of his hotel room. He opened it to some "ferocious-looking men" and found himself staring down the barrel of a large, ancient weapon known as a horse pistol. Cunningham, a feisty Irishman, once shocked *Today* listeners after a dockside interview with British Prime Minister Anthony Eden by telling an intrusive French journalist to shut up or he'd knock him on his ass. But whatever emotions churned through Paul's system this time, he eyed the formidable-looking weapon and decided to go quietly.

As the soldiers led him outside, Cunningham kept asking "Where are we going?" to no response. As they got into a car, Cubans gathered around, cheering, and the morose soldier with the pistol began to loosen up and play to the crowd, grinning as he put the weapon to Paul's ear. Paul figured he was regarded as a Batista stooge and was on the way to a firing squad. Instead, they drove him to a house, led him upstairs, sat him next to a young man with a beard and said, "Interview him." With that, Cunningham realized that the revolutionary forces wanted publicity, not American hostages. So he struck out later with his camera crew and interviewed the officer who led the capture of the Presidential Palace.

Laden with film, Cunningham chartered a private plane to the mainland, only to discover at the Miami airport that he couldn't get a seat on the plane to New York, due to the post-Christmas rush. Paul explained that it was essential that he get his film back to NBC.

A young lady overheard the conversation, tapped him on the shoulder, and said, "I'd be happy to take your film to NBC. I used to work there. I'm Barbara Walters." When Cunningham offered Barbara a drink, she said she'd settle for a Coke and excused herself to go to the ladies' room.

"I waited and when she came back, I saw that she was transformed," Paul recalls. "A pretty girl when I first saw her, now she looked smashing. Instead of having her hair pulled tightly back and fastened at the nape of the neck, it was now fluffed out and she'd added some things to her face. I remember that I was quite taken."

Barbara apparently knew which way she was headed before her plane took off. Her first question was right to the point: How, she asked, did one go about getting a client on the *Today Show*? Barbara was not only interested in whom to contact for a *Today* appearance, she also wanted to know who was who these days at NBC. Pretty and tense, as Paul recalls, Barbara waved away a cigarette, saying she only smoked when nervous. Then she reconsidered and took the smoke anyway.

Paul was finally confirmed on the New York flight, and the two of them flew back together. Barbara kept up her acquaintanceship with Cunningham and was soon submitting suggested scripts for the show. Her first "score," though, came indirectly. She wrote copy for a series of short public service features, which were sponsored by S&H Green Stamps, a Tex Com client, and broadcast on the *Today Show*.

Barbara's scripts were narrated by Anita Colby, a comely woman-about-town known as "The Face." According to a *Today* writer, Anita "could barely enunciate," but Barbara's scripts were good enough to attract notice at *Today*.

Fred Freed, the producer whose reign began and ended in 1961, signed Barbara on as a freelance writer for the show. The union permitted several of the eight writers then assigned to the show to be freelance contributors. This meant that they could be fired without notice at the end of thirteen weeks, the standard broadcast contract interval. They received no pension or other fringe benefits, but they were better paid than the regulars. Not a bad deal for a young person with few responsibilities. When Freed left the show, Shad Northshield began the first of his two terms as *Today Show* producer. He liked Barbara—a lot. He began to give her regular film assignments.

Shad gave Barbara her first major break by sending her to Afghanistan to cover Jackie Kennedy's trip to the Orient. It was obvious when she returned that she had not been ready for this kind of assignment. Two *Today* staffers who looked at her film footage were appalled.

"She hadn't really done this kind of thing," one explains. "When she came back, Tom Galvin and I told her how bad it was and explained what she should have done. We went into some detail, and she listened to us. She didn't like it one damn bit at first, but she *did* listen to us. And the next time she went out on a film assignment you could see that she had listened to Tom and me. That's what I admire about her."

On the other hand, Barbara could be difficult, and John Dunn drinks to that. Writers had to be film directors as well as scripters. When a film spot was to be done, the show sent the writer who had prepared the spot to direct it.

"Now Barbara got the feeling she knew more than the writer, and in some cases she was right," Dunn says. After all, Barbara was a writer for the show. But her duty when she was on camera was to accept direction from whichever writer wrote the spot. "She sometimes could be a problem. I remember doing a film spot with her some years later. I happen to be one of those who taught her. On this occasion she started telling the cameraman what to do and I said, 'Barbara, you and I have got to have a little talk before we start.' I took her aside and said, 'I don't want to embarrass you, but either I'm directing this film or you're directing it. If you want to direct, you can direct. I am ready to go downstairs and get a cab back to NBC. I don't give a good goddamn; it doesn't matter to me, but I set this thing up, I've written the script, and now if you want me to direct it you can keep your mouth shut.' She did.

"She's smart," Dunn adds. "Vanity really doesn't count with her. I'm sure I'm vain too. But when it comes to the crunch she wasn't going to have me go back to the office and have Morgan ask, 'What the hell are you doing here?' The point is she did have the intelligence to keep me there. There were no more problems, I ran the show. Other writers have come back embittered. I used to say to them, 'Why didn't you stop her? Tell her. She'll listen. Barbara is a very sensible person.' "

After Maureen O'Sullivan left *Today* in the summer of 1964, there was a lively debate within the *Today* company over the merits of Barbara Walters' well-known aspiration to become a regular member of the on-camera family.

Her friend Barbara Gordon, then a *Today* staffer, says, "I told Al Morgan I thought her wonderful, different, *menshy.*"

Others put down Barbara Walters as too aggressive and brassy. They argued that she was too Jewish for middle America. And there was that lisp that Al Morgan was afraid would grate on the public if she was seen five mornings a week.

Barbara was, of course, determined to get the job, after having been passed over when Pat Fontaine came in and again with Maureen. Al Morgan wasn't opposed to Barbara—he had been overwhelmed by the professional job she did in a non-stop *Today* broadcast of President Kennedy's funeral—but he still leaned to casting someone who would project Broadway or some other sector of the performing arts. This time, however, it wasn't his decision to make. Hugh Downs says he disapproved of pulling someone in from another medium, feeling that TV was mature enough by 1964 to develop its own talent. He believed that Barbara proved this point, and he wanted her for the job.

One *Today* source states that while Morgan likes to say it was he who brought Barbara in, it wasn't. "Morgan was in a corner on a girl, there was no one waiting to step into Maureen's place—so when Downs said it's going to be Barbara, Morgan couldn't argue. He said yes." Some say had Morgan another candidate, he might have withheld the prize one more time.

Barbara, meanwhile, realized what was at stake. While she was told that she could go back to writing if she didn't make it on camera, she wouldn't have been able to accept the demotion. Nervous she undoubtedly was. But she was certainly not afraid. She was confident she would make it. She knew she had learned her lessons well.

Once she was on camera regularly, it was inevitable that Barbara's assertiveness would become an issue. She would grow impatient when she felt that a guest was being mishandled or let off the hook by Downs, but for a while she kept her peace.

"Barbara sat there morning after morning while interviews went down the drain," Al Morgan explains. "One day she finally decided to step in and do *his* job. She's taken a bum rap ever since for being very aggressive."

Hugh Downs himself concedes that Barbara was good at things he was not, saying, "Barbara was magnificent at specifics." To some, that was another way of admitting that Barbara was prepared when Downs was not. Certainly she would have been put in her place had Downs wanted to keep her back. But not having done his homework, Hugh was willing to let Barbara ask tough questions.

The first few times Barbara waded in—with concise, well-thought-out questions—the guests were anything but happy. Many were famous people used to pleasantries and pap. Barbara socked it to 'em. Since she hadn't had the usual *Today* Girl build-up and was very different from the teacup dollies anyway, the reaction was "Who is this nobody who is embarrassing me coast to coast?"

Downs was somewhat displeased in private, but he decided not to make an issue of it when he noticed the ratings beginning to climb. No harm done, Downs thought, as he continued to begin and close all interviews he was involved in, thus appearing to be genial, cooperative, and very much in charge. But Barbara Walters had begun to establish herself as an important TV personality.

CHAPTER 19

The Up Years with Downs

The Hugh Downs years, from 1962 to 1971, are considered by many to be the *Today Show*'s peak in terms of quality, influence, and power. By the mid-1960s it seemed that everyone wanted to appear on *Today*—from athletes to zoologists, actors to Zen Buddhists.

Take writers, for instance. Many of them are important people, with stature and dignity. But few could be found, then or now, who were unwilling to humble themselves in just about any way to get their books a hearing on the show. For in the world of books, the *Today Show* is Everest. All other interview shows that authors frequent are smaller peaks—and some are valleys. A legend, based at least partially on fact, persists that a *Today* appearance is good for 5,000 hardcover sales.

Writers and publishers, therefore, constantly prostrate themselves before even the lowest functionaries at *Today*. Book companies commonly agree not to have an author appear anywhere else until he has had his shot on *Today*.

Yet important as the show has been to publishers and authors,

books have been of relatively little importance to the show—
except in emergencies. Happenstance has often played a major
role in *Today*'s exposure of books.

Under the system that Al Morgan instituted in 1962, every
Friday at 11 A.M. the producer sat down with the staff and
assigned responsibility for the shows to be aired in the week
ahead, a different *Today* writer for each day's broadcast. The
writer would later fill the allotted schedule with the important
fare—an astronaut, perhaps, just getting his feet on the ground;
a Senator with his bill in the hopper; an important educator
with his head in the clouds; and, say, a European microbiologist
to talk about a strange disease terrifying Peoria.

If, however, the European scientist cabled to beg off, citing a
death in the family, an author would probably be selected to fill
the gap. The *Today* writer would pluck a book out of a stack
of new works that arrived in the mail each day, and prepare
to make it possible for the interviewer to seem to have read the
book. Barbara Walters was conscientious and would sometimes
burn the midnight oil in an effort to prepare for last-minute
author visits. But even she couldn't read most of the books
thrown her way on short notice. And Hugh Downs hardly
ever tried.

Ambitious young staffers would generally be asked to read
the books being considered for the show. The ones who proved
to be good at summarizing what they had read were depended
upon to carry some of the load—if the author's book was
scheduled far enough in advance. But if a *Today* writer got an
unread book at 1 P.M. for the show coming up eighteen hours
later, nobody seriously thought he was going to read it. One
writer says: "I know what I did under such circumstances. I
started with the press agent's release, which summed up the
book, and then I read the book jacket. Next I would leaf
through the book, skimming and looking for things the *Today*

audience cares about—the broker in Topeka; the nurse in Sausalito."

Sometimes the *Today* audience was persuaded that the host had read the book and sometimes it was not. This often depended on how well the writer had prepared questions. A former *Today Show* managing editor comments: "All I had to do was look at the script and I could tell if the show's writer had read the book. I like to think the viewers weren't quite so perceptive."

More important to the show than authors were the people in positions of power who watched and appeared on *Today*. And many very powerful figures did both. *New York Times* critic Jack Gould once said that during Lyndon B. Johnson's years as President any bureaucrat with a brain knew that the best way to get a "memo" to the boss was to wangle a visit to the *Today Show*. For Johnson recognized that the show was a major influence on American thought. Lyndon Johnson himself first appeared before a *Today* camera in 1955, when he was Senate Democratic leader, and after becoming President, he was a regular viewer and an occasional critic of the show.

Once, NBC's Ray Scherer answered a telephone in *Today*'s Washington studio after completing an interview with Ambassador-at-Large Averell Harriman. The caller said, "You don't look as good as he did . . . the lighting on you wasn't good." Scherer recognized the voice as that of LBJ. Another time, while Jack Dempsey was being interviewed on the show, writer Joe Gottlieb got a telephone call in the control room. "The President is calling," an operator said. "What president?" asked Gottlieb. "The President of the United States," replied the White House operator. Busy and skeptical, Gottlieb replied, "Well, he'll have to wait," and with that put the call on hold. At the commercial break, Gottlieb picked up the call again and, red-faced, put the Chief through to Dempsey. LBJ wanted to invite him to the White House.

Being the visible center of all this power, it is not surprising that the *Today* host evoked extremes of both praise and disdain from his lesser known colleagues on the show. One *Today* staffer, for instance, called Hugh Downs a "prick by omission." It wasn't that Downs set out to be mean. He was universally pleasant—always a gentleman. But some felt that in furthering his career Downs unconsciously stepped on other people. While this could be said of many who make it to the top in the hard world of television, a star's slights or demands can cause unpleasantness for associates.

One problem was that Downs seemed to see himself as the center of the universe. Once on a remote visit to Holland, his wife, Ruth, demanded that Hugh not take the window seat in a bus about to travel across a sparsely populated section of the country. His millions of Dutch fans might discover him and mob him, she explained. Hugh agreed and took an aisle seat.

When this author attempted to elicit high points of the Hugh Downs years on *Today* from the former host, Downs replied with enthusiastic reports on how the show made it possible for him to do so many interesting things. He took some astronaut training at Wright Patterson in Dayton, experiencing weightlessness, and some aquanaut training in the Virgin Islands. Hugh also explained how he got to take flying lessons for a series of broadcasts on the subject. He obviously enjoyed these experiences in part because they were all free.

Prompted to recall experiences that had profound effects on others besides himself, Hugh finally remembered a broadcast in the early 1960s in which Adlai E. Stevenson eloquently defended his performance as Ambassador to the United Nations. But it wasn't he who invited Adlai, Downs explained. Stevenson, fearing the impact of a critical magazine article then hit-ting the stands, had begged to make an appearance because he recognized that the show was widely watched by official Washington. And he succeeded, receiving reaffirmation from the White House right after the show.

The trouble with Downs, basically a top-notch commercial salesman, was that he was an interviewer only because the *Today* hosting job demanded that he be one. Interviewing political figures was not his strong point. Producer Al Morgan especially deplored Downs' lack of preparation and his occasional bumbling on interviews.

Morgan also liked to make light of Downs' favorite fallback expressions, "Mercy!" and "Oh, I see!" The latter expression was the object of one of Morgan's most elaborate jokes.

For weeks the *Today* staff counted "Oh, I see's" for an office pool with the reward going to the participant who came closest to guessing the daily "Oh, I see" harvest. Morgan and others then impishly decided to make Downs the first recipient of an award by the fictitious Organization of International Communicators—the "OIC." According to Morgan, the conspirators wrote Downs on special stationery printed for the occasion and asked if they could give him the award on the air. The letter was signed, of course, with a phony name. Downs asked Morgan if it would be okay, and Morgan deadpanned, "Sure."

"We hired Al Kelly, the double-talk guy, to present the award," Morgan explains. "But it played straight, since Downs never guessed that he had been ripped off. Mercy!"

Morgan was outspoken in his scorn for Downs, referring to him as "the idiot." When this inevitably got back to the *Today* host, it fueled the discord between the two men. And Morgan's opinion of Downs has remained unchanged over the years. He enjoys recalling, for instance, the side benefits Hugh reaped from the show, suggesting that a trip through the Downs household would have provided a virtual trade show of all the products represented by *Today* sponsors. On location, Downs always demanded and got the best stereo available installed in his hotel suite. And when Hugh and Ruth Downs left a remote, says Morgan, the place would seem to have been "sacked by the Visigoths."

One writer remembers that once in a while Hugh would take him across the street after the show to Cromwell's drugstore for coffee and a danish. They were there so that Hugh could "keep on top of things," and each writer in turn would get the invitation. But at the conclusion of such visits, Hugh would ask for two checks. "He wasn't going to pay for your coffee," the writer says.

Barbara Gordon, a former *Today* staffer who now does documentaries for WCBS-TV in New York, says separate checks would have been fine insofar as Barbara Walters and she were concerned. According to Gordon, in many years of going with Hugh after the show to have coffee "or eggs and a drink, Hugh would leave before coffee. Barbara and I used to have to pick up the tab."

The Downses' Christmas gifts came from wholesale or discount stores, always wrapped in brown paper. "One year we all got ugly, black men's umbrellas," says Barbara Gordon. "Not only were the gifts cheap, they were very elitist. All people in a certain job got the umbrellas and those higher up got something else. There was never a note, just your name written on the brown paper and signed Hugh and Ruth. We used to joke that they didn't want to spend twenty-five cents for a card."

Al Morgan says that Hugh was conscious of the fact that people thought him cheap, but he defended himself. Downs claimed that his salary, which with the show *Concentration* reached half a million dollars a year at his peak, was almost wiped out by 90 percent income taxes; he got to keep only ten cents of every dollar he earned. And besides, he would complain, NBC wouldn't pay for Ruth's travel expenses on remotes. That cut further into the Downs kitty.

Actually, taxes topped at 70 percent in the late 1960s, and anyone as careful as Hugh Downs must have found ways to trim federal imposts through tax shelters, which were widely available to people in the upper tax brackets. Salaries are more heavily taxed than many forms of investment income, but there were ways to reduce the levy substantially below peak levels. "Let's face it," says a staffer, "generous he ain't."

For all the harsh things many of his colleagues have to say about him, Hugh Downs was not a man without convictions, and he showed them on *Today* when he felt strongly about a subject. If a guest with whom Downs differed was evasive on the air, viewers could tell Downs was getting annoyed. Without raising his voice he would begin calling the guest "sir"— softer but reminiscent of his old boss Jack Paar's sarcastic "pal." And despite his weaknesses as an interviewer, he could occasionally rise to a subject.

When Downs interviewed this author on *Today*, just before air time he asked, "Why is the stock market acting so badly?" It was at the nadir of the worst bear market in a generation—on May 27, 1970. The author said, "Wall Street is blaming Nixon." Downs asked, "Will you say that on the air?" and when the author said yes, Downs threw away the script. The market was discussed in terms of presidential indifference, which made for a much livelier interview than if Downs had stayed with his prepared questions.

In an effort to keep a dialogue going with his son Hugh Raymond during the late sixties' period of youthful revolt, Downs smoked marijuana with him. With characteristic thoroughness concerning things that commanded his attention, Downs studied the drug and became convinced that its harmful effects had been considerably overstated. The *Today Show* thereafter invited a government official to talk about marijuana. Downs was at his best, for once asking tough, concise questions when the official parroted the party line about the drug's disastrous consequences even with light use.

But Hugh Downs' finest hour came at the Democratic Convention in Chicago in August 1968, the conclusion of several of the most tumultuous months in American history. The Vietcong's Tet offensive in February disillusioned tens of millions of Americans who until then had believed in the correctness of the Johnson Administration's Vietnam policies. Then anti-war candidate Senator Eugene McCarthy made an impressive showing against President Johnson in the New Hampshire primary, thanks largely to the efforts of thousands of anti-war youths who still believed in working through the system. Within the next few months, Johnson announced his withdrawal; Robert Kennedy entered the race; Martin Luther King, Jr., was assassinated, triggering riots in ghettos throughout the country; and Robert Kennedy was assassinated.

As the convention began, Vice-President Hubert H. Humphrey, closely tied to LBJ's Vietnam policies, held a commanding lead over McCarthy, though Humphrey had entered few of the major primaries. Allied with the Johnson-Humphrey camp was the nation's toughest, most successful regional politician, Chicago mayor Richard Daley. He planned to rule the convention city with an iron hand. Fences and barbed wire were installed around the convention area.

When the *Today* company arrived in Chicago they found an armed camp. Youthful McCarthy supporters and anti-war demonstrators were herded to Grant and Lincoln Parks, far from the convention grounds. Some of the protesters, who numbered about 10,000, were violent and threw rocks. Most were peaceful and unarmed. Perhaps violence was inevitable, but most observers insist that the police initiated it. Television mobile units covered the demonstrations, and when police advanced on the throng at Grant Park the demonstrators taunted them with shouts of "The whole world is watching! The whole world is watching!" (This became the title for a novel that Al Morgan wrote.)

When the unarmed demonstrators began a protest march on the convention site, the police beat them back with nightsticks and sprayed them with tear gas and Mace. Scores of them fell wounded, some to be taken away in ambulances, others to be loaded into paddy wagons. In addition to the demonstrators, twenty-one reporters and photographers were injured by the police. Almost everyone on the *Today Show's* remote staff was gassed, and Aline Saarinen was Maced. Warned in advance that the police would tear-gas demonstrators, the staff had walked across Michigan Boulevard to sit quietly and share the punishment with the crowd.

The entire *Today* company was radicalized by the Chicago experience. Joe Garagiola, a great respecter of authority, was no exception. He had been talking with a well-behaved group in Lincoln Park—college kids who deplored violence but felt they must protest a convention they believed to be rigged. Joe watched in stunned surprise as the police lobbed tear gas at the peaceful demonstrators. He then went on the air and, his voice breaking with emotion, ad-libbed that we go around telling kids to be honest and true and then this happens to them.

For once Hugh Downs forgot about winning friends. He read a strong statement on *Today,* written by Al Morgan, which condemned the police brutality. The Chicago cops were not pigs as the youthful demonstrators had contended, he said. Rather, they were far worse than that. Downs was so stirred by the events that he ordered five thousand sandwiches for delivery to the demonstrators. He paid for the food himself and reportedly sent it anonymously. Al Morgan, Downs' most vociferous critic, insists that Downs wanted it both ways— "Just like always!"—letting the demonstrators know he sent the sandwiches while trying to keep the establishment in the dark. No so, says another frequent Downs critic. For once, he was mad enough to spend money and not claim the credit.

There was one final and important interview for *Today* in Chicago—with the triumphant nominee, Hubert Humphrey. Downs did not ask the loaded question written by one angry writer: "What did it feel like on the greatest night of your life to see all those young people on the other side of the barricade?" But Downs did ask about the violence that injured so many un-armed citizens. Humphrey, who by his silence during the con-vention was regarded by the *Today* staff and millions of voters as having condoned the police brutality, said that he deplored violence on all sides. His statement seemed little more concilia-tory than that of Mayor Daley, who said, "Nobody got killed."

The *Today Show* had the final word. During the credits at the conclusion of its last Chicago broadcast, the old Frank Sinatra tribute to Chicago—"that's my kind of town"—was played as vocal background to films of police wading in on the demonstrators, nightsticks flailing.

The mail was overwhelmingly against *Today*'s accent on the street violence, and the NBC Chicago station raised hell with the network over the *Today* coverage. But the staff was closer, perhaps, than it had been in many a month. Except, of course, for the running feud between Downs and Morgan.

According to Al Morgan, one character in the *Today Show* company was such a lush that his nickname was "Huckleberry Drunk." When the author asked what that man's none-too-sober associate was called, Morgan quipped, "Very rarely!" John Dunn says there was no way on earth to beat Morgan in verbal combat. He and Morgan were once stymied by a prob-lem that was basically Morgan's responsibility. Dunn said, "I wouldn't be producer of this show for a million dollars a year."

Without losing a beat, Al Morgan said, "That's exactly what I'm getting." It is not surprising that a man so quick-witted was able to dream up a means of extracting a final fat paycheck from NBC when he left the show.

By October 1965, Downs was so furious with Morgan and his put-Downs that he demanded Morgan's head as a condition for signing a new three-year contract. But Morgan had already signed a new three-year contract months before, having arrived on the show in 1962 four months before Downs did. The network not only was on the hook with Morgan, he also had a powerful friend in Bill McAndrew, the NBC News executive. NBC looked for an alternative solution. They sweetened their offer to Downs until it became irresistible. Downs signed the three-year contract, saying, "Okay, but next time, you're not going to be able to buy me off."

Morgan was confident that he would outlast Downs in their fight to the finish. Like some other producers in network television, Morgan sometimes felt like a ventriloquist. He believes it is the producer's talent that makes a show succeed, not the on-camera personality, despite his superior pay. If Morgan provided quality grist for Downs, the star looked good. A strong star would do better, but even a weak star could survive if he got strong backing from the production staff.

Some say that Morgan was guilty of a classic blunder in failing to recognize the enormous power of the on-camera personality. You just didn't win against a star. On the other hand, a writer for *Today* says that Morgan claimed in early 1968 that he had won and that McAndrew had finally decided to replace Downs.

It never happened. In May 1968, just before Morgan's contract was up, McAndrew, then aged fifty-four and apparently in good health, entered the hospital. According to the report *Today* received, he had slipped in his bathtub and broken some ribs. Several days later, totally unexpectedly, he died. "Nobody even went to see him," says Morgan. "He was to be in the hospital only a couple of days." Morgan later dedicated his novel *The Whole World Is Watching* to McAndrew.

Morgan had to negotiate his new contract without McAndrew's support. He demanded substantially more money, even though he knew Downs would enforce his "Morgan goes" edict shortly. Says an associate of the era, "I admired Morgan for this. He had the balls of a brass monkey. A lot of guys would have thought the jig was up and just let the contract run out and take the blow."

In the fall of 1968, when it came time for the management to negotiate with Downs, they again tried to buy him off. No soap. Downs said, "Look, I told you the last time: no more Morgan."

Morgan's firing, like that of so many on the show, was poorly executed. His managing editor, Al Smith, was at home the day it happened. "It was Yom Kippur," Smith remembers, "and Al Morgan called to ask, 'Having a miserable day?' I said, 'Well, it *is* a day of atonement.' Morgan said, 'I'll give you something to be miserable about. I've been fired. At least that's what they tell me it says in *Variety*.'"

Morgan had gotten a call from someone who said he was sorry to hear about it. Only when he asked, "What are you talking about?" did Morgan find out about the *Variety* item. It was the only Wednesday in years that the weekly show business newspaper hadn't been delivered to the *Today* offices.

Morgan went down the hall to the *Tonight Show* offices and learned from someone there that he had been reassigned. He then went to Don Meany, the new vice-president to whom he had been reporting following McAndrew's death. Al asked what was happening. Meany reportedly snapped his fingers and said, "Oh, yeah, I've been meaning to talk to you about that."

Badly done or not, Morgan was certainly prepared for the

ax with his fat new three-year contract. "They put Al Morgan in a fur-lined dog house," John Dunn explains. "They gave him some phony title, a secretary, and an office without any windows. He had everything he needed except something to do."

Morgan was, of course, restless and finally managed to get a settlement after about a year. "I got all the money stipulated in the contract," Morgan says. "NBC had cooled me off [as a producer] and that's what they wanted."

Al Morgan had reveled in the power of the job, though he did become bored with it in the last two years of his six-year command. He regards the position as the "last monarchy," conferring the power of a great newspaper publisher, a power to shape events as well as chronicle them. Morgan says that producing the show was, in a paraphrase of Orson Welles, "like owning the biggest, most expensive set of electric trains in the world."

It was in Al Morgan's era that the *Today Show* abandoned its earlier corniness, despite the basic corniness of its host. Judith Crist, *Today*'s movie critic during the Morgan years, says with feeling, "Al Morgan *invented* the *Today Show*." Instead of featuring so many beauty contest winners, *Today* concentrated more on the great events of the era—civil rights demonstrations, the radicalization of American society by the war in Vietnam, the assassinations of the Kennedy brothers and Martin Luther King, Jr.

When Al Morgan went, so did Al Smith. *Today*'s associate producer as well as managing editor, Smith was too closely associated with Morgan to survive. When Stuart Schulberg got Morgan's job, Smith says, Stu had orders to "get rid of the smell of Morgan."

Not that Smith's departure was widely mourned. Like every other producer, Morgan needed a "yes" man and Smith evidently filled the role ad nauseum. One writer of the era remarked that Smith "spent hours on his expense accounts" and added facetiously, "it was the only important work—the only creative writing—he ever did. But the day he became associate producer—in the waning months of Morgan's reign, by the way—his first official act was to veto his ex-roommate's expense account."

Today editor John Dunn survived the turnover. Dunn liked and respected Morgan—"We are adults with each other" —but saw no need to go further. When Downs came to Dunn and asked if he was loyal to Morgan, Dunn said, no, he was loyal to the show. He could have told Downs that he wasn't loyal to him either.

Among the telephone calls Al Morgan received after he was fired was one from Mike Dann, a CBS vice-president, and before that, an NBC vice-president. Reflecting upon the wild salaries drawn by broadcasting's amiable no-talents, Dann told Morgan, "It'll be hard to find a job for you. You're no $50,000-a-year bum!"

The Hugh Downs era of the *Today Show* ended in October 1971, when Downs quit voluntarily, citing his desire to do things that he couldn't do while chained to Manhattan. Al Morgan remarks that Downs had always said he would quit when he had enough money. "That's what he did, and I admire him for it," says Morgan grudgingly.

Apparently bored by his retirement life in Carefree, Arizona, however, Downs made one television comeback. He became a host on Barbara Walters' syndicated *Not for Women Only*, as Barbara cut back an intensely busy schedule. The program treated subjects in depth for a full week—the nation's changing sex mores, abortion, women's rights. It was not Hugh Downs' metier, nor was he willing to do the homework. After a few months on the show, Downs quit.

In August 1976, while Downs was still doing the show, the author called the show's home station, WNBC-TV in New York, which shares the same switchboard with the network, and asked for him by name. The operator said, "Who?"

"Hugh Downs."

"What's the first name?"

Didn't the operator know the man who now worked on an important show on the local station—the man who had hosted *Today* for nine years?

"Never mind that. What's that first name?"

Sic transit gloria mundi.

CHAPTER 20

The Star

Barbara Walters was a *Today* original; more so, perhaps, even than Garroway in his prime. Garroway represented informality in a formal age and seemed to have the affection of almost everyone. Barbara, on the other hand, was strong, acerbic. She was loved by millions and not loved by millions of others. But as producer Stuart Schulberg said, "Whether they loved her or hated her, they sure did watch her."

She was a star, and a most unusual one. She was not from show business, and she wasn't from newspaper journalism. Television newsmen, who mostly came from newspaper backgrounds, were bewildered that someone who hadn't apprenticed in their sacred crucible could do what she did so well. They resented her—especially since she had once worked in that odious handmaiden to their craft, public relations. In news parlance, Barbara had been a "flack," and for most in the business that ended it. Barbara complains that this is a "bum rap," pointing out that she had been in PR only eight months, but it is a rap that has stuck to her.

Judith Crist, a traditional journalist who began doing hard-nosed movie reviews on *Today* at the time Barbara became a regular, analyzed her journalistic ability more objectively: "Barbara, I discovered, was not bedazzled by the glamour of Jackie Kennedy. Barbara saw Jackie just as the other news-people did—a voracious society broad, a snob without any social instincts. Barbara said of her Indian tour, that Jackie was totally involved with herself. If they gave Jackie a choice of posing on a baby elephant or opening a peasant craft show, Jackie would always opt for the elephant. Barbara's reaction to Jackie won me."

Yet Barbara sometimes "paid off." President Nixon, shortly after his first inaugural, discovered Barbara in the White House Rose Garden interviewing a member of his family. He walked out and invited her to breakfast with his closest sup-porters. It was a major coup for Barbara.

"She was smart enough to grab it and to realize what she had," says *Today* editor John Dunn. "It was the first time any reporter had a live thing in the White House."

But Dunn snorted at the payoff: What was your impression of Mr. Nixon? reporters asked, and Barbara said that she found him "sexy." Another first for Barbara, says Dunn. He added that Barbara would use Eunice Shriver on *Today* for some "little publicity thing" because Eunice was "very important to her . . . she may want something from Eunice sometime. Eunice may invite her to the right kind of party—not neces-sarily to have fun or to get news—but because Barbara likes to be important."

There is a softness about Barbara as well, and she had many fervent supporters at *Today* who insist that she is the most sensitive of human beings. Jim Gaines, *Today* director, says, "If you went in and told Barbara that you beat up your wife, she would say, 'You're an idiot'—you'd get an opinion, but she'd listen. She had the biggest shoulders in the world. I've often wondered whose shoulders she cries on—we've all cried on hers.

"Once I was here and my wife was in West Virginia," Gaines continued. "Barbara said, 'What are you doing for dinner?' and took me to her place for the evening with her and Jacqueline [Barbara's adopted daughter]. Later I called my wife and said, 'You'll never guess where I had dinner tonight,' and she said, 'Yes I can—Barbara's.' "

Doreen Chu, a *Today* writer, experienced Barbara's solicitude under unusual circumstances. Barbara was traveling with the *Today* cameras in India and Doreen was along as her writer. Doreen became sick and began to run a fever. As far as Barbara was concerned, only the ranking doctor on the trip was good enough for Doreen—Vice-President Spiro Agnew's doctor—and Barbara saw to it that Doreen got him. With Doreen out of commission, there was much more work. Barbara handled Doreen's writing chores and did her own work as well. At the same time, she fed and bathed Doreen and dispensed TLC.

When a *Today* friend needed help, it seemed to make no difference how busy Barbara was. Once she dropped by the studio late one day on the way to a formal dinner. She discovered a *Today* secretary in anguish, head on typewriter. The woman's doctor had found a lump in her breast that afternoon. Barbara canceled her plans, got the best specialist she could find, and stayed to help the woman through the night.

Judith Crist is another who sees Barbara Walters as a basically warm person.

"When an individual reaches a certain point of success—financial and professional—a hard shell develops," she says. "This is especially true for women, who have had to be even more aware of who's behind them than men. Women are far more vulnerable. Say a man is a tough cookie and that is complimentary; but say that of a woman and you are calling her a hard bitch. I don't think that hardening has taken place in Barbara at all. I still find her to be the sweet, warm, vulnerable, and strangely innocent person she was when I first met her."

Writer Bob Cunniff, who shared an office with Barbara on the *Today Show* for several years, remembers many occasions when Barbara's aggressiveness, which in a male would have been called competitive fire, was dismissed as the efforts of a "pushy broad." He remembers an incident in Miami Beach that explains how Barbara reached eminence. In 1968, with Richard Nixon's nomination for the Presidency a foregone conclusion, an associate producer was dispatched to set up the Miami Beach convention remote and had managed to organize an opening show guaranteed to drive viewers to *Captain Kangaroo*. Late Saturday night, about twenty-eight hours before the first Miami show was due to air, Cunniff's phone rang. It was Barbara. She said she couldn't believe how dull that first show looked. What was the point of going to Miami Beach if we didn't care how the show was? Would Cunniff join her at breakfast to try to persuade producer Al Morgan to throw out that first show and replace it with something to catch the excitement of a convention, even if it was just a Nixon convention?

Cunniff agreed and at breakfast, after frantic badgering from both Barbara and Cunniff, Morgan gave in. The scheduled show was abandoned and within an hour the staff had been notified and dispatched all over Miami Beach, covering, with film crews and tape units, a series of stories showing the maneuvering that precedes any convention. It was a fast, exciting program. Morgan congratulated the staff for great zeal under fire, but never mentioned that Barbara had been responsible.

"Barbara never stopped working and she really gave a damn about *Today*," Cunniff remembers. "And while I certainly had my differences with her about the handling of my material on the show, I can't remember anything but great fun with Barbara when working on the show. She's a great gossip, funny and quite aware of her own vulnerabilities. She was fun to be around and I'd hate to think of that show without her during the last months of the Morgan years when he was bored stiff."

Those exposed to Barbara's warmth certainly have found it to be appealing. A magazine writer was put at ease by her solicitude, and was charmed by her reaction to a telephone call that delayed his interview with her. "Why are you keeping me waiting?" Barbara said kiddingly. "Don't you know that I'm a star?"

After the author of this book did a *Today* interview on the stock market with Hugh Downs, Barbara stopped him to say, "I don't know anything about finance, but when you were talking, I somehow felt I was getting it." It was a spontaneous gesture and certainly a winning one.

Yet there are those in the *Today* company who rarely saw this warmth, or seeing it, distrusted it. They remembered Barbara's insensitivity. Frank Blair complained publicly about Barbara's assertiveness. He said staffers would observe as Barbara bore in relentlessly on a guest and mutter, "Oh, shut up, Barbara, and let him talk."

Barbara was temperamental at times, too, and impatient with incompetence. Threaten Barbara's performance through a lack of professionalism—bad lighting, a garbled script—and she could strike back with a vengeance.

Helen Marmer, an NBC newswoman who is bitter about what she considers *Today*'s unkept promises concerning her job on the show, remembers Barbara at her worst. After a *Not for Women Only* broadcast, a staffer brought a ten-year-old boy forward, having told him that Barbara would autograph his cast. But instead, according to Helen Marmer, Barbara started yelling that if she signed one cast she would have to sign them all.

"The kid turned crimson and looked as though he wanted to die," says Helen. "Every time I find myself turning sympathetic toward Barbara, I think of this devotion to career at the expense of other things."

Most of Barbara's detractors respect her as a woman who made it in a man's world through hard work, tenacity, and grit. But they are suspicious of the way she mixes glamour-girl opportunist, warm-hearted woman, and hard-boiled reporter, on and off the air, for her own ends. Barbara herself becomes defensive at the suggestion that she somehow seems softer off the air. When the author brought it up, she bristled, then finally accepted the assessment that there was a "seductive" quality that is missing on broadcasts.

Former *Today* producer Stuart Schulberg says that Barbara exudes femininity and sex appeal, and adds that these are qualities she does use, to a point. "But when the camera goes on— all that turns off," he says. He goes on to defend this approach. Stuart notes that Marguerite Higgins, a seductive war correspondent, entertained a Red Army general for days near the end of World War II to the grumbling of shut-out male correspondents. She got ten news beats, says Schulberg, and rightly so. It is unfair, he insists, to accuse women of using feminine wiles when men use their wiles as well.

Whatever it was that Barbara used, it was successful. Schulberg regards the Hugh Downs-Barbara Walters-Joe Garagiola period as the most successful in the show's history, and the period when Frank McGee took Downs' place as very good too. Largely this was because Barbara was distinctive enough to fascinate the public—as an unpleasantly outspoken maiden aunt to some, as a comforting presence to others. "The great audience," says the newsman and one-time Walters associate

Jim Fleming, "wants someone they feel is strongly *there*." Walters filled this role in the difficult wake-up hours. And with her penchant for asking tough questions, she frequently elicited headline news—even when the questions were trivial.

Barbara asked Mamie Eisenhower if she was aware of rumors about her drinking. Mrs. Eisenhower answered that she was and insisted that it was not alcohol but an inner-ear problem that caused her to appear to be tipsy. Barbara asked Lady Bird Johnson if she was jealous of her late husband's reputation as a ladies' man. Mrs. Johnson took the impertinence well and said no.

Barbara reached a point at which she was sometimes bigger than the story she covered. Dr. Edgar Berman discovered a hard-as-nails adversary when he argued on *Today* that women would be unfit for the presidency because of "raging hormonal imbalances." Barbara frosted him, saying that her questions were right to the point because "it's not my time of the month."

She didn't always win these exchanges and sometimes faced guests who were openly hostile to her questions, which *Newsweek* once characterized as "dum dum bullets swaddled in angora." Walters dealt with a mute Barbra Streisand until she mentioned the fact that both were career women facing the added responsibility of raising children. Thereafter, the two chatted engagingly about kids. On the other hand, Warren Beatty, early in his acting career, was so infuriatingly cool that Barbara blew up on the air, ending the encounter by throwing up her hands and saying, "Oh, let's forget the whole thing."

She also lost a round to Oscar Werner, the Austrian actor who scored brilliantly in a movie based on Katherine Anne Porter's *Ship of Fools*. Werner was one of Barbara's first major interviews and he loafed through it, though he presumably was there to plug the movie. Exasperated and looking

for a way to get the interview off dead center, Barbara remarked that she had heard Werner was difficult to work with.
In an aggressively seductive tone, Werner replied, "How
would you know? We've never had an affair." Barbara flushed
and stammered, and was unable to get the next question out.
"Our producer said he wanted to walk on camera and throw
a pail of cold water on me," she recalls.

She has said that the Werner interview was the only one in
which she completely fell apart on the air—but it wasn't the
only time she was embarrassed. Leo G. Carroll, who played
the terribly British spy in *The Man from U.N.C.L.E.*, appeared at the studio early one morning, sleepy-eyed and yawn-
ing. Barbara told him that her signal to wind up comments prior
to a station break was a touch on the knee—out of camera
range, of course. Carroll evidently wasn't listening. When
Barbara gently reached over and touched the actor's knee, he
raised his eyebrows and said sharply, "Young woman! What
are you doing crawling up my thigh?" Barbara made a weak
stab at an explanation—to Carroll and a national audience—and
was not amused as the *Today* crew snorted and chortled.

Sometimes there was no way to answer an unexpected response to a tough question. Burt Reynolds, star of *Deliverance*
and a wise-cracking actor with more spirit and intelligence
than most, had long been involved in a well-publicized relationship with Dinah Shore. "How are you and Dinah getting
along, and do you plan to marry?" Barbara asked. Reynolds
answered heatedly, "That's a stupid question! I wouldn't ask
you about your divorce." (At the time, Barbara was still getting over her parting from Lee Guber, which was done so
quietly some didn't even know there had been a final break.)

Barbara had a similar experience after she asked David Kennerly, the White House photographer, about his reported
romance with Susan Ford. Kennerly's retort concerned Barbara's rumored romance with Senator Edward Brooke, Repub-

lican of Massachusetts. Barbara brushed past that one to her next question and put the interview back on an even keel. Rumors that she plans to marry the Senator, who is black, have surfaced recently, and Barbara has denied them.

It isn't always the tough question that brings the unexpected response. While Barbara is probably as well informed a generalist as anyone in the business, she has on occasion revealed certain gaps in her knowledge. She asked the author of a book about Albert Schweitzer how the doctor was doing. "He's dead!" said the unhappy author.

Today editor John Dunn used to deplore Barbara's tendency to ad-lib when she didn't know what she was talking about, with sometimes painful results. He remembers an episode that reveals one of Barbara's basic weaknesses.

"In some things, Barbara was as astute as anybody," he says. "But she is not an intellectual. Hard, real things are easy for her. Concepts are not. They were outside her experience. I had a man on the show from Harvard University who had pulled off a great hoax to explode the I.Q. myth. He got an agreement with the board of education of a West Coast grade school. Without informing the faculty, he set up a phony testing program and let the teachers know how individual children 'performed' in the test. The school had a mixed population of whites, blacks, and Chicanos. He faked the results so that a higher percentage of Chicanos and blacks were in the promising group. And to everyone's surprise, that is the way they performed thereafter. Once the teachers believed that certain of the children were bright, they nurtured them, and the test became a self-fulfilling prophecy."

Dunn explains that Hugh Downs was supposed to do the interview, but that Barbara felt she didn't have enough to do that morning. So she persuaded an associate producer to let her come in on the Harvard interview.

"She missed the point completely," says Dunn. "It was a

concept that was foreign to her middle-class mind. She took the experiment to mean that we don't demand enough of our children. That our expectations are too low. She kept hammering away at this guy with 'What'll we do to get more performance?' and finally he just quit trying to explain. While Downs was shrewd about these things, I'm not sure he understood this one either. At the time, I thought I had done a bad job. Now I'm convinced that it was Barbara's inability to deal with concepts that killed the interview."

Today writers were amused at the amount of time both Walters and Downs spent talking about themselves during interviews. A friend of one of them, Jack Orr, satirized their egocentrism in an article published in *TV Guide* in February 1969:

HUGH DOWNS: Well, folks, you've seen my pumpkin-pie message, and now I have an interview with one of the giants of the American theater, playwright Tennessee Williams. Last time Mr. Williams was here, unfortunately for him and me, I was on vacation. I was, you may know, climbing a mountain in Colorado, a state in western United States with a population of 1,975,000 and with an area of 104,247 miles. Were you here, Barbara?

BARBARA WALTERS: No, I wasn't, Hugh. I was in Hollywood taping some promotion material for NBC shows. I interviewed Barbara Eden, Phyllis Diller, Ray Charles and Simon Oakland. It was pretty thrilling stuff, too. I stayed at the Hollywood Roosevelt because there was a mix-up about my reservation at the Beverly Hilton.

HUGH: That happened to me once.

BARBARA: I remember Mr. Williams' work, though. When I was in college at Sarah Lawrence we used to sit around in the dorms and talk about how accomplished he used to be in exploring the passions and frustrations of our society—that is, I mean how accomplished he still *is* in exploring the passions and frustrations of our society. Beg pardon, Mr. Williams. As I was talking to Phyllis Diller out in Hollywood, I suddenly remembered that he was going to be on *Today*, and, I must say, it gave me a thrill and a glimpse backward to the time when I was young and hanging around backstage at the Latin Quarter. I was always carrying a copy of *The Glass Menagerie*. You ever read that, Hugh?

HUGH: Indeed, I did, Barbara. I have read it and reread it. In Chicago when I was doing those remotes on WMAQ . . . and when I was doing the *Home* show and the *Paar* show . . . and I read it when I went around the world in my little skiff . . . and I think I even had a copy with me during my hair transplant. I read Mr. Williams a lot . . .*

Egocentric or not, Barbara managed to corral many important people for *Today* interviews, among them Secretary of State Henry Kissinger. Some are convinced it was Barbara's weakness as an interviewer rather than her strength that led Kissinger to grant the *Today* interviews.

An NBC critic comments, "I remember one Kissinger interview where she failed to follow up with a very important point because she didn't know enough about foreign policy. Any interviewer in her position needs to know a little about a lot of things and a lot about a few things—politics and economic history.

"If you don't know how nations interact and the economic motivation for their actions, you won't know how to deal with a Kissinger or a Nixon. Ed Murrow didn't have a news

*Reprinted with permission from TV GUIDE® Magazine. Copyright © 1969 by Triangle Publications, Inc. Radnor, Pennsylvania.

background either, but he learned economic determinism through hard study and extensive reading. Sure Kissinger liked to be interviewed by Barbara, because she didn't know enough to ask the jugular question."

Perhaps Kissinger was using Barbara. But in any event, the news she did elicit was important enough for the newspapers to give heavy coverage to several occasions. And Barbara's scoops were the envy of other electronic journalists.

Through jealousy or professionalism, journalists deeply resented Barbara's way of becoming a part of the story. During Nixon's China trip—one of the biggest news stories of the decade—Nixon was often behind closed doors and the only spontaneous news centered on Pat Nixon. With every new print coming out of the developer, it appeared that Barbara was standing next to Mrs. Nixon. In Shanghai, angry photographers went to Barbara's hotel room and dumped a week's worth of useless film on the floor. She angered the hard-news men as well. Once she refused to take her turn and file a pool report. Later she said that she did so due to deadline pressure, but the correspondents thought she was just being snobbish.

Whatever her shortcomings, Barbara Walters at *Today* was a journalistic phenomenon: a broadcaster of extraordinary skills and charisma, the leading practitioner of her trade. One way or another, she did get those interviews. She once kept an Israeli cabinet minister waiting in her outer office so long that he left in a fury; Barbara had been busy working to line up some more important interview by telephone.

If Hugh Downs was the laziest host ever to run *Today*, Barbara was certainly the hardest-working. Barbara Walters had emerged as one of the nation's leading journalists—and as a star.

CHAPTER 21

The Ballplayer and the Batboy

In a competitive environment like the *Today Show*, it's not surprising to find some negative opinions by colleagues of almost everyone who worked there for any period of time. There are exceptions, though. Everyone, it seems, likes Joe Garagiola, who was an on-camera regular for a decade, and Bernie Florman, the show's prop man since 1959.

Affable, wise-cracking Joe Garagiola was born and raised in St. Louis, the son of an immigrant Italian bricklayer. He spent eight years in baseball as a catcher for the St. Louis Cardinals, the Pittsburgh Pirates, the Chicago Cubs, and the New York Giants. "I thought I was modeling uniforms for the National League," he said—a sally typical of those that endeared him to *Today* audiences. Viewers liked him, says Al Smith, managing editor when Joe became a regular, because of "his ability to cut through the horseshit and ask the one question you and I would like answered."

Once, says Smith, as Downs finished asking a stuffy and famous lawyer some "convoluted" questions about torts, Garagiola popped up with "It always seemed to me that lawyers do little and charge a lot. How come?"

When Joe became a regular on the show in 1967, those bull's-eye questions—the ones a cab driver might ask—became his trademark. The gentlemanly Hugh Downs, the astringent Barbara Walters, and the happy-go-lucky Joe Garagiola proved to be a very successful mix for the show.

Joe's office at NBC contains an old jersey from his St. Louis Cardinal days. It has the same lived-in look as the tan knit suit he wore for an interview with the author. The European-cut suit—a button missing, baggy at the knees, and in a decidedly unchic state of mild disrepair—looked as though Joe had worn it defending home plate against hard-sliding base-runners. In person Joe is as comfortably informal as his knit suit. He sprinkles baseball jargon and other slang into his conversation with abandon. *Today*'s prop man Bernie Florman, says Joe, would have made a "great designated hitter" and is "the best blow-out patch I've ever seen."

Joe's role on the show grew like no other supporting role in the history of the production. Soon after Garagiola became a regular, Al Morgan was handing him book assignments. More diligently than any other save Barbara Walters, Joe read the books in advance. He was also assigned to interview guests who were representing his Roman Catholic religion. But if that faith's party regulars thought this meant Joe was a patsy, they simply weren't paying attention.

Once after he had endured several minutes of unresponsive answers from a high figure in the Knights of Columbus, a Catholic men's lodge, Joe began to be annoyed. For one thing, the man kept looking away as he gave his answers and, for another, he addressed the interviewer as Joseph. "My sixth-grade nun was the last to call me that!" Joe said. "Then I

looked over his shoulder and saw he was reading from a prepared speech. I reached over, grabbed it, and said, 'Now, let's
visit.' We got going and I said, 'What is the K of C doing
now?' "

The K of C representative offered something innocuous and
Joe, who could see that the time was running out, said hur-
riedly, "You've got to get more involved. There is divorce,
mixed marriage, poor housing and right now there is a Synod
of Bishops in Rome."

With that, the show switched to a commercial. The producer ran out in a panic and said, "What did you say? What
did you call the Pope—a son-of-a-bitch?"

"My wife told me later that she swallowed her coffee and
choked on that Synod of Bishops line," says Joe. "Naturally,
when it came time to wrap this guy up, I was uptight. I finally
said, 'Who runs the K of C?' and he said, 'An organization in-
corporated in Connecticut.' I said, '*What?*' and '*Thank you
very much.*' "

The hate mail descended like locusts. Joe's name was spelled
every conceivable way except the right way. (A friendly
critic once wrote Joe putting the ballplayer's picture on the
envelope and no address. It arrived at *Today* in two days.)
Even the K of C joined in, damning Joe in its newsletter.

Joe is quite religious, but has no tolerance for cant. One
pompous priest on the show, who "was giving the impression
that he had fallen right out of the Twenty-third Psalm," finished by thanking Joe and saying, "Please pray for me." Joe
retorted, "Wait a minute! Pray for *you*? You're in management, *you* pray for *me!*"

Even the Protestants got their knocks. When Norman Vin-
cent Peale told of a man fleeing oppression who picked his
daily route by opening his Bible to a random passage each
night, Joe said, "How can you have faith in that kind of thing
when people are trying to kill you?" Even the *Watchtower,*

the Jehovah's Witnesses' publication, joined those heaping abuse on Joe after that one.

Basically conservative, Joe is no admirer of the drug culture, but he was keeping his peace when Timothy Leary, the former Harvard professor, extolled tripping on *Today*. Leary was talking with Hugh Downs and Joe was off to the side, uninvolved in the interview, when Leary wheeled on him and said, "Look how uptight *he* is." Later, Leary wheeled again and said, "Look at those expressions!" At that, Joe grabbed Leary by the shoulder and said, "Hey! You're the guy who is uptight. You're the guy walking around with a pigtail!"

No one ever knew what Joe would say next. He was a refreshing iconoclast who found joy in down-to-earth people—including athletes, black and white. Typical of the kind of hate mail Joe often received after interviewing a black athlete was one from a semi-literate who addressed him: "Dear nigger-lover, you dago, ginnie bastard."

Joe has always been fair and generous toward everyone on the show. While many on *Today* are more than willing to knock Hugh Downs now that he's gone, Joe isn't. "My description of Hugh Downs," he says, "is this: Picture us at the desk and on the air and the studio bursts into flame. I would jump up and say, 'Let's get out of here.' Hugh would tell the viewers, 'The reason for the fire is spontaneous combustion,' and he would then do the commercial, excuse himself, and leave.

"Hugh was the kind of guy who would reel you in if you were drowning. He wasn't one of those guys who would hit you with an anchor or row out fifty-five feet and stop when you were out a hundred and say, 'I met you more than half-way.' If I was doing an interview, Hugh was my ace in the hole. He would be there."

Though Garagiola could rile some of the audience occasionally with his directness, *Today* viewers loved him—as they made clear with their supportive responses. Joe wears a wedding ring on his left hand and his World Series ring on the other. He left the two rings at home for a stretch—at 4 A.M. it's easy to forget—and he got a concerned letter asking if he was having trouble at home. But it was the death of Joe's mother that really brought the audience to his side. Notes and letters arrived by the hundreds from viewers offering prayers and masses.

Somehow people care about Joe—on unimportant things as well as important ones. They even identify with Joe's baldness. Joe once interviewed bald linebacker Ray Nitschke of the Green Bay Packers, who planned to sell toupees in the off-season. The two put on "rugs" during a commercial and admired themselves in the monitors when the cameras came back. It was during the Vietnam War, and that same day General James Gavin, who was thinking of running for President, was a guest. Gavin had advocated a de-escalation of the war and was popular with the anti-war forces. The mail count after the show: 1,800 pieces for Joe (to toup or not to toup) and 20 pieces for General Gavin.

Former managing editor Al Smith sums up the feeling about Joe within the *Today* company, saying, "Joe is a beautiful person. I don't know anyone who had an ax to grind with Joe. In any unit there is going to be some backstabbing. But I never heard it with Joe—either directed toward him or coming from him. He is truly a lovely man."

Known as the miracle worker, Bernie Florman has been backstage for three-quarters of the *Today Show*'s run. Officially, he is the prop man, but that only begins to explain his function. Bernie knew who liked whiskey in the morning and would quietly supply it; for years one important *Today* figure drank Scotch rather than coffee from his styrofoam cup. Request a prop—however difficult to obtain—and it would be there in time for the show.

Garroway would often say, "You can find anything, Bernie." Once the show needed a license plate from Georgia the next day. Bernie got it. A Sherlock Holmes pipe was called for—and there it was clamped in Garroway's teeth on the next broadcast. An old-fashioned milk can turned up on schedule, as did a replica of Gainsborough's *Blue Boy*, an old beer pail—even an electric chair.

Bernie loved working with Garroway. When Dave called in from a stay on Long Island to set up a gag shot, Bernie responded eagerly and worked it out. On the next show Garroway came on carrying a suitcase. "I never saw so much fog as on my vacation," he said. "I'm going to show you what I mean." With that, Garroway opened the suitcase and the studio filled with "fog"—from a smoke candle Bernie dredged up.

When Garroway came back from Italy, he complained about the ferocious coffee in Italy. Bernie brought in a glistening espresso maker, and Garroway said he would demonstrate to viewers what he meant. Dave opened the coffee valve and as the hot fluid landed in the coffee cup, the cup dissolved. Bernie had ordered one made of sugar from a candy factory.

Downs enjoyed Bernie's tricks, too, and used him when a customs inspector appeared on the show to warn of the seriousness of smuggling and how futile it was. The inspector was then presented with a filled suitcase and was told that somewhere among the contents were thirty diamonds. The inspector searched the suitcase confidently, but grew frantic when he found nothing. He took apart an alarm clock—again nothing. He hefted a flashlight and pressed the switch. It lit. Finally he gave up in disgust. With that, the flashlight batteries were removed and one was opened. There, among what was left of the carbon, were the thirty diamonds. The inspector was not amused. He left fuming, and Hugh turned to Florman and said, "Bernie, never try to leave the country."

Once newscaster Frank Blair was scripted to refer to a picture of George Washington on the first President's birthday, and say with a smile, "I am just like him. I cannot tell a lie." Frank was startled when he said it—the picture fell off the wall: another Bernie Florman production.

If Bernie was a necessary man at Rockefeller Plaza, he was absolutely indispensable on the road. He catered meals on remotes and always managed to find someone to help him even in the most sparsely settled location. Bernie once fed sixty people in a forest in Michigan, assisted as usual by a local gofer. He had gone out the night before and bought six charcoal grills and five hundred pounds of fuel. He had 125 TV dinners of all types plus soda picked up in the usual conveyance—a station wagon rented at the airport, Bernie's first transaction on any remote.

Abroad, he would "adopt some poor native child" to help with the lemonade—or an older individual, a "wonderful, warm human being like himself," an associate reports. If there was rain, yellow slickers and appropriate-sized boots would appear as if by magic, and the *Today* camp would be sheltered from the elements.

Bernie provided shelter from all kinds of problems. Jim Gaines, a *Today* director, arrived in Puerto Rico with his ulcer kicking up. He called out, as usual, "Where's Bernie? I need some milk." This time Bernie was *really* ready for Jim. Bernie led a borrowed cow out from behind the *Today* mobile unit, complete with sign: "For Jim Gaines only."

On that same remote, Bernie had to adjust to one situation he didn't like. Gaines came over to him and said, "That man over there looks tipsy. Let's get rid of him." Bernie pulled a local guard aside and asked, "Can't we lose this fellow?" and the guard said, "Better not. He's the Governor's son and he carries a gun."

Bernie got along with everyone on the show, and they responded. He remembers Barbara Walters with particular affection. Once Barbara needed a scarce item in a hurry—Bernie doesn't say what, but nothing sinister about it, just personal. Bernie knew that a friend of his could get the item, and the friend came through. But the middleman was then pressured to get Barbara to make a speech in a distant city.

Bernie explains: "He called Barbara and said, 'Barbara, could you fly out here?' Barbara said, 'Gee, I've got a tight schedule.' The middleman then said quietly, 'Barbara, if you don't it's my job.' She caught the next plane."

Bernie regarded it as a point of honor to deliver on all requests, no matter how unusual. Staffers remember only one time when he couldn't deliver. The show was doing a piece on the praying mantis. Unfortunately, it was past the season for the ferocious-looking three-inch green insects with the outrigger eyes and craning necks. "Bernie called all over the United States and various parts of Argentina," Al Smith says. "He could not find a live one. Regretfully, he finally gave up. Al Morgan used to say he never wanted to see Bernie's basement because it undoubtedly was loaded with improbable items. Al didn't want to be disillusioned."

CHAPTER 22

The Oklahoma Kid

Frank McGee, Hugh Downs' successor as *Today* host in 1971, had done a brief stint on the show before. Though Al Morgan thought he did fine, McGee might never have gotten the job had Morgan lasted as producer until Downs left. In Morgan's view, Frank McGee was "always a very unpleasant man."

McGee's early stint happened when Downs went on vacation and Morgan's usual fill-in, Jim Daly, was unavailable. Morgan reluctantly turned to the NBC news department for a replacement, though he was always wary of the journalist's heavy hand. He found McGee to be so natural and so good that "he surprised the hell out of me."

In appreciation, Morgan sent McGee a case of Scotch. "At *Today* we were great flower senders, great Scotch givers," Morgan explains. "I wanted him to say thank you, but he never acknowledged the gift. I thought maybe he didn't get it. But then Bernie Florman checked the receipt, and it was signed by Frank. I thought it was a very rude thing to do. I never liked him, and I think very few people did."

McGee did have an abrasive, messianic quality which he himself described as that of a "misguided Baptist minister." It showed on the *Today Show*. Shortly after he joined the production, Barbara Walters, tough under the bland Hugh Downs, began to seem warmer and more feminine. The producer, commenting on the role shift for Barbara, noted that it was reflected in the mail. Letters would say, "Frank McGee was rude to so-and-so" or "God bless Barbara Walters for being nice to so-and-so."

Said McGee in acknowledging his hard-nosed quality, "I'm like a collie puppy. I come bounding into a room all fat and grinning and I expect everybody to like me. If they don't, I bite them."

Frank McGee was always like that—fierce and determined, even at the expense of his own interests. When he was in high school in Norman, Oklahoma, his teacher gave a fellow student a dressing down for disagreeing with her over the Civil War. Frank, outspoken even then, accused the teacher of dictatorial methods. When Frank refused to apologize in front of the class, the teacher flunked him. Thus, though he lacked but a half point to graduate, Frank never got his high school diploma.

While in the Army in the Aleutian Islands during World War II, McGee had a heated argument with his first lieutenant. He was promptly busted from sergeant to private. When he was discharged, he enrolled in the University of California at Berkeley, and again his uncompromising nature asserted itself. He took a course in speech therapy. The therapist studied Frank's diction and spoke of a "cavern" inside his mouth that rattled the sound. It could be corrected, the therapist said, by repeatedly stage-whispering "cool green salad." At that, McGee came up with a scalding phrase from the barracks, and shortly thereafter his GI Bill subsidy was cut off. Frank and his wife, Sue, retreated to their native Oklahoma, and Frank landed a job at a TV station. He learned to report, film, and edit his own stories, including one that traced a raindrop through the water system and out the tap at home. He was good and soon got attention.

NBC hired McGee and sent him to Montgomery, Alabama, where he covered the early days of the civil rights movement. He was the first to give national exposure to a determined young minister from the Dexter Avenue Baptist Church in Montgomery—the Reverend Martin Luther King, Jr. He gave the first national coverage to a story that began when a weary black seamstress in Montgomery, Rosa Parks, refused a command that she move to the back of a bus. Her defiance led to a year-long boycott on the part of the black community in Montgomery.

McGee, whose broadcast station worked hard to earn the trust of the black community, emphasized the hypocrisy of "separate but equal" playgrounds by filming a black playground, which, as Frank explained, was "nothing but one fire hydrant sticking out of the ground."

When McGee learned that an ambulance driver had left an accident victim in the street because the victim was black, McGee called the dispatcher to ask what was going on. The dispatcher denied that discrimination was involved, and then expressed a few clearly racist opinions.

"Look, I don't care what you think," McGee said. "I just want to know your policy."

"Would you want to be in an ambulance after it's been hauling some nigger?" asked the dispatcher.

"Okay," McGee said. "Now we know what your policy is." He talked about the incident on the air that night, and the policy was later changed.

When McGee became host of *Today*, it quickly appeared that he either was jealous of Barbara Walters' skills and accomplishments or, purely and simply, was a male chauvinist. He was so uncivil to Barbara that, she has said, he wouldn't speak to her when the TV lights went out. On the rare occasions when he did speak to her, he was condescending—speaking as journalist to non-journalist. When Barbara was especially good, the best Frank could summon up was, "We'll make a reporter out of you yet." Never mind that Barbara had interviewed President Nixon, Henry Kissinger, Egypt's Anwar Sadat, and Israel's Moshe Dayan and Golda Meir by the time McGee arrived at *Today*. McGee saw himself as the only heavyweight on the show.

From Walters' near-equal status with Downs, McGee downgraded her as much as possible. He insisted on signing on and off for *Today* and asked the first question of every guest Barbara snared for an appearance on the show, thus giving the impression that it was he who had scored the coup. He would even barge in at times, taking over Barbara's interviews if he felt like it. This gave Barbara's enemies perverse pleasure, remembering her interruptions of Downs.

In an interview some months after he began as *Today* host, McGee explained to a reporter the various roles on the show. His comments revealed some of the already developing tension between himself and Walters. "Friends have been asking me, 'When are you going to gut Barbara Walters?' My answer is, 'Never.' There's room for both of us," he said.

McGee's interpretation of Joe Garagiola's role was much friendlier, though it showed a bit of condescension. "Joe's a great big hunk of pulsating humanity," Frank said. "He responds to the warm, the gentle, the furry, the jockstrap side of America that's very real and very there. He asks questions that I wouldn't ask, out of professional vanity. I've found myself fudging up to a question in diplomatic Washington language and Joe busts right out with a blue-collar taxi driver kind of question. Joe's marvelous. He's honest. He says just what he believes."

Whatever the strains between them, the McGee-Walters team came across very well to the viewers, it seems. The show's ratings were not much less than they had been during the best months of Walters-Downs.

And guests on the show, who had often heard about the tough quality of McGee and Walters, were sometimes pleasantly surprised by the two. Thomas Thompson, author of the recent best-seller *Blood and Money*, told of a McGee-Walters interview, occasioned by his earlier book *Hearts*, in a December 1971 *Life* magazine article: "My first impression was that Barbara Walters is extraordinarily pretty—in burnt orange and jangling necklaces that morning—and she spoke in a voice so soft that one wondered how it could be heard.

"She and McGee worked cleverly together. *He* went after the news, *she* pried out the human anecdotes that, had I been watching, would have made me more interested in *Hearts*. How could I have felt apprehensive about that wonderful, sensitive woman? They seemed a team that had sat together for years, certainly not as Miss Walters had described them before the show. 'Hugh Downs and I were side by side for nine years,' she said, 'and we had an uncanny instinct for knowing just what the other would think and say. Now, with Frank, it's almost like a second marriage. We're still feeling each other out.' "

Walters was keeping her peace—and she was to keep it for many years, until long after McGee was gone. Meanwhile, McGee was in command, doing tough interviews and, when the subject appealed to him, light feature pieces. Anyone who came into contact with him quickly discovered that Frank McGee was hard as nails and willing to go for broke.

CHAPTER 23

The Short Happy Romance of Frank McGee and Mamye Smith

Outwardly, Frank McGee was happily married. When not putting in his long work days at NBC, he spent most of his free time with his wife, Sue. The two of them had built their lives around each other ever since high school in Norman, Oklahoma.

Frank McGee certainly didn't seem a man who would waver from his high personal or professional standards. Though a heavy smoker, he wouldn't buy cigarettes at the substantial discounts available to *Today* people through advertising channels. He was so proper in his relationships that few suspected him capable of an affair, though opportunities for liaisons abounded at *Today*, where staff camaraderie often led to intimacies.

But at fifty-two, Frank McGee was ailing and apparently lonely. He had known since before coming on the *Today Show* that he had cancer. He knew it would shorten his life, though he didn't know by how much. His son and daughter were grown, and Frank and Sue lived dull lives at home. With the exception of Gene Farinet, the show's news producer, hardly anyone at *Today* was a regular visitor. Sue apparently preferred things that way. There may have been a friend or two who sensed Frank's discontent, but it didn't appear to be a subject for comment in the gossipy offices of *Today*.

Mamye Smith, a production assistant, knew only that Frank enjoyed the conversations between herself and his secretary, Mary Wagner, which usually took place in McGee's office after *Today* signed off. Mamye, Mary, and other chums called themselves "the never-go-home crowd." They spent many hours in nearby singles bars, flirting with men they usually viewed as "losers." Mamye and Mary shared a sense of the ridiculous, and would exchange entertaining tales of the past evening's encounters. Frank was a good listener and was amused by the stories.

Mamye would say, "Frank, you ought to come with us sometime," and Frank would say, "Sure, sure . . ." but he never did. Mamye says the invitations obviously included Frank's wife: "We didn't care. We only knew that she was nice and assumed they were in love. We all did." Sometimes Mamye, Mary, and Frank would talk more seriously about life. "He always seemed to be on the same wave length," says Mamye. Frank and the women didn't always agree, but "there was never an 'I don't understand you' kind of thing from Frank."

When Frank broke his leg skiing, Mamye and Mary kidded about it. Mamye would threaten to close the door on Frank's leg, and he would smile and say, "You'd better be fast on your feet!"

It was fun, and it was platonic—even those good-natured embraces typical of the easy informality at *Today*. If someone in Mamye's tight circle of friends was down, Mamye explains, "We used to say, 'Let me give you a hug, you've had a hard day.' "

One day Mamye told Frank about a guy at a bar the night

before. She said, "This weirdo walked up, said hello, told me his sexual preferences, and added, 'Besides, I'll take you to a party.' " Mamye and Mary laughed. Frank did not. Mamye remembers that he seemed to take it seriously: "I said, 'You're not fun anymore,' and Mary said, 'Yeah, that's right,' and I walked out." A couple of days later, Mamye asked Frank why he had been upset. Was he afraid she might get hurt? He said quietly, "Sorry, I was just in a bad mood."

There was less unrestrained laughter after that. But Frank would still say, "Mamye, come give me a hug." One day, Mamye sensed that Frank wasn't just giving her a friendly hug—there was more meaning than that. She confronted him, asking if there was something going on she was unaware of, and Frank laughed it off. Mamye said, "Okay . . . just asking," relieved because she had no desire to become a homewrecker.

Nevertheless, Frank apparently thought it was understood that Mamye was his special friend. He once got angry, accusing her of being with someone else. More deeply involved by now than she had intended or wanted, Mamye denied the accusation. "But he didn't believe me," she says. "I was angry because I don't really lie. I blew up and said, 'Don't you ever do that to me again!' I just walked off, and he came back and said, 'What do you really want?' and I said, 'I want you out of my life.' He said, 'Okay,' and went away. Then he came back ten minutes later and said, 'That's not what you are going to get.' "

This was in 1973. Later that year Frank McGee, the host of the *Today Show* and a man whose understated delivery in reporting on the world's calamities was a steadying influence for millions, spoke his feelings to Mamye Smith. Frank asked Mamye to meet him for breakfast after the show. Over eggs and coffee he told the comely and warm-hearted woman, who was half his age and happened to be black, that he loved her. He added that he had had those feelings a long time, possibly since the first day he met her. And then he said something that again made Mamye angry. He told her that he had informed his sister that he was leaving his wife to be with Mamye.

"He didn't *ask* me," Mamye says. "It wasn't like he said, 'Is this what *you* want?' It was like he decided. I got sick and I wasn't sure why. I was especially shocked that he had told his sister about me without first asking me what *I* thought. I know he didn't mean it that way. He was a very decisive man. After I calmed down a bit, I told him he had no right to do that without asking me. What a hell of an assumption!"

Nevertheless, Mamye wouldn't deny that she shared Frank's feelings. She did say to him, though, "You can't do this. You can't leave your wife."

"I realized that sometimes people see only what they want to see," Mamye says. "I realized that there would be quite a few complications if he did it. I don't know why, but I was kind of wondering whether he was aware of them. Frank lived and functioned on one level of the establishment. Everybody likes you, but that's deceptive. They love you as long as you are doing what they want you to do, but they won't like you if you don't.

"I knew that some of his *Today* friends wouldn't go along," she explains. "They wouldn't go along because I'm black. And they wouldn't go along because he was married. Before this, they'd sit around and say nasty things about his wife, but that didn't mean they liked her or didn't like her. It's hard to say what motivates people to say what they say. But anyway, their attitude was 'Frank, you can't leave her!' "

One of the married men on *Today*, who called himself Frank's friend, dated a *Today* secretary for eight years while carrying on another affair with a second NBC woman. He was outspoken in his opposition to Frank's decision and hostile to Mamye. Mamye was not surprised by the man's attitude, nor by the slights of others at *Today*, especially those involved in office romances.

"It was *their* business," she says. "I had no ax to grind." While she was uncomfortable as the cause of Frank's marital break-up, she was prepared to accept the consequences: "I make the decisions for my life. If I make decisions, then I have to accept responsibility for what I've done. I don't ask anybody to accept what I've done."

Many at *Today* were perplexed over Frank's decision to leave his wife, popular though Mamye had been with staffers. It was easy to keep affairs from husbands and wives in *Today's* closed society, and no one could understand why Frank needed to dissolve his marriage. Perhaps it was male menopause, some mused. Or, more likely, Frank's last desperate fling—a reaction to the bone cancer that eventually would kill him. Few were able to accept the obvious: that Frank had fallen in love with a woman he found intelligent, warm, amusing, and physically attractive; a woman he cared enough about to want to marry.

Stuart Schulberg, the producer in 1973, was one of those who was baffled. In the first place, Stuart couldn't take Mamye seriously: "You laugh too much," he'd say. "What's so funny?"

Mamye sensed a resentment on Stuart's part, and it was mutual. "Stuart liked people to say how great he was. That wasn't my temperament. When Frank and I got together, he seemed to feel there was some kind of usurpation of power," Mamye says. "His line with me had to do with my being black—as though I was an authority. He would ask me about living conditions in Harlem. I used to look at him, like "What are you talking about?' I lived in Brooklyn. I never played up to him, never joked with him. I was indifferent to him."

Despite Stuart's apparent distaste for Frank's decision, he was practical when Frank came to the office to tell him he had left his wife. What, Stuart asked, was Frank going to wear?

Where were his clothes? Where was he going to stay? Stuart offered his brother Budd's East Side apartment, which was vacant. Frank and Mamye stayed there about a month and then moved to Gracie Plaza at 89th Street and York Avenue.

It was a joyous move as Mamye remembers it. Despite Frank's condition, there was no sense of impending doom. "Frank was in no pain. He knew four years earlier that he had trouble. But he didn't know he would soon die. It didn't interfere with his life. He skied and rode horseback. We played tennis together. There was nothing he couldn't do."

Frank was a good dancer, and they went to the Americana, the Rainbow Room, places where they could ballroom-dance. Frank liked jazz, too, and they went to the Half Note. Mamye likes country music, and they listened to that too. "We were doing all the things Frank had always wanted to do and had never done," Mamye says.

One day, Frank left for Ann Arbor to conduct an interview at the University of Michigan. Suddenly he became seriously ill and had to be taken to a hospital. Mamye got a call from Stuart, who told her that Frank wanted her to come to Ann Arbor and to bring some things. When she arrived, she was taken aback. Frank was in bed and didn't move from it the whole first day. They played gin. The second day, Mamye teased him, saying, "Get your happy ass out of bed. You can't stay there all day!" Frank was sicker than Mamye knew, but he got up and several days later he was released to fly back to New York. Though he was on medication, including a pain-killer, on the flight back, he enjoyed the trip. His doctor in New York prescribed long walks—at least four miles a day—to help keep his body going.

At 5 A.M. thereafter, Frank and Mamye walked together some two and a half miles to the *Today* studio. In the evenings, Frank would precede Mamye home from work. When she arrived, she would insist on another walk—usually to midtown and back. They looked in the shops and joked as Frank worked to ease the frequent pain he now felt in his lower back and joints. Despite his problems, Mamye remembers that he was warm and selfless.

"One day we were walking and saw a man fall down in the street," she says. "Frank helped him up and asked if he was all right. The man said yes, and then said, 'Aren't you Frank McGee?' and Frank said, 'That doesn't matter, are you all right?' Frank shouldn't have done that—exert himself so—in his condition."

Sometimes Frank was in considerable pain at *Today*. In the spring of 1974, members of the *Today* company noticed that his condition was deteriorating and that it could take several minutes for him to rise from his seat after the final sign-off. Mamye insists that Frank was neither worried nor irritable, as some have suggested. The way to irritate Frank, Mamye says, was to "screw up"—jeopardize a telecast through carelessness. She had once done it, before they became lovers. She left a script on his desk without informing him, and minutes before the show he stormed out of his office demanding to know where the script was. Mamye gave him a copy, and Frank later discovered he had thrown the original script in the waste-basket. He apologized, but Mamye insists it was her fault for rushing off without telling him what she had left.

In April 1974, Frank was clearly growing worse. One night, he couldn't get to sleep and suffered from chills. Mamye called the doctor, who suggested additional blankets. The doctor came by in the morning and thought it better if Frank went to the hospital. "Doctors don't let you know how serious things are," Mamye says. "But I knew it was serious because I had never seen him that sick before. He was really very, very sick."

Mamye continued to go to her job, and would leave as soon as she could to go to Frank's bedside. Producer Stuart Schulberg was, in Mamye's view, no help. "Stuart used to bug the hell out of Frank, calling him on the phone and asking when he'd be back. Frank said to find someone to fill in, saying he wasn't sure when he'd be back. Stuart used to call every day and would say, 'Mamye, I'm relying on you to tell me what's going on.'"

Recalling those days is still painful to Mamye. As she talked she was moved to bitterness and tears, saying, "Do you know what else that bastard would do? Stuart wouldn't give me my scripts on time so that I could get to the hospital. If Frank hadn't been on the show and I was dating someone else, I would probably have taken time off. I never took a day off, I was at the studio every single day. I would call Frank from there when he was very sick."

One day Mamye got a call from the nurse, who said Frank wanted her at the hospital and could she leave work? "I went. I was there with him all day. The doctor said that the most crucial time would be the next twenty-four hours. They were taking cultures and fluid from his lungs."

Frank's daughter Sharon and her husband, Peter, had asked if they could come to the hospital, and Frank said yes. Though he hadn't told them about Mamye, they knew anyway. Mamye recalls that the three of them found Frank in good spirits and that they teased him. She adds that Frank did not, as was widely believed, know that he was dying. "I think he might have had some idea, but the doctors never said, 'You've got six months to live.' He'd always told them he could handle it, should it come to that. They did say that if they didn't get the illness under control he would die within two years. But they never told him that they couldn't get it under control."

Soon Mamye became alarmed as Frank's breathing grew labored and his lungs began to fill with fluid. The doctors came with oxygen and an injection. Now Mamye wonders if the injection was to make it easier for Frank to breathe—or easier to die. Even so, Frank was awake and concerned about those around him. "He kept saying to me when we were alone, 'Are you and Sharon getting along?' and I said, here he is sick, and what does he care if she's being nice to me?"

Frank McGee died at five in the morning on April 17, 1974. Mamye called Schulberg and told him, adding that she was going back to the apartment. Peter and Sharon dropped her off, and they went home. That was Mamye's last contact with the McGees.

"I didn't go to the funeral," she says. "He was buried at his farm in Virginia. Sharon and Peter said I could come, but I would not have gone. I went to my brother's funeral and my grandfather's, but I doubt if I'll ever go to another one.

"They [some *Today* people] were worried that I would come to the *Today* memorial for Frank, but I couldn't have gone even if I had wanted to get back at them. I had the worst problem dealing with hospitals thereafter. I used to cry at the mention of the word. My older sister got very sick and I couldn't bring myself to go. I called her and said, 'I can't.' I guess she understood."

Things were different for Mamye at *Today* after Frank's death. She sensed that she was regarded as an embarrassment and resented it. There *was* some publicity—a write-up in the *Amsterdam News*, for one thing. But by and large, she said and did little to call attention to herself.

There was, of course, the grief. Even to this day, Mamye says, she isn't sure she has dealt with this. Like many who suffer loss, she can't accept Frank's death. There were bad moments at work. Her friends on the show were very supportive. She remembers Edwin Newman with particular affection. Once he went by her office and said, "Mamye, are you all right?" Mamye said, "Yes, I'm all right." Newman walked a step or two, then came back to her doorway and said deliberately, "No, I mean are you all right?"

Another time, Mamye went to the newsroom to seek out a friend there who wrote for Ed Newman. She didn't see him, so she stopped by Newman's office and asked. When Ed said the man was off that day, Mamye's eyes clouded and tears ran down her cheeks as she said, "Why is it he's never around when I need him?" Newman jumped up and pulled Mamye inside, closed the door, and told her she couldn't go out looking as she did. He kept her there while she composed herself.

Mamye was sure Stuart Schulberg wanted her off the show, and they argued frequently. She resented his attitude in view of her long service and what she regarded as her excellence on the job. Once Barbara Walters had come over to her at a party where Mamye and friends were laughing and having fun, and in a misguided attempt at humor said, "You got your job because you're black." Mamye said with some heat, "No, I got my job because I'm damned good!"

Nevertheless, her performance on the job became an issue. One day Stuart came back from lunch in an ugly mood, as Mamye recalls it, and summoned her to his office. Their conversation degenerated into a "shouting match" as mutual resentments boiled over. At length Stuart told Mamye she was incompetent and fired her. Stuart later apologized, and suggested that she would be happier if she transferred to another department in NBC. Mamye refused the apology and the suggestion, and instead regarded herself as fired.

She hired lawyers and charged racial discrimination before the Office of Equal Employment Opportunity. There were affidavits. Mamye mentioned racial slurs. Joe Garagiola admitted to some slurs in "good fun," and Mamye accepted them as such—from Joe. If Mamye asked Joe for something, he'd say, "You've moved into my schools, my neighborhoods, when will you people stop?" and everybody laughed. Mamye had never tried to answer the ebullient Garagiola: "He had so much mouth, I couldn't think of anything to say. He'd say things for me and answer again before I came up with anything."

What mostly concerned Mamye were her treatment following Frank's death and the charges of incompetence, which to her reflected intolerance. She recalls in bitterness that Barbara Walters called after Frank died to express sympathy but then filed an affidavit in the suit saying she "could not always rely" on Mamye's judgments and consequently had to give extra work to a second production assistant. Stuart's affidavit said that Mamye had trouble performing under deadline pressure and that she spent a great deal of time away from the office and was "not completing her work." The news producer in his affidavit said that Mamye had difficulty adjusting to and working on the program when it deviated from the normal *Today* format.

Mamye was stunned by the affidavits. She had been on all overseas remotes during her service and had never known about dissatisfaction with her work. It irked her when the defense made much of Stuart's proffer of his brother's apartment as evidence of a lack of animosity: "What he didn't say was that we paid the rent while we were there."

Mamye's friends at *Today* wrote letters to help with her case, but she withheld them out of fear they might get in trouble. One found the need to write "bewildering," the charges of Mamye's "incompatibility" being "silly as hell." Another found her pleasant, responsible, and very cooperative, adding: "There has seemed to be a concerted effort to beset her with obstacles, in an attempt to hinder the performance of her duties and to delay her daily departure from the *Today* offices; this would appear to constitute a personal vendetta against her, since others were somehow given their material earlier in the day and were therefore able to leave at an earlier hour. Despite adversity, the quality of Ms. Smith's work had never faltered, for she has remained steadfast in completing the tasks required of her, and her capabilities are certainly not to be questioned."

Not everyone on the staff agreed, however. One man referred to Mamye as a "country girl from Brooklyn." Another said, "If you wanted her you had to look high and low, but you couldn't complain because McGee would have your head."

In any event, Mamye's complaint was not upheld by the OEEO, though it was irrelevant by then. Mamye had been hired by an NBC documentary unit in the meantime. Her long travail was at an end, though she was seriously in debt. The lawyers, who had told Mamye an appearance before the OEEO would cost $300, charged $3,000 in all. She was shocked, and is still paying.

Frank left Mamye nothing. "There had been a general understanding that we would be married," Mamye says, "but with the understanding that if either of us became unhappy, we would have the good sense to say it hadn't worked out and not feel trapped because we had made a decision."

Frank had mentioned money many times but Mamye waved him off, saying there was plenty of time to think of that. Frank went so fast that he didn't provide for her, though it was perfectly clear to Mamye that he intended to do so.

But the prospect of money meant little to Mamye. What she regrets is the loss of *Today* associations, the camaraderie, and, most of all, the man she loved and who loved her in those brief months of his final illness.

CHAPTER 24

Endurance

Today producers have mostly found the job exhilarating, but also a pressure-cooker experience. Gene Buck, an ex-leatherneck who carried the producing responsibilities for a time, was turned off by the negatives and went out in a shower of expletives. The soft-spoken Bob Bendick also exploded at last, and he too got the ax. Like Bendick, Shad Northshield got two cracks with the whip and used foul language to work off his frustrations.

Al Morgan thrived by avoiding the pressures of the broadcasts themselves, watching the shows on his bedroom TV rather than at the studio. While most producers percolated either internally or visibly, Morgan kept his cool, and he kept the job for six years. Morgan's successor Stuart Schulberg lasted the longest, with an eight-year reign—a third of *Today's* history to that time—but he was a walking advertisement for coiled springs.

An incessant smoker, Schulberg sipped from a styrofoam cup, had high blood pressure, and paced like a tiger. Said an observer of his habits, "Stuart is so nervous he'd find room to pace in a closet."

The goateed Schulberg had a professional mien some called pompous. He liked to be "yessed," ruled the show with an iron hand, and paid as close attention to detail as to strategy. One veteran writer who missed the autonomy of the Morgan years said, "Stuart wanted to ring up the whole thing—like some self-important cashier at a five-and-dime in Paducah."

Adds another writer, "Think of a predictable idea, and you'll have thought of a Schulberg *Today* feature. You *knew* what you could get on the show with Schulberg—and that was just the trouble..."

That is not to say that Schulberg was a poor choice for the job. A third writer, Christian Brown, not only liked Stuart but found him to be the "most literate executive type and producer I've ever known in television." Brown remembers an advance visit to Rumania—before a *Today* remote—during which cumbersome translation stymied communication. Stuart, who was educated in part in Swiss schools, said something in French, got a reply in kind, and the meeting waltzed forward fluently thereafter.

Stuart's father was B. P. Schulberg, head of production at Paramount Pictures under the legendary Adolph Zukor and a rare intellectual in Hollywood during Tinseltown's golden age. His mother is a show business agent, and his brother is the novelist Budd Schulberg, author of *What Makes Sammy Run* and *On the Waterfront*.

Chris Brown can't remember anything the unusually knowledgeable Stuart Schulberg didn't know something about. He was at ease with sophisticated companions and waiters. He had also rubbed elbows with down-to-earth athletes as a sports writer in Washington, D.C. During World War II, he served in the Marine Corps and, using his knowledge of German, also worked for the OSS.

Brown acknowledges the difference in Schulberg's approach from that of his predecessor and agrees that Schulberg would "agonize" over the smallest detail. But he argues that his scripts were improved by Schulberg's touches. Stuart brought impressive credentials with him to *Today*. He had won prizes for NBC documentaries, including, in 1966, *The Air of Disaster* and *The Angry Voices of Watts: An NBC News Inquiry*; and in 1968, *American Profile: Somehow It Works*.

Schulberg's hypertension was, however, a burden not only to himself but to those he worked with. He was jealous of his authority over his subordinates, a trait that worked to his disadvantage and at times demoralized the staff. One writer complained that when he was assigned to a spot another writer wanted and they then agreed to trade assignments, they invariably would run into a stone wall with the producer. Schulberg would reject the switch with the words "Who's producing this show anyway?"

"I found it a shame," says the writer. "Stuart was a very intelligent, cultured man who gave the show a good appearance and represented it well to the VIPs—executives at NBC and important people the world over. But in some pathetic way he lacked the saving grace of a sense of humor. Even when he laughed, it seemed an embarrassment to him."

The writer said that Stuart's stiffness came across as insensitivity when he dealt with blacks. Stuart, who had a "great and obvious social consciousness," devoted considerable coverage on *Today* to problems of racial equality, but he nevertheless patronized individual blacks. "I am convinced that he didn't mean to be that way, but several people on this show and elsewhere have been hurt by this," the writer said.

Schulberg, the writer believes, was essentially "anti-writer" and this showed in story conferences. Another critic remarks that Stuart loved individual writers at first. "Then you could see the marriage going sour. You could see Stuart's blue eyes chilling. Suddenly in those meetings, the writer would say something and Stuart would ignore the remark. The writer would become less and less sure of himself."

One writer in particular found it impossible to work with Schulberg. He was a veteran radio man, and regarded as extremely conscientious. "He tried very hard to please and did a good job," a friend notes. But his personality led to a clash with Schulberg.

"He was the kind of guy who could never leave well enough alone," his friend explains. "He would say to Stuart, 'Look, I've got a spot and I'm doing it this way.' Schulberg would say, 'Okay.' Then he would come back in again and say, 'Look, I think I was wrong, we ought to recast this and do it like this . . .'

"This drove Stuart up the wall, and he eventually fired him from the show. That didn't mean the man was fired from NBC —he was given a different job until retirement—but he lost $110 a week, and it affected his pension benefits to a certain extent. It was too bad. He was a very competent writer, but his personality worked against him with Schulberg. But then, hell, so did mine."

Dealing with writers was just one more source of tension that kept Stuart on cigarettes and lunchtime martinis. There were also the raging world events that Schulberg felt demanded his constant attention. He would conduct exhausting all-night work sessions following late-breaking events of world impact. While the *Today* crew were in Washington during the inauguration week in 1973, former President Lyndon B. Johnson died. Stuart was tossing a *Today* cocktail party and prop man Bernie Florman had just laid out a spread of food and drinks, including a six-pack for a writer who rarely drank hard liquor and champagne for a staffer who preferred that beverage. The staff quietly set down their drinks when they heard the news and turned from fun to the anxieties of a twelve-hour work session.

Stuart often felt frustrations in relations with the show's sometimes temperamental stars. Barbara Walters, says Schulberg, "could not have been more supportive and kind whenever I had a personal, private problem. But she could be awfully damned tough and self-centered when crossed or frustrated or, in her opinion, not supported on the air or otherwise. I didn't mind her outbursts in private, but I resented them in front of the production crew and in front of guests."

Stuart put up with this because it went with the job and because Barbara was, in his words, "truly phenomenal and unique." Yet she contributed to Stuart's tensions, as did the uneasy truce between Barbara and Frank McGee. Even the guests on the show could bring him to a boil. It happened, for instance, when Woody Allen appeared, according to Schulberg, in sneakers and light nylon jacket in the dead of winter to say that the yet-to-be-accused President Nixon flew out of the White House at night to suck blood.

Others at *Today* felt that Schulberg was bothered most by the increasing interference from the NBC executive suite. NBC producers often mutter about vicepresidentitis at NBC and how it hamstrings creative effort. A few insist that as a result NBC is suffering from an incurable and worsening paralysis.

Stuart found that he would have to deal with second-guessers early on. While he insists that his meetings with nice guy Don Meany of News were "relaxed and civilized," there were two or three such meetings a week concerning *Today* and what it was programing. Schulberg is more outspoken about his relationship thereafter with Lee Hanna, the next News executive in charge of *Today*, whom Stuart dealt with for two and a half years.

Hanna, says Schulberg, became "terribly involved with the physical look of the show. He was awfully concerned about sets, gizmos, graphics, and set decoration." Schulberg concedes that Hanna was a "very smart fellow" but he asserted himself "in a manner we were not accustomed to." Hanna, no doubt to Schulberg's relief, did not get involved in programing matters, but he ruled the housekeeping department. Schulberg says that the set Hanna substituted for the old familiar one was a "splendid modernistic one" but that a lot of people found it too cold, too sterile. *Good Morning, America*, then coming up fast on ABC with David Hartman, seized on the change to counter with a homey American living room set, which many people found more comforting.

As the pressures mounted and the years wore on, Stuart apparently became somewhat bored with his responsibilities. He began to talk longingly of moving to Haiti, his favorite island, and running a hotel there. He confesses that toward the end he was doing too many public service items, for which he "had a thing," and that these were sometimes dull. Others contend that *Today* itself had grown tired—obviously so as the ratings dropped steadily following the death of Frank McGee and the unfortunate choice of Jim Hartz as Barbara Walters' co-host. Stuart was still on the job when Walters resigned. He told friends that he planned to stay, but he didn't.

Stuart denies that he was asked to resign. To the contrary, he says, he was approached by CBS to become a documentary producer, and when NBC heard of it, they asked him to stay and do documentaries for them. Stuart accepted NBC's offer.

Interviewing Stuart Schulberg in his corner office at NBC left this reporter with a feeling that he was not so much relieved to leave *Today* after eight years as wistful. Perhaps, though, the last word on Stuart's change of jobs belongs to his doctor. At his annual physical check-up, after leaving

Today, the doctor took Stuart's blood pressure. The doctor then asked him to lie down so that he could take the blood pressure again. When he seemed puzzled, Stuart grew alarmed. "What's the matter?" he demanded.

"I'm not sure," the doctor replied. "But it's the first time in eight years your blood pressure has been normal."

CHAPTER 25

Today *Today*

It was January 15, 1977—the twenty-fifth anniversary of the *Today Show*—and to long-time viewers *Today* looked very much as it did on that first broadcast a quarter-century earlier. The show began in black-and-white. Lionel Hampton played "Sentimental Journey" on the vibraharp. Dave Garroway said hello in the old manner, introducing his companions, Jack Lescoulie and Frank Blair, on a set very similar to the original. The three old-timers seemed somehow smaller than life, looking tired and jaded. Their appearances were in marked contrst to those of the current principals, who, the camera revealed, were seated nearby basking in living color. Tom Brokaw, the thirty-six-year-old host, and Jane Pauley looked that morning like dutiful collegians, squiring their bewildered elders around the campus on alumni weekend.

Blond and perky Jane—affectionately "Janie" at times on the show—said that back on January 14, 1952, in Indianapolis, she was still completely bald and was struggling to walk—struggling, it can be assumed, almost as hard then as Jack Lescoulie and Frank Blair were now to steady themselves following several visits to a party spread set up for a post-broadcast bash. The two men had been accustomed to holding forth at Hurley's Bar near Radio City for years after each *Today* broadcast, and they wasted no time renewing their convivial relationship.

Garroway revealed glimpses of his old self but was not at his best during most of the broadcast. At one point, with past and present cast crowded around, he commented that the show had been "made for him," then he ducked as though J. Fred Muggs might spring from the wings to nip him on the cheek. Asked if Muggs really did bite, Garroway warned, "You're going to be sued," and said there were twenty-two entries in the NBC dispensary for anti-tetanus shots.

Many of the reminiscences seemed equally exaggerated, as did word that autobiographies by Lescoulie, Blair, and Garroway were all within months of publication. Garroway said there would be only one chapter on *Today* in his tome, adding that he was now at work on chapter 26. Lescoulie gave his crony Frank the old "hee-haw" when Blair said proudly that his work would be called *Let's Be Frank About It*.

There were filmed shots of young J. Fred Muggs demolishing Lescoulie's desk and a clip on National Doughnut Week twenty-two years earlier with Garroway testing a "pinky" rester for doughnut dunkers and a more functional but equally unlikely gadget, a doughnut retriever.

Pat Weaver also appeared on the anniversary show and lived up to his name, weaving back and forth in his chair as he told about his inspiration and its early success. He glossed over the near-misses of the NBC ax in *Today*'s shaky early history.

As the broadcast ended, the camera panned to the party spread and Garroway lunged, sinking a long knife into the heart of a birthday cake—as though to make a statement. It was more than a little embarrassing, but at least it was over. The *Today Show*, a Methuselah in the evanescent world of television, had something more to celebrate that day besides a silver anniversary. It was finally on the upswing again after a long slide toward disaster.

The slide began, most believe, with Frank McGee's death. After a long talent search and periodic consultation with Barbara Walters, now officially co-host, *Today* chose Jim Hartz to succeed McGee.

Hartz regarded McGee as his mentor. McGee, Hartz remembers, was a "legend" in Tulsa, Oklahoma, where Frank did early TV work and Jim Hartz was raised. When Hartz came to New York, McGee took his fellow Oklahoman under his wing and influenced him greatly. But Hartz, whose boyish charm seemed too bland to viewers and critics, did not have McGee's bite. Perhaps that is why Barbara liked him. He had, she said, "the ease and charm of Hugh Downs and the newsman qualities of Frank McGee." He also had at least a substantial part of McGee's salary as his reward for winning the talent search. He earned an estimated $250,000 a year as Barbara's co-host.

What Hartz didn't have in sufficient numbers was fans. When Barbara said good-bye to *Today* and left for ABC, Hartz was not seriously considered to remain as co-host. The ratings had dropped alarmingly with the two, as *Good Morning, America* climbed fast in the national early morning sweepstakes. Jim reportedly kept his ransom money but was replaced by Tom Brokaw, an NBC reporter who had turned down the *Today* assignment before Hartz got the job. At issue was Brokaw's refusal to do commercials—"needless cross-fertilization," growled the newsman—even though Frank McGee had done them, as had all previous hosts except John Chancellor.

Tom was a veteran Washington correspondent, or "political junkie," as he called himself, and a terrier who had nipped at the Nixon heels through three years of Watergate reporting. When he finally became *Today*'s host, he brought with him an intense curiosity, plus a contract that stipulated no commercials by the star. He also offered impressive work habits, in the hard-working tradition of Barbara Walters and Stuart Schulberg.

An activist who was determined to shape the broadcasts personally, he read the important newspapers and the Washington newsletters, and he fired off telegrams to VIPs and politicians asking them to visit the show. On his first broadcast, on August 30, 1976, he featured a low-keyed presidential aspirant speaking from a rocking chair, with a plowed field in Plains, Georgia, as the incongruous backdrop. Critics and viewers alike yawned over the product in the early weeks of the Brokaw reign. At least one critic predicted more gains for *Good Morning, America* on ABC.

And it happened. Brokaw with his South Dakota drone seemed too stiff and flat for the role of *Today* host. Gene Shalit, resident clown and all-around *Today* critic, began goading him to loosen up. (When Shalit first appeared on *Today*, his walrus mustache and afro hairdo caused one viewer to write that he thought "you've brought back J. Fred Muggs . . . but he *has* developed.") Brokaw tried, and he does have a good sense of humor, but at first his witticisms were received as flatly as they were delivered. When Jane Pauley joined *Today*—as a member of the cast but not as co-host, though she received a salary estimated at $100,000—Brokaw brought her into his jokes. Once he told Jane and Gene to take paper and pencil in hand and record the numeral "10," then the letters "US" and "NE" followed by the numeral "1."

"Tennis anyone?" asked Brokaw—an actual license plate out west, he explained limply. Pauley, very much on trial, smiled indulgently. Another Brokaw written quiz in September—9/8/76—got a similar pained response when Brokaw noted that such a descending series of numbers in a date occurred only once every decade. Shades of dunking doughnuts.

The show not only wallowed in disarray, it continued to sink. Princeton man Paul Friedman, the new producer—executive producer right off the bat, to the dismay of NBC critics who noted that the engaging youngster was only thirty-one—claimed the distinction of having taken *Today* to the very pits. "Under my expert tutelage we reached an all-time low of 2.7," he said.

That was the bottom, and then things began to improve. Brokaw, growing more familiar with his surroundings and his colleagues, became more relaxed in front of the cameras. Even his jokes improved, as the company began to work toward a more informal style. A new production format was tried, with success. Fewer scripts were prepared. Instead, the writers would brief the on-camera talent once on a preliminary basis, then again after talking with a guest before the show. The talent would take notes, which they would use in conducting interviews. New books were assigned far enough in advance so that the talent could at least skim them before the author walked into the studio and sat down. By that time, the talent would have word of the strong points in the author's spiel, and where he was weak or dull.

Most items, however, were not locked into the schedule more than a day or so before the actual broadcast. "TBA" notes—"to be announced"—speckled the show's calendar for the next week when this author looked at it in Friedman's office.

The writers sensed a new freedom. They found Friedman to be a man capable of instant decisions—a needed quality for the job—and one who could be argued out of a "no" if the writer was insistent. He told one, "When I tell you 'no' on a spot and you feel strongly about it, come back and argue with me. But if I say 'no' again, forget it."

The writer went fuming back a second time after Friedman rejected an art show item and got an okay. But Friedman still had misgivings and said, "When it's over I will play back the tape and show you why you were wrong." Instead, he wrote the writer a note saying he didn't know whether the spot had worked or not. Memos, in this regime, fly like leaflets at a political convention.

Friedman seems to the staff to have Schulberg's intelligence and good taste, and a further quality Schulberg lacked—an easy, informal confidence in dealing with the staff—and this has reduced frustration and resentment. One writer says he likes Friedman's "off-hand Bogart approach. 'Don't think I'm soft,' Friedman told me, 'but I'm going to do something nice for you.'"

The behind-the-scenes tranquility helped bring a more human quality to the broadcasts. And middle America—always the biggest audience, with several times the viewership of New York and Los Angeles—obviously liked the geographical backgrounds represented by the talent. Tom is from South Dakota. Lew Wood, who does sports and weather, is, like Jane Pauley, from Indianapolis. Newscaster Floyd Kalber, who was Jane's co-anchor at NBC's Chicago station, comes from Omaha, Nebraska. Shalit's sassy New York Cityese adds spice.

A Princeton student who authored a trivia book was put on the show by Friedman "for the fun of it" and to show off Brokaw's sharpened delivery and wit. Light items like these began to poke through the smog of heavyweight interviews that had dominated the show for years.

Viewers warmed as they learned that the new cast wasn't afraid to giggle or to look uninformed from time to time. Brokaw referred constantly to his brown, leather-bound notebook and his neatly penciled witticisms, which began to go over better and better: "This is the beginning of national procrastination month . . . Tell you more about that tomorrow." "A worm farm was robbed last evening and sheriff's deputies are questioning a five-hundred-pound robin."

The cast began to have fun—even the portentous, fashion-plate newscaster Floyd Kalber. A Kalber critic notes that some have called him "the midwestern John Chancellor," adding that Kalber would tell you that "Chancellor's the Kalber of the East." Still, Kalber has been solid and thoroughly professional. He moved smoothly into the job after Lew Wood went to weather and sports—and commercials. Only Wood and Shalit do commercials—along with Barbara Hunter, who does sports from time to time so that sponsors who use Hunter can console themselves that she actually has a role on the show.

Jane Pauley, who sailed far above the competition in her tryout, will never forget the anxiety she experienced one day during her tryout stint after awaking from a nap to discover it was six o'clock. In her rush to dress and get to the studio, she put a foot through her last pair of pantyhose, then discovered it was 6 P.M.—not 6 A.M. Her winsome, bubbling personality enlivens the show, and though she's still not a good interviewer, she is learning, disproving the Chicago critic who accused her of having the I.Q. of a cantaloupe.

Jane does suffer from nervousness. She has started smoking thirty Kools a day and has had a succession of colds, thought by some to be psychosomatic. Her boyfriend, an Indianapolis *Star* reporter and "the best friend I have in the whole world," was said by a gossip columnist to be eyeing another attractive TV personality back home. Jane commutes to him on some weekends.

Whatever the problems of adjustment, *Today* has come back fast. And strong. As this book went to press, *Today* ratings were topping 5 and a fraction—or within a whisker of their highest levels. More important, *Today* is once again swamping the competition after a vigorous rally by ABC's *Good Morning, America*. In a record cold week early in 1977, when America turned on the TVs to follow the mercury, *Today* jumped to a 5.5 rating and a 33 percent share of the viewing audience. CBS, with gravel-voiced Hughes Rudd, posted a 2.4 and a 17 share, and ABC, a 3 and a 19.

Today clearly remains America's favorite electronic drink of java. As Pat Weaver puts it, "You couldn't kill that show with a baseball bat."

What is the meaning of *Today* in the national scale of values? To John Crosby, the critic who years ago at the *Herald Tribune* gave early shows those scathing reviews, *Today*—along with *Tonight*—now represents the "only true television."

Crosby says the so-called practical men who came to the network after Pat Weaver was canned for being "too impractical, too head-in-the-clouds" then filled NBC with "rubbish which promptly sank out of sight, while all of idealistic, impractical Pat Weaver's ideas persist to this very day, enriching NBC beyond calculation."

The program's importance, as seen by Jack Gould, retired television critic of *The New York Times*, is "less in the numbers of those watching than in the quality of the individuals watching."

True, Presidents have made it a habit, and most of official Washington sees the show.

Thomas Thompson, author of *Blood and Money*, the bestseller about murder motivated by gain, probably spoke for millions of Americans who watch *Today* when he wrote in

Today *Today*

Life magazine on the occasion of the program's twentieth anniversary:

"*Today* is very much a part of the only constant ritual of my life. When I am at home in New York, I awake . . . make instant coffee, fetch *The New York Times* from the front step, turn on *Today* and get back in bed to savor an hour of indolence. Somehow it is comforting to see the *Today* people there beside me, already dressed, already at work, faces washed, minds percolating. If *they* can do it, so, perhaps, can I."

The show remains a staple for millions—in the cities as a supplement to the daily newspapers, and in backwater towns and villages where the newspapers often fail to inform. It is these millions—Presidents, politicians, pundits, and just plain people—who give *Today* its reason for being.

AFTERWORD:

A Tribute to Johnny Dunn

He was tall and cadaverous, with a weathered face. He wheezed with emphysema—like an old prospector too long on the trail. In telling a story, his voice shifted easily from an excited piping to dramatic, melodious lower register. Recalling a choice moment or a joke, he would dissolve into laughter—a dirty "heh heh" or an open "ha ha" if the matter was absurd enough. ("Nixon *sexy*? Ha ha ha!") His wife called him "Johnny" and so did the writers on *Today*. He was a delight at home and at work—but hardly a pushover.

John Dunn was *Today*'s editor—the conscience and resident intellectual for the show for most of its history, even after he retired. Following his farewell party, someone let a doctor argue on *Today* that people shouldn't eat any sugar at all. After the outrage died down, Stuart Schulberg rehired Dunn as a consultant on all medical matters. But he was invaluable in other ways as well, as a former *Today* writer explains:

"Al Morgan could scream and yell, and Stu Schulberg could scream and yell, but the bad stuff that didn't get on the air failed to because John Dunn was smart enough to know it was b.s. and keep it off."

Paul Cunningham adds: "He could spot baloney in news copy or a press release as fast as you could read the lead sentence. Then he would deliver a short lecture explaining why the story didn't stand up. Sometimes the reference was personal—'I knew that bum when I was working on the copy desk of a newspaper in Ohio . . .' "

John Dunn learned journalism the old way. He used to say that Andrew Carnegie was the nation's most important educator because of the many libraries he built across the land. John Dunn visited dozens of them, devouring information as he knocked about the country, writing for newspapers before he came to New York City to write for television.

Dunn loved to talk and, an associate says, would come up with the "damndest fact or story concerning anything from medicine to literature to politics."

Al Smith remembers sailing in the Greek islands with John Dunn on the Metaxes liquor company yacht. "Johnny liked to drink, but didn't drink that much and didn't hold his liquor well," Smith says. "He was drunker than a lord and was giving me a magnificent lecture on Greek philosophy and the Greek wars. He would point out an island and say that was where the Greek fleet hid before a battle."

Al Smith doesn't remember which battle, but John Dunn did. His memory was quite phenomenal, as Paul Cunningham attests: "Sometimes in arguing a point he would actually quote word for word a script I had written months before.

"Not that he was always patient," Cunningham adds. "He had a helluva temper, and he told me off more than once in the most picturesque words. Yet he was most kind. He worried about a lot of people—old friends who might be out of work. He was always a soft touch.

"He had a marvelous way of getting close to people, of having them accept him warmly. I remember that he had the assignment once of organizing a television remote in a small town in Puerto Rico. The morning we dropped him off, he had a huge straw hat covering his bald head from the sun and we saw him heading for the nearest coffee shop.

"When we returned to do the remote broadcast a week later, he not only had it organized perfectly but seemed in danger of being elected mayor of the town. Everybody knew him as we walked down the street with him, just about everybody had a smile and a wave for 'Juan.' "

But it was as a copy editor and censor that John Dunn put his unique stamp on the *Today Show*. Al Smith remembers him as "most literate" and "extraordinary," adding, "You never objected to anything he took out—there was a reason for it."

Cunningham spoke of Dunn's war on ambiguity, convoluted sentences, and fancy words: "He loved the language and insisted that its prime use was to communicate simply and clearly, not to try to impress anybody. He would take a piece of my copy which I would hand him with some pride, peer closely at it for only a moment or two, make a few deft slashes with his pencil, perhaps insert a word or two and hand it back with such words as 'You were saying the same thing too many times.' Of course, he was always right, and when you delivered the copy on the air you knew it was John Dunn making you look good."

John Dunn spent hours with the author recalling important events and humorous episodes in *Today Show* history. He was the necessary connective tissue that made this book possible. Shortly after a long first interview, he wrote a letter to clarify a couple of things he had told me, because "I want to be certain." The letter was marked with several copy-editing changes, including a sentence written at the bottom and referenced to a point high up in the typewritten letter. Below that handwritten sentence was another one that read: "God pity me: I can't help editing even when it's my own copy."

John Dunn died after a short illness some months before this book was completed. News-reporting methods are capricious. Had the editor of *The New York Times*, the Washington *Post*, or some other leading newspaper died, the obituary would have commanded prominent space in the important newspapers in the land. But when the editor of the *Today Show* died—a production with a bigger impact than twenty newspapers—the *Times* carried a mere five paragraphs.

But those writers who worked for him at *Today* haven't forgotten Johnny Dunn. Paul Cunningham, now with NBC in London, writes: "Disconcerting thing. I still do my reports and find myself wondering what John Dunn will think of them. Perhaps it's just as well that despite his departure, I still write for John."

Bob Cunniff, who remembers the embarrassment John Dunn saved the show, believes the old newspaperman and raconteur put his stamp on the production more than any other individual. He says simply, "John Dunn was the show."